LAW
and the
COMPUTER

LAW
and the
COMPUTER

Michael Gemignani

CBI Publishing Company, Inc.
51 Sleeper Street
Boston, Massachusetts 02210

Library of Congress Cataloging in Publication Data
Gemignani, Michael C.
  Law and the computer.
  Bibliography: p.
  Includes index.
  1. Computers—Law and legislation—United States.
I. Title.
KF1890.C6G45   346.73′024   81-396
ISBN 0-8436-1604-0   AACR1

Copyright © 1981 by CBI Publishing Company, Inc.
51 Sleeper St. Boston, Massachusetts 02210.

All rights reserved. No portion of this book may be reproduced without the specific written permission of the publisher.

Printed in the United States of America
Printing (last digit): 9 8 7 6 5 4 3 2 1

To Bill Harvey, Dean when I started; Tom Read, Dean when I finished; and to all of the administration, faculty, staff, and students of the Indiana University School of Law at Indianapolis, I gratefully dedicate this book.

CONTENTS

Preface		ix
1 A BRIEF INTRODUCTION TO THE NATURE OF LAW		1
Where does the law come from?		1
Of courts and lawyers		3
The purpose and scope of this text		4
2 CONTRACTS		7
What is a contract?		7
The typical vendor contract		8
Breach of contract		19
Contract remedies		23
Misrepresentation, fraud, and other shields and weapons		36
Some suggestions concerning computer contracts		41
3 COMPUTER TORTS		45
Negligence and malpractice		45
Strict liability		56
Additional topics in product liability		61
Other torts		65
4 LEGAL PROTECTION OF SOFTWARE		79
The nature of the problem		79
Copyright		84
Patents		93
Trade secrecy and contracts		109
Possibilities for the future		114
5 CRIME		121
The nature of crime		121
Theft		127
Other state and federal statutes		136
New legislation		142

6 EVIDENCE 153

    Discovery 153
    Evidence at trial 163
    Trial and after 170

Appendix 1: A Brief Guide to Legal References and Citations 177

Appendix 2: *IBM* v. *Catamore Enterprises* 183

Appendix 3: Selected Sections of the Copyright Law of 1976 192

Appendix 4: *Parker* v. *Flook* 195

Appendix 5: *Data General Corp* v. *Digital Computer Controls, Inc.* 207

Appendix 6: *Monarch Federal Savings* 213

Appendix 7: *United States* v. *Russo* 219

GLOSSARY 225

INDEX 237

PREFACE

Computer science, in the few decades since the first stored-program computer was built, has evolved at a rate that has outstripped society's ability to deal with the novel issues this technology has raised. In no area is this fact more evident than in the law which is just now beginning to recognize that its classical concepts and rules literally cannot "do justice" with regard to much actual and potential computer-related litigation. There can be little doubt that vendors, buyers, operators and other computer professionals have proceeded until now without more than at most a nod toward major legal issues, if not, indeed, a total ignorance of such issues.

This book is intended to acquaint those who work with computers, but who have no training in law, with basic legal concepts and some of the principal issues of law relating to computing. Because the law, even computer law, is so vast in its scope, only selected materials can be included in a single text. And because this area of law is developing so rapidly, much of what this text contains may already be out-of-date. Nevertheless, the fundamental legal concepts and the necessity for the computer professional to be aware of those legal issues which significantly affect his work remain. Just as Business Law has long been a core course in the business administration curriculum, so too computer law must certainly become a central part of the education of anyone who holds a position of responsibility in computing.

Much of material in Chapters IV and V appeared in the RUTGERS JOURNAL OF COMPUTERS, TECHNOLOGY AND THE LAW and the INDIANA LAW REVIEW. I thank Robert Macek, my editor, who was of considerable assistance as I wrote this book, and I thank as well the unnamed reviewers for their thoughtful comments.

LAW
and the
COMPUTER

1

A BRIEF INTRODUCTION TO THE NATURE OF LAW

WHERE DOES LAW COME FROM?

It is probably fair to say that most citizens' ideas about the law are negative. The law orders us *not* to drive 40 miles per hour in a 30 mile per hour zone. If we choose to disregard this negative command, then we risk suffering penalties. The law commands us not to steal or murder under pain of suffering serious punishment. The law tells most businesses that they must file numerous reports and forms with the federal government, certainly something that businesses do not view in a very positive way. We may say to ourselves, "The law ought to be simple and readily understood so that all persons can understand and follow it," yet the law's complexity seems to increase at an ever-greater rate so that even lawyers have difficulty comprehending it. Yet the popular view of a perhaps unpopular legal system encompasses but a small part of that system. Before beginning a discussion of computer-related law, it is necessary to have some idea of what "law" in general is and where it comes from.

Despite the belief of many that law should be, and can be, made much simpler than it is, law as it exists today is highly complex. The concept of "law" as used here will not include a variety of legal processes and functions. A municipal ordinance which forbids driving at a speed greater than 25 miles per hour in a certain zone is part of the law; and the officer who arrests a speeder in that zone is performing a legal function, but that function is part of a broader notion of law than will be employed in this text. Likewise, the process of a trial is different from the positions that the attorneys representing each party in the trial will try to convince the judge is really the law governing the

Rules of law

case being tried; and each of these remains distinct from any questions of fact, that is, questions about what really took place, which a judge or jury may have to determine. The law this text deals with is really the rules of law, the rules that try to determine who has a right to what property, who has the power to do what things, what is wrong, and what is right in the eyes of the legal system.

Sources of law

The rules of law come from three basic sources: the federal and state constitutions and statutes, case or common law, and rules and regulations of administrative agencies. The broad outlines and fundamental principles of government and law within the United States are spelled out in the Constitution. Each state has its own constitution, but these may not contradict the Constitution of the United States. The Congress and state legislatures pass statutory laws. None of these statutes should contradict the federal Constitution and no state statute should contradict the constitution of the state that adopts it. In many areas, states are not free to pass statutes because the federal government has declared that area to be under its sole control because of powers given it by the Constitution. No state, for example, is free to declare war on another state or country.

Statutes and general rules of law are not always clear; it is not always obvious what they mean or when they apply. Nor is it always clear whether or how some rule of law applies in some specific situation. There may even be a question whether a given statute or rule of law was adopted in an improper manner or contradicts an even higher rule of law, and, hence, is invalid. Who then is to make this decision how to interpret a certain law, or even whether a given statute is void? This is the role of the courts. Very simplistically, the legislative branch of government passes laws in the form of statutes, and the courts interpret those laws, thus sometimes making new law in the process.

A state larceny statute may declare, for example, that the subject matter of larceny—that is, an object that is capable of being stolen, in the eyes of the law—is "something of value." The phrase "something of value" could be interpreted as requiring that some specific value be proved for some object in order to be able to convict someone accused of stealing it; or it could mean that it suffices for the prosecution to prove that the item in question just has some value, however small or uncertain, in order to establish the item could be an object of theft. It would be up to courts, unless there is some express and clear intent on the part of the legislature concerning the matter, to determine whether some specific actual value must be proved, or a mere proof of some real, though wholly unknown, worth was required.

Case law

When deciding an issue of law, that is, giving an interpretation of the law, a judge or group of judges usually produces an opinion, which is a written statement setting forth the reasons behind the decision reached. These opinions are an important source of information about the law, because they inform us what the courts believe the law to be. Because courts are likely to be guided in the future by what they have said in the past, these opinions offer a guide as to how the courts issuing them will act when presented with various questions of law. The body of interpretations of the law handed down by the courts forms the case, or common, law.

No one should believe that courts are unfettered in what they can do or in the conclusions they can reach about the law. A lower court can be overruled or reversed by a higher court. No court, high or low, can act outside its proper jurisdiction. There are many laws that bind the courts, but this is not the proper text to discuss this matter. Nevertheless, it is important to understand that the courts themselves are a source of law. They also remain those bodies to which citizens must resort to redress real or imagined grievances that cannot be settled outside the courtroom, and to which they turn to seek many clarifications of the law.

In addition to the legislatures and courts, there is a third source of law, an area of government that shares aspects of all three branches of government—executive, legislative, and judicial—and that source is the administrative agencies. An administrative agency is established by legislative action under broad guidelines to provide rules and regulation in some important area of society, such as interstate commerce. Administrative agencies can be involved in both adjudication and fact-finding as well as rule-making, and the rules that an agency makes generally have the force of law. Administrative rules and findings are often subject to review in the courts. This is, however, a highly technical and complicated subject and, again, not one which is appropriate to explore at length in this text. But because administrative law undoubtedly affects computer professionals now, and will affect them even more in the future, we must deal with this area to some extent in later sections.

<small>Administrative agencies</small>

OF COURTS AND LAWYERS

The role of a good attorney is not simply to defend his or her client in court when that is necessary, but to keep the client out of court in the first place. Someone resorts to a court after a conflict has arisen which cannot be resolved in any other way than formal litigation. The good lawyer should try to keep the client from such conflicts. But because in this country anyone can file suit on any one of numerous grounds it is too much to expect that an active business man or woman will never be in court. The next best thing to never being brought to court is to have one's adversary's case dismissed by the court as being insubstantial as a matter of law. The good lawyer should try to make his or her client's position as genuinely unassailable as possible, thus effectively blocking anyone wishing to bring the client to court before the matters in question get to trial. That too, of course, is not always possible.

A law student learns a great deal of law in three years of law school, but the purpose of law school is not primarily to teach the law. There is so much law in so many different areas that no one, not even the most capable and famous of all attorneys, ever really knows more than a small fraction of it at any one time. What law school teaches the future attorney is to review a particular situation, identify the special legal issues and problems that the situation presents, and then to do the research necessary to address the issues and propose solutions to the problems.

<small>Rarely one solution</small>

Rarely does a legal problem have only one solution. Our legal system is adversarial in nature. Cases do not come before courts until there is some conflict, and there is more than one party in any conflict. Each party in a case believes in the rightness of its cause. The lawyer for each party will of course attempt to argue as persuasively as possible for the court to adopt his or her client's view of the facts and the law.

In rendering a legal opinion for a client, then, a lawyer must anticipate what opposing positions might be, because these are the positions that will be argued if the matter is ever litigated. It may seem that an attorney always hedges his or her bets, never coming down solidly on one position or another. A lawyer can support any legally defensible position, but must keep in mind that there may be, and usually are, other lawyers willing and able to defend an opposing viewpoint. For better or worse, that is the system of justice, of arriving at the "truth" in the courtroom, that we have in this country.

The lawyer, in short, analyzes his or her client's situation, and suggests and if necessary defends the position which he or she feels is both lawful and most beneficial to the client. The lawyer is trained to spot issues of law and to find the required answers.

THE PURPOSE AND SCOPE OF THIS TEXT

This is not intended as a text that will enable computer professionals to be their own attorneys. It is not intended as a do-it-yourself legal kit, but to

1. Acquaint the reader with some basic legal concepts and terminology, as these relate to computing;
2. Enable the reader to recognize more easily and more quickly potential legal problems in his or her work, and thus know when the help of an attorney might be required;

3. Aid the reader in communicating more effectively with an attorney. This includes both explaining the potentially or actually troublesome situation as well as understanding more clearly the attorney's response.

The reader should expect few clear-cut answers to any legal questions in this text. There are many good reasons for this. First, each computer user's situation is individual and unique. Any attempt to generalize to fit all situations is foolish and dangerous. Sometimes minor differences in a fact pattern can make a major change in how the law views a certain situation. Second, much of the law relating to computing is state law, and state law differs from state to state. What may pertain to trade secrets in California, for example, may not be valid in Virginia. Local attorneys know best what the local law is. Third, and perhaps most important, computer law is a very new and rapidly evolving area of the law. There is simply no settled body of computer law anywhere. No doubt major decisions will be reached and laws passed, even as this text is being published, which will make some of it obsolete before you even read it. Yet the basic legal issues will still be relevant. You should be able to identify these so that you then can go to an attorney to find out what the latest state of the law actually is.

Understanding now what this text is and what it is not, let us get on with the business of exploring some of the important legal concepts and questions as they pertain to computing.

Few clear-cut answers

SOME GENERAL SOURCES ON COMPUTER-RELATED LAW

The *Rutgers Journal of Computers, Technology and the Law* (until recently the *Rutgers Journal of Computers and the Law*) is a law review that is largely dedicated to computer-related law. It also regularly publishes book reviews and bibliographies in this area. Its editorial and business offices are located at the Rutgers Law School, 15 Washington Street, Newark, NJ 07102. The *Computer Law Service* and *Computer Law Service Reporter* are a loose-leaf and reporter series published by Callaghan and Co., 3201 Old Glenview Road, Wilmette, IL 60091; the editor is Robert Bigelow. An early survey text is *Your Computer and the Law* by Robert Bigelow and Susan Nycum, published in 1975 by Prentice-Hall. Survey articles appear from time to time in various journals; see, for example: R. Raysman, "DP and the Law," in the "In Depth" section of *Computerworld*, March 10, 1980; and John Lautsch, "Computers and the University Attorney: An Overview of Computer Law on Campus," *Journal of College and University Law*, Vol. 5, No. 4 (1979) (this entire issue is devoted to Mr. Lautsch's article).

The Computer Law Association (address: c/o Michael Yourshaw, 1776 K Street, NW, Washington, D.C. 20006) publishes proceedings of conferences on various topics of computer-related law.

Roy Freed (address: c/o Powers & Hall, 30 Federal St., Boston, MA 02110) is a prolific computer lawyer who has privately published a compilation of articles, opinions, and miscellany on a wide variety of topics. The Fifth Edition of *Computers and the Law: A Reference Work* came out in 1976.

Jurimetrics, the journal of the Section on Science and Technology of the American Bar Association (address: ABA, 1155 E. 60th Street, Chicago, IL 60637) often contains excellent material related to computer law. The Spring 1980 issue is completely devoted to "Digest and Analysis of State Legislation Relating to Computing Technology" by John Lautsch.

2

CONTRACTS

WHAT IS A CONTRACT?

In essence, a contract is a promise that the law is willing to enforce. As is true of most legal concepts, however, there is no simple definition of contract, nor any certain test to see whether any given agreement rises to the level of a contract. Yet the contract has for a long time been one of the notions at the very core of business law.

There are at least two parties to any contract: the party that promises to do, or refrain from doing, something, known as the promisor, and the party to whom the promise is made, known as the promisee. A contract implies a meeting of the minds of the parties, an agreement concerning the terms of the contract. It also implies that something of value, known technically as consideration, passes between the parties. The courts will generally not enforce a purely gratuitous promise. Thus, if you say to a friend, "I am going to give you $50 tonight," and there is nothing to be given in return, such as a power saw or stamp collection, then the friend is unlikely to be successful in a suit for the $50 if you do not pay. One common form of consideration is a return promise; for example, "I will write a program to enable your computer to keep your accounts if you will promise to pay me $5000 when the job is completed." A promise to do certain work is exchanged for a promise to pay when the work is completed.

<small>Essentials of a contract</small>

The formation of a contract generally begins with an offer made by one of the parties; for example, "I will paint the fence around your house for $50." The contract is created if both parties understand the terms of the offer and the second party accepts the offer; "All right, I will pay you $50 if you paint the fence around my house." A problem arises, and there may be no contract formed, if the parties understand

<small>Formation of a contract</small>

quite different things by the offer. For example, if the party accepting the offer is speaking about the fence that surrounds his 500-acre country estate, but the other party offers to paint a fence for $50 believing the fence in question is the picket fence enclosing the offeree's small town cottage, then there has been no agreement, and hence no contract, because the two parties have not been able to agree on the fence to be painted.

All this may seem somewhat elementary. After all, to have a genuine promise, you need someone to whom the promise is made. If one person is to give something to another, then it is not unreasonable to expect that other person to give something in return if he or she wishes to enforce the original promise in a court of law. And if two people cannot agree on what they are to exchange, then it hardly seems right to make them go ahead with the exchange anyway. If all contracts involved painting fences, life and the law would be much simpler indeed.

But, of course, problems do arise that do not have easy solutions. The contractor may begin building a house only to find that an underground river runs through the basement, and insists the job cannot be completed at the agreed-upon price because of the unforeseen complication. A saleswoman claims that the paint will not peel for at least five years, but the written contract expressly states that no promise is made concerning how long the paint will go without peeling. The seller tells the buyer to pick up his piano at the factory in Walla Walla although the buyer in New York assumed it would be delivered to his home: no mention is made of the place of delivery in the contract. These are but a minute fraction of the dilemmas that anyone doing business can face each day in the area of contracts.

It is axiomatic that each party to a contract wants the better deal for him- or herself. Each party will therefore attempt to have the contract drawn with as many clauses and terms favorable to him- or herself as possible, and, conversely, with as few clauses and terms favorable to the other party as possible. The next best thing to scoring a point yourself is avoiding letting your opponent score against you. The typical computer or computer services vendor contract is usually roundly laced with terms highly protective of the vendor.

THE TYPICAL VENDOR CONTRACT

There are three principal tools a vendor will use as protective shields should anything go wrong with his or her product. These are disclaimer of warranties, limitations on remedies, and integration clauses. We consider each of these in order.

Disclaimer of warranties

A warranty is essentially a guarantee that some product or service will live up to certain expectations. A computer vendor may warrant less than a certain percentage of downtime. If the downtime exceeds the warranted amount, the vendor may be in breach of warranty and be liable for damages caused by the excessive downtime.

Warranty

Warranties can be either express or implied. An express warranty is one which the warrantor spells out expressly. "This car will go 50,000 miles without any repairs," is an example of an express warranty. Express warranties can be created in several ways. Below is quoted Section 2-313 of the Uniform Commercial Code; the code is a vitally important piece of legislation adopted in some form in every state except Louisiana.

Express warranties

1. Express warranties by the seller are created as follows:
    a) Any affirmation of fact or promise made by the seller to the buyer which relates to the goods and becomes part of the basis of the bargain creates an express warranty that the goods will conform to the affirmation or promise.
    b) Any description of the goods which is made part of the basis of the bargain creates an express warranty that the goods shall conform to the description.
    c) Any sample or model which is made part of the basis of the bargain creates an express warranty that the whole of the goods shall conform to the sample or model.
2. It is not necessary to the creation of an express warranty that the seller use formal words such as "warrant" or "guarantee" or that he have a specific intention to make a warranty, but an affirmation merely of the value of the goods or a statement purporting to be merely the seller's opinion or commendation of the goods does not create a warranty.

Note that this section of the Uniform Commercial Code (UCC) speaks of a warranty created by a *seller*. Article 2 of the UCC, of which the section quoted above is a part, deals only with "transactions in goods." Services are not considered to be goods according to the UCC. Because much computer equipment is leased rather than sold, and because many computer-related contracts or purchases deal with services (such as maintenance), it is far from clear that this section of express warranties can be applied in any but very special circumstances, specifically, where something that is recognizable as goods, such as hardware, is actually sold. Despite this seeming drawback in the express wording of the section, many courts are willing to apply the principles of the section, and of Article 2 generally, by analogy to leases and provision of services; but not all courts are willing to do this.

Note too that the seller does not have to make formal reference to the word "warranty" in order to be held bound by an express warranty. The salesperson, who is usually considered to be an agent of, and able to speak for, the seller can make express warranty simply by asserting that the product is capable of doing thus and so. If a salesman says that a particular system has sufficient memory to solve a particular class of problems, that may constitute an express warranty binding the seller if the ability to solve problems of that class is one of the principal reasons the buyer chose that particular machine. If the salesman points to a picture of an IBM 370/158 and says, "My Ipswitch 001 does everything that machine does," he has made an express warranty if the reason, or one of the basic reasons, why the buyer chooses that machine is that she wants the capabilities of an IBM 370/158. If the Ipswitch 001 can't live up to the warranty, then the seller may be liable for damages in breach of warranty.

One of the most important forms of express warranties is the Warranty of Fitness for a Particular Purpose. Basically, this warranty arises when the seller knows that the buyer is relying upon the product to do a particular task and upon the expertise of the seller in selecting a product that can do the job. If a businessman comes to a computer vendor and describes the requirements of his particular business, and relies on the vendor to suggest an appropriate machine to fill those needs, then by suggesting a particular computer system, the vendor may make an express warranty of fitness for a particular purpose; in this case, the purpose is to satisfy the computing needs of the business-purchaser.

Implied warranties

Express warranties are thus rather strong promises, at least in the eyes of the law, that a seller makes stating that a product will perform in a certain way; these warranties must be stated explicitly in some form in order to be enforceable, or even to exist at all. The law, however, also provides some implied warranties. An implied warranty is one which automatically attaches to the goods sold unless the seller successfully disclaims it.

One of the most important protections any buyer has is the implied Warranty of Merchantability. Again, we quote at length from a section of the Uniform Commercial Code:

§2-314. Implied Warranty: Merchantability; Usage of Trade
1. Unless excluded or modified, a warranty that the goods shall be merchantable is implied in a contract for their sale if the seller is a merchant with respect to goods of that kind. . . .
2. Goods to be merchantable must be at least such as
    a) pass without objection in the trade under the contract description; and . . .
    b) are fit for the ordinary purposes for which such goods are used; and

c) run, within the variations permitted by the agreement, of even kind, quality and quantity within each unit and among all units involved; and
   d) are adequately contained, packaged, and labeled as the agreement may require; and
   e) conform to the promises or affirmations of fact made on the container or label if any.
3. Unless excluded or modified other implied warranties may arise from course of dealing or usage of trade.

Observe that merchantability includes having all of the properties described in (2), not merely one or two of them. Probably the most important of these properties, however, is set forth in (2)(c). A computer, to be merchantable, must be fit for the ordinary purposes for which a computer is used; that is, it must compute. It may even reasonably be expected to compute without undue downtime or excessive mistakes caused by operating systems failure. Merely to sell a computer does not make someone a "merchant" with respect to computers, a condition required to make this section applicable to the sale. But anyone trying to sell a computer will almost always be either a merchant with respect to computers, or else someone who has purchased a computer and then simply wants to get rid of it. A sale by the latter will almost always be on an "as is," or "buyer beware" basis, while a sale by the former of even a used computer may include an implied Warranty of Merchantability.

From the vendor's viewpoint, warranties are points scored by the "opponent," the purchaser; therefore the vendor will try to avoid making any warranties. Express warranties might be avoided by not saying anything very specific about the product. A mere statement that "This is a good computer," or "This machine will please you," does not create an express warranty. On the other hand, the implied Warranty of Merchantability is present in every sale unless the vendor takes some positive action to get rid of it. The Uniform Commercial Code permits vendors to disclaim the Warranty of Merchantability. Section 2-316 of the UCC reads in part:

Disclaimer of warranty

   2. Subject to subsection (3), to exclude or modify the implied warranty of merchantability or any part of it the language must mention merchantability and in case of a writing must be conspicuous, and to exclude or modify any implied warranty of fitness [for a particular purpose] the exclusion must be by a writing and conspicuous. Language to exclude all implied warranties of fitness is sufficient if it states, for example, that "There are no warranties which extend beyond the description on the face hereof."
   3. Notwithstanding subsection (2)
      a) unless the circumstances indicate otherwise, all implied warranties are excluded by expressions like "as is", "with all faults" or

other language which in common understanding calls the buyer's attention to the exclusion of warranties and makes plain that there is no implied warranty; and

b) when the buyer before entering into the contract has examined the goods or the sample or model as fully as he desired or has refused to examine the goods there is no implied warranty with regard to defects which an examination ought in the circumstances to have revealed to him; and

c) an implied warranty can also be excluded or modified by course of dealing or course of performance or usage of trade.

We will return to warranties later; in particular, we will want to know what a buyer can do to be protected against attempts by the vendor to avoid any warranties. For the moment, we simply note that although the UCC provides warranty protections for a buyer, it also permits the seller to take them away if he or she goes about it properly. The typical disclaimer clause in a vendor supplied contract reads:

> Vendor does not make any express or implied warranties, including, but not limited to, the implied warranties of merchantability and fitness for a particular purpose.

If you are a computer purchaser or buyer of computer services, a clause such as the above is clearly not in your best interests. It is particularly disconcerting to find such a clause in the written contract after a salesman has been promising you that the machine or service will be everything you really want and more. This subject will be returned to later.

Limitations of remedies

Remedy

A second vendor protective device in common use within the computer industry is limitation of remedies. A remedy is something the law supplies to make an injured party "whole." If a cement plant next door to your home is spewing huge amounts of dust and noxious gases into the air, making you cough and ruining your furniture, one remedy may be a court order, or injunction, which tells the concrete plant to close down. Or the remedy may be an order to the plant to pay you money to compensate you for the inconvenience and the decreased value of your property caused by its operation. If your computer crashes and causes a major loss of business records, for example, then you may reasonably believe that you are entitled to some remedy if the failure is traced to the design or construction of the machine or its operating system. You may believe that payment for the cost of reconstructing the records is a just and suitable remedy in that situation. Naturally, the vendor who sold you the machine may believe otherwise.

Part (4) of Section 2-316 of the Uniform Commercial Code, quoted above in connection with disclaimers of warranties, reads:

> Remedies for breach of warranty can be limited in accordance with the provisions of this Article on liquidation of damages and on contractual modification of remedy.

UCC—
Limitation
of remedies

In the vendor's eyes, the next best thing to making no guarantees at all concerning the product is having to pay as little as possible if something goes wrong. One means of effecting this is through a provision for "liquidated damages." Liquidated damages are some specified sum of money, agreed to at the time of contracting, that will be paid in the event of injury caused by the product. The sum to be paid is fixed in advance and does not depend on what any actual losses might be. The seller of a fire alarm system might set liquidated damages of $50 if the system fails and a factory burns to the ground, even if the overall value of the fire damage may run into the millions of dollars.

The law is not totally unreasonable and there are severe restrictions on the use of liquidated damages as a means to limit liability. The amount of liquidated damages provided for in an agreement must be *reasonable* in the light of *both* the anticipated harm and the harm that actually occurs. Moreover, there must have been some good reason for resorting to liquidated damages in the first place. The contracting parties may expect great difficulties in proving any loss, or there might be substantial inconvenience or difficulty in obtaining some "adequate" remedy.

By way of example, consider the following. A service bureau contracts with a business to keep track of its inventory. In the service bureau's form contract is a clause that limits any liability it may have, in case of failure to do the job properly, to exactly the cost of three months' fees. Inasmuch as the provision of services of this sort is not a transaction in goods, the contract probably would not fall under the state UCC provisions. As pointed out before, however, a court might be willing to treat the situation by analogy to UCC provisions, that is, extend the terms of the UCC to provision of services. In any event, the law relating to liquidated damages is fairly well settled even without reference to the UCC. The service bureau will argue that liquidated damages are appropriate if they fail to provide adequate service because it is impossible to estimate ahead of time what sort of damage a failure on their part would cause, and because much of the damage claimed by the business in the event of inadequate service is likely to be too speculative to actually prove. The business might state that it could have sold 1000 additional gross of widgets if the bureau had kept proper stock of its inventory, but a claim concerning future unmade sales is necessarily speculative. If the business relies heavily on the bureau for purchasing decisions and suffers loss because the bureau fails to provide reliable information, the damages may be far and away more than the bureau's fees for three months. Should such a misfortune befall the business (and such misfortunes have occurred), it would argue that the liquidated damages provided in the contract bear no rational relationship to the harm caused by the bureau's malfeasance and that the damages here, or at least part of them, are easily provable. Who would prevail in such an instance? Actual cases have gone both ways and the law concerning such economic harm caused by software failures is not settled.

What vendors of computers or computer services fear most are claims for so-called consequential damages. Consequential damages follow later as a result of the direct harm done by some injury. For example, lost sales due to downtime in a computer are consequential damages. If a factory burns to the ground, the wages lost by unemployed workers are consequential to the destruction of the factory, as are profits lost to the shareholders who owned the factory in the first place. As large as general damages caused by an injury may be, for example the value of the factory destroyed because of faulty wiring, the consequential damages may be even larger and extend into the indefinite future as well. Moreover, a vendor may have little or no idea how the product will ultimately be used. A computer used to monitor the vital functions of patients in an intensive care unit has greater chance of threatening life in the event of a malfunction than a similar computer in the hospital billing department, yet a vendor may know only that he or she is selling a machine to a hospital, and not at all how it will be used once it is installed. Vendors, therefore, often make a special point of disclaiming any responsibility for consequential damages, and the UCC permits this:

> Consequential damages may be limited or excluded unless the limitation or exclusion is unconscionable. Limitation of consequential damages for injury to the person in the case of consumer goods is *prima facie* unconscionable but limitation of damages where the loss is commercial is not.

This quote is taken from Section 2-719 of the UCC. Generally speaking, a computer used in a business would not be a "consumer good" so that consequential damages for personal injuries might be limited in a vendor contract. A typical vendor contract clause limiting remedies reads:

> The Customer agrees that Vendor's liability hereunder for damages, regardless of the form of action, shall not exceed the total amount paid for services under the applicable Service Estimate or in authorization for the particular service if no Service Estimate is made. This shall be the Cus-

tomer's exclusive remedy. In no event shall the Vendor be liable for any consequential damages, even if it has been advised in advance of the possibility of such damages.

Translated into simple language, this reads:

> If anything goes wrong for whatever reason, the most the Vendor is obligated to do is give the Customer his or her money back. This is true even if the Customer fully informed the Vendor of damages he or she would suffer if Vendor's product did not perform as expected.

Once again, however, the law does not always take such obviously one-sided conditions as valid and enforceable, and the customer may have more remedies than the seller is willing to concede. We will return to customer's rights later in this text.

The vendor may further seek to limit a remedy by specifying a definite time within which a remedy must be sought; the buyer who failed to seek a remedy within the time allotted would be barred from ever seeking a remedy under the contract. If the time period within which a remedy can be sought is too short, a court will not allow the provision to stand; but one year is usually considered adequate. Thus, a vendor may place a clause in the contract that states that any party to the contract must seek a remedy for breach of contract or breach of warranty under the terms of the contract within one year after the contract is formed, or lose the right to any remedy later. Unless there is some good reason for not honoring the clause—for example, deliberate concealment by the vendor of some defect in the product—courts are likely to find this clause valid, especially in a commercial setting.

Time limitations

Integration clauses

A written contract, of course, is intended to embody the agreement reached by the parties to the contract. Conflicts can arise if one party claims that some part of the agreement is not contained in what has been written down, or when a party claims that something that is written down is contrary to what was actually agreed upon orally. For example, the former situation would occur if the buyer of a computer system alleges that the vendor promised her complete installation by July 1, but there is no mention of any specific installation date in the written contract; the latter situation would occur if the contract stated that installation had to be completed only by September 1, despite the buyer's claim of having been promised an earlier date.

Vendors in particular will want to avoid any rash promises or claims that might have been made for them by sales representatives.

Integration clause

They also have worked out their form contracts carefully and do not want changes or additions made by oral agreement between sales staff and customers. Therefore virtually every computer contract has what is known as an integration clause. The following is a typical such clause.

> There are no understandings, agreements, representations, or warranties, express or implied (including any regarding the merchantability or fitness for a particular purpose), not specified herein, respecting this contract or equipment hereunder. This contract states the entire obligation of the seller in connection with this transaction.

This is called an integration clause because it declares all of the agreements that form the entire contract between the parties have been integrated into the writing. The writing then is the exclusive statement of the terms of the contract.

Parol evidence rule

The presence of an integration clause has special importance because of a very old rule of law known as the Parol Evidence Rule. This rule in its classic form states that no oral or written evidence of agreements prior to, or contemporaneous with, the creation of the written contract can be introduced if such evidence contradicts, varies, or modifies an unambiguous written contract that the parties intend to be a final and complete expression of their agreement. This rule, despite its antiquity or perhaps because of it, is a legal swamp, and its harsh effects have been softened by the ways that many courts interpret or even ignore it.

If the Parol Evidence Rule were applied strictly, then a written contract whose integration clause contained a provision that no maintenance would be provided free at any time would prevent the buyer from introducing a letter from a salesman, written before the contract was signed, which promised that maintenance would be provided free for six months and that the no-free-maintenance clause in the standard contract would not apply to him. Such evidence might be introduced in court for some other reason, for example to show fraud, but it could not be introduced solely to prove that maintenance was to be provided free. Fraud, misrepresentation, and various other nasty things that might arise in a contract dispute will be discussed later.

The more modern views hold that all evidence may be introduced to show the intention of the parties. Courts too may be quick to find ambiguities, and thus no unambiguous contract, from the mere fact that there is a dispute among the parties. Or a court may find that the written contract is not really a final or complete expression. It may not be final if some matters are yet to be settled after it is signed, nor is it complete if there are terms that are yet to be agreed upon. A finding that the writing is incomplete or not final will take it at least partially out of the coverage of the Parol Evidence Rule.

What happens if a written contract, or even an oral one, simply fails to provide for some important element, such as time or place of delivery or even the price? Prior to the Uniform Commercial Code, if some critical point was left undetermined, the contract might well be null and void, because it would be assumed that the parties had not really concluded their dickering to the point of actually reaching an agreement at all. If it was clearly the intention of the parties to have a contract, the Uniform Commercial Code and many courts will supply the missing terms, usually substituting something like "reasonable time" or "reasonable price" for the missing term. There are likewise rules for resolving terms which may be ambiguous. Courts, for example, will look at any performance under a contract offered and accepted without dispute, prior to the dispute that brought the parties into court, for an indication of what the parties intended in the way of performance.

Gaps in contracts

The disclaimer of warranties, the limitation of remedies, and the integration clause are three important "weapons" that the vendor will try to use as a shield against the disappointed customer. These are formidable weapons, to be sure, and in many instances well respected by the courts. But the customer is not left defenseless by the law to the mercies of the vendor. Later we will see some of the buyer protective devices.

We close this section with a brief look at a classical business situation, the "Battle of the Forms." What happens when one business makes an offer to another business using its form and all the provisions that form contains to protect the offeror, and the second business accepts the offer on its own form which, of course, contains many protective provisions of its own, some of which conflict with the terms of the offer? Whose form wins out in case of a dispute?

Battle of the forms

It must be pointed out that in virtually all instances in which a contract is formed by the exchange of offer and acceptance forms, no conflict ever arises. Company A orders 1000 widgets from Company B, specifying in fine print on the back of the order form that they have the right to cancel the order without penalty for 90 days after acceptance, and Company B accepts the order and fills it, even though its fine print reads that there can be no cancellation of the order following acceptance thereof. The 1000 widgets and the payment are exchanged, and no one even bothers to read the fine print in either form. This is the way most business is done.

According to classic contract law, if an acceptance of an offer included terms different from those of the original offer, it was not really an acceptance at all, but a counter-offer that needed a separate acceptance by the original offeror in order for a contract to be formed. Therefore, according to classic contract law, an exchange of forms that were not mirror images of one another did not create a contract. The companies involved might be doing business quite frequently and harmoniously, but they were doing so without a contract. The modern trend, and definitely that of the Uniform Commercial Code, is to protect intended contracts and not to void them on the basis of technicalities. If an offer and acceptance vary in relatively minor ways, then it seems natural to let the major area of agreement stand as the basis for the contract. The actual section of the UCC (2-207) that deals with this problem reads as follows:

1. A definite and seasonable expression of acceptance or a written confirmation which is sent within a reasonable time operates as an acceptance even though it states terms additional to or different from those offered or agreed upon, unless acceptance is expressly made conditional on assent to the additional or different terms.
2. The additional terms are to be constructed as proposals for additions to the contract. Between merchants such terms become part of the contract unless:
    a) the offer expressly limits acceptance to the terms of the offer;
    b) they materially alter it; or
    c) notification of objection to them has already been given or is given within a reasonable time after notice of them is received.
3. Conduct by both parties which recognizes the existence of a contract is sufficient to establish a contract for sale although the writings of the parties do not otherwise establish a contract. In such case the terms of the particular contract consist of those terms on which the writings of the parties agree, together with any supplementary terms incorporated under any other provisions of the [Uniform Commercial Code].

As reasonable and as well-intentioned as this provision is, its principal effect may have been to make businesses redesign their forms. Company A will now send a form offer that includes a clause stating that the offer expressly limits acceptance to the terms offered; Company B will reply with a form that gives its own additional or conflicting terms. Now the parties still do not have a contract. But they will probably act as if they do, and this action, at least in the case of a sale, suffices to establish a contract at least as to those parts of the forms on which they find themselves in agreement. What happens when there is no sale or no transaction in goods is for the courts to decide in each case.

We have dealt thus far primarily with the making of a contract and with some of its possible terms. We now explore what happens when the promises embodied in a contract are broken.

BREACH OF CONTRACT

What is "breach of contract?"

It is necessary and useful in a text such as this occasionally to remind the reader that the treatment of the law herein is by no means exhaustive. Merely the highlights of the law are touched upon, and not even all of those. Breach of contract seems at first glance to be a comparatively easy concept. One party breaches a contract by failing to live up to its terms, that is, failing to keep the promises made in the agreement. One should certainly be able to readily determine whether a promise has been fulfilled. But what if the promise has "almost" been fulfilled, as when 4999 widgets have been delivered instead of the contracted-for 5000? And what if one party says to the other, "I know you promised to deliver the goods by July 1, but you may have until August 1," yet the contract states in clear and certain terms that what has been written in it constitutes the whole and entire contract and cannot be changed? There is even a problem at times in determining precisely what promises have actually been made. Consider the following situation.

A is having a new computer system installed for the purpose of offering computer services to businesses. A expects installation of her system to be completed by July 1. A contracts to supply services to B, and in their contract is included a clause, "A's computer system is to be up and running not later than July 1." What are the consequences if A's computer system is not up and running by July 1? Whether or not there is a broken promise, and hence a breach of contract for which A may be liable to B for damages, depends on whether or not the clause in question embodies a promise in the first place.

The clause, "A's computer system is to be up and running not later than July 1," may be interpreted as a promise, that is, as an agreement by A that her computer system will be operative by July 1. It might also, however, be interpreted merely as an express condition that must be fulfilled before the contract becomes fully effective. With this interpretation, it should be read, "*If* A's computer is not up and running not later than July 1, then there is no duty to perform on the part of either party." The clause might even be taken merely as a statement of intent, "A expects her computer system to be up and running by July 1," which does not go to the heart of the agreement at all, the real agreement being that A will supply services to B as soon as her system is up and running.

One thing to look for then when it appears that a contract has been breached is the presence of conditions. Conditions can be of various sorts. There are conditions that must occur before the parties have an obligation to perform their respective duties; these are known as con-

Breach

Conditions precedent and subsequent

ditions precedent. If a condition precedent does not occur, then usually both parties are absolved from performance. There are also conditions that will void the contract if they occur. Such conditions are known as conditions subsequent. These are rather rare in contracts and of little practical importance. With a condition precedent, the condition must occur first before the contract becomes operative; in the case of a condition subsequent, the contract is operative unless the condition occurs, at which time it then becomes of no effect.

_{Conditions express and implied}
Conditions are also characterized as express or implied. An express condition, like an express warranty, is one that is set forth explicitly. An implied condition is one that is reasonable in light of the overall terms and intent of the parties to the contract. If A is to supply computer services to B, then it is incumbent upon B to cooperate with A and supply A with such data and information as A needs to properly carry out the task. If B refuses to cooperate, then the failure of that condition excuses A's performance, although it may constitute a breach of contract on the part of B. The contract does not have to state explicitly that B should cooperate with A in a reasonable way. The law expects parties to act in good faith.

It would really be more correct to say that the failure of a condition precedent makes the contract voidable by a party for whose benefit the condition has been included, rather than simply void. B may wish to have A supply computer services even if the installation of A's system is late; B would then not wish to cancel the contract despite the failure of the condition precedent. It should also go without saying that A cannot in bad faith avoid the contract by interfering with the occurrence of a condition precedent. For example, if A sees that the contract with B is likely to result in a loss, A cannot refuse to have the system installed so as to make performance impossible or avoid the July 1 date, at least unless the contract gives her this right.

Implied conditions are also known as constructive conditions. They are law-created conditions intended to make contracts reasonable and fair. From a purely practical point of view as well, it is usually impossible to cover every eventuality in a contract, and some provisions of an agreement must be understood as dictated by the very nature of the agreement or by fair play and common sense. There is the possibility, as will be seen later, of being too clever in drafting a contract.

Just as the law wants to see justice done in the interpretation of a contract by the imposition of implied or constructive conditions, so too the law does not favor one party to a contract taking unfair advantage of the other party, or being unjustly enriched by invoking some technical breach.

_{Material breach}
A material breach of contract is one which permits the aggrieved party to cancel the contract entirely, avoid performance on his or her

part and sue the breaching party for "total" breach. If the breach is not serious enough to be material, then the injured party may still sue for damages, but may not avoid his or her obligations under the contract.

Unfortunately, there is no hard and fast test to determine when breach is material. John Calamari and Joseph Perillo, two leading experts on the law of contracts, list at least five factors to be considered:

1. the extent to which the contract has been performed at the time of the breach;
2. whether the breach is willful, as opposed to caused by negligence or outside forces;
3. how serious the breach is in a quantitative sense;
4. the degree of hardship that would be imposed on the breaching party if he or she were considered in total breach, as well as the benefits that would flow to the injured party; and
5. the degree to which the injured party may reasonably be compensated for damages if the breach is considered to be partial.

If a contractor has built 90 percent of a house and then stops work, it is doubtful that any court would consider the breach to be material and allow the owner of the property to avoid all payment for the work that was done. On the other hand, if the contractor had just begun to lay a foundation for the house before he stopped work, that would very likely be held to be a material breach and the property owner would not only be able to avoid any further payments to the contractor, but could sue for return of any payments she had already made.

The opposite of material breach is substantial performance. A general rule might be that a party has substantially performed if whatever performance has not yet been completed on his or her part does not effectively destroy the value of the contract to the other party, or if the intent of the parties concerning performance has basically been satisfied.

Substantial performance

Thus far we have not addressed the question, "To what is an injured party entitled if the other party has breached the contract or warranties, or somehow caused damage by not living up the contract terms?" The issue of evaluating the damages to which someone is entitled will be discussed at length later on. It is, of course, a very important question. If someone is able to recover only $500 in damages, but it costs $3000 to pursue the claim, it may not even be economically practical to sue for damages.

Before proceeding to discuss remedies for breach of contract, including assessment of damages, we pause briefly to look at two legal notions closely related to contract, but where no real contract is present. The first of these notions is promissory estoppel.

22 LAW AND THE COMPUTER

Promissory estoppel

As was pointed out much earlier in this chapter, the law is not willing as a rule to enforce gratuitous promises. If I promise to lend you my lawnmower Saturday, you cannot go to court to force me to lend you the mower because my promise was merely a friendly gesture and I received nothing in return. On the other hand, if I promise to lend you my lawnmower on Saturday in return for a commitment on your part to mow my lawn as well as your own, then the promise is no longer gratuitous and a real contract is formed. Sometimes it is not clear whether a promise is genuinely gratuitous. For example, if I promise a nephew who is about to graduate from college a trip to Europe when he graduates, the promise might be read, "If you graduate from college, I will give you a trip to Europe." But here the graduation is something that my nephew would do anyway; the graduation is merely a condition and not a return promise. If I had said to my son who does not want to go to college, "I will give you a trip to Europe if you graduate from college," and my son elects to go to college and does graduate, then I owe him a trip to Europe because he has done something he did not otherwise have to do. He has made a commitment and fulfilled it and I must fulfill my commitment in return.

Suppose, however, that I told my nephew who was about to graduate from college anyway that I would give him a trip to Europe upon his graduation, and he acts in good faith upon my promise and makes all the arrangements for the trip, incurring substantial expenses in the process. If I then break my promise by refusing to provide the trip, my nephew is not merely left in the same position as he would have been had I made no promise at all; he is worse off because he has actually made commitments of his own he would not have made and spent money he would not have spent had it not been for my promise. In such an instance, the law says that I am "estopped" to deny my promise, and the nephew's justified reliance places him in much the same situation in the eyes of the law as if an actual contract had been made for me to provide him a trip to Europe. I will probably wind up having to reimburse the nephew for his expenses even if I do not actually have to give him the trip.

Quasi-contract

The law has also invented a remarkable and reasonable notion called "quasi-contract," which it uses to prevent unjust advantages coming to a person where no formal contract exists. Suppose Ann tells Charlie to paint her living room. Charlie does so even though the two of them have not agreed on the price. Ann cannot now come to Charlie and say, "We had no contract because we never agreed on the price, therefore I won't pay you anything." On the other hand, Charlie cannot tell Ann, "Because we had no agreement concerning the price, I am free to charge you anything I want to." In an instance where one party has provided goods or services to another party, although without a contract, and it would be unjust to allow the party receiving the benefits to keep them without having to give something in return, the law will imply a contract and treat the situation much as if a contract had been made. The law will assign a reasonable value (one based on market conditions) to what is rendered, and make the benefitted party pay that amount for what was received.

It should be clear that an implied contract does not arise every time someone does something for someone else. If someone sends you unordered merchandise in the mail, you are generally free to keep it and treat it as a gift. But whenever someone has provided you with something of value, or you have provided someone else with something of value, without a contract, payment might be required in quasi-contract.

The discussion now turns to a more detailed discussion of various contract-related remedies, both in general and under the Uniform Commercial Code.

CONTRACT REMEDIES

Remedies—the vendor's side

This section examines a variety of vendor responses to an actual or potential breach of contract on the part of the buyer. As has been mentioned earlier, the contract itself can provide for remedies in the event of breach. For example, A may agree to purchase a computer from B with an express provision in the contract that if A later changes her mind and does not wish to take delivery of the machine, then the sole remedy will be a payment of $5000 from A to B. In effect, the contract gives A a limited right to revoke the contract for a set price. Many contracts will not attempt to limit remedies to only those mentioned in the contract, if any are mentioned at all; moreover, courts and the Uniform Commercial Code tend to interpret attempts to limit remedies very narrowly and will seek to provide additional remedies where they seem needed in order to do justice.

What can the seller do if the buyer says, "The deal is off; I won't go through with it. Keep your 5000 widgets." One response of the seller could simply be to say, "OK," and cancel the contract. The parties, by their mutual agreement, are free to cancel the contract if they wish. The seller may, of course, also withhold delivery of the widgets in order to protect his investment.

Possible responses to a breach

The vendor might also try to convince a court to order the buyer to go through with the sale, or fulfill the contract. This is a remedy which is rarely granted to the seller of goods or services because the seller can usually be made whole, that is, be awarded adequate compensation for his or her injuries caused by the breach, through the payment of money damages. Forcing a party to go through with a contract is an unusual remedy, which will not be granted if there is a satisfactory way to repay the seller in money for any losses.

The vendor might also resell the goods he or she was to deliver to the buyer and then sue the buyer for any difference between that new sale price and the contractual sale price. If the goods are sold for as much or more than the old contractual price, then the most the seller can hope to recover from the breaching buyer is the additional expenses caused by the extra sale. The breaching buyer has no right, though, to any excess profit the vendor made by selling the goods at a higher price to another.

Special orders

Special problems are presented if the vendor is doing work or furnishing goods especially customized for the breaching buyer. For example, if the vendor is writing a special computer program of use to one particular company and the company decides that it does not want the program after all, then the vendor will, or course, have some problem unloading the program at almost any price to another buyer. In this type of situation, the injured seller would usually be able to choose from a selection of remedies. These would include to

1. sell the product as it is when the buyer breaches;
2. sell the unfinished product for scrap (hardly a viable option in the case of a computer program); or
3. complete the work and then try to sell it in some completed form.

The seller needs to exercise reasonable business judgment as to the course of action selected. He or she cannot merely stop work on the special order and try to sell the used computer print-outs for scrap if a small amount of modifications in the project will enable him or her to complete it and sell the modified project at little or no loss to another customer.

Action for the price

The vendor has other options in the way of remedies. In certain limited instances, the Uniform Commercial Code permits an "action for the price." If the vendor has goods especially made for the buyer that cannot be sold to others, even at a loss, the vendor can seek a judgment for the contractual price of the goods in issue, which he or she must then provide to the buyer if the suit is successful and the price is paid. If the buyer has materially breached the contract, then, in effect, the vendor is also free to treat the contract as void and may sue the buyer in quasi-contract for the fair market value of the work done or goods provided up until the time of the breach. If, for example, the contract called for software development at a price of $50,000, but the vendor has actually spent $75,000 on the development at the time of the breach, the vendor can sue the buyer for the $75,000. The buyer should therefore consider well before breaching. In some instances, it may be cheaper for the buyer to complete an unwanted contract than to breach and have the expenses of a lawsuit and a judgment that may exceed what he or she would have had to pay under the contract.

The Uniform Commercial Code in Section 2-706 states the principles that a court is likely to apply in assessing damages against the breaching buyer:

> [When the buyer is in serious breach of contract], the seller may resell the goods concerned or the undelivered portion thereof. Where the sale is made in good faith and in a commercially reasonable manner the seller may recover the difference between the resale price and the contract price together with any incidental damages allowed under the provisions of this Article (Section 2-710), but less expenses saved in consequence of the buyer's breach.

Section 2-710 referred to above reads as follows:

> Incidental damages to an aggrieved seller include any commercially reasonable charges, expenses or commissions incurred in stopping delivery, in the transportation, care and custody of goods after the buyer's breach, in connection with return or resale of the goods otherwise resulting from the breach.

It should also be noted that if the resale is made in good faith, the substitute buyer will take the goods free of any claims of the breaching buyer. If the vendor of a computer sells a computer ordered by one buyer to another buyer in the reasonable belief that the first buyer has breached the contract of sale, the second buyer should not have to worry about losing the computer and its purchase price to the first purchaser. If there is a dispute at law, it will be between the original contracting parties.

Rights of substitute buyer

It will probably help to go through an example to clarify the provisions of the Uniform Commercial Code quoted above. Baker contracts with Ace Programming Services for Ace to write a program to run on Baker's PDP 11/45 to keep track of Baker's inventory. Ace begins work on the program and has spent $5000 when Baker calls the entire deal off. Ace learns that Charlie wants a similar program to run on his DEC system 20 and offers to sell him for $10,000, a package similar to the one it would have sold to Baker, even though Ace realizes that some modifications will have to be made because of the change in systems, and because Charlie's accounting needs are somewhat different than Baker's. The original contract with Baker called for a payment of $10,000, and it would have cost Ace an additional $3000 to complete the work for Baker. Charlie pays the same $10,000, but it costs Ace a total of $9,500 to complete the work to Charlie's specifications (including the initial $5000). In addition, Ace spent some $500 finding Charlie and selling him the program. Ace then sues Baker to recover damages for breach of contract. What, if anything, can Ace recover?

One measure of damages would be this: When Baker canceled, had Ace stopped work at once on the project, it would have saved an additional $3000 in costs. The contract price was $10,000. Therefore, under traditional contract theory, Ace could recover

$10,000	contract price
− 3,000	savings for work not done
$ 7,000	recovery

Ace chose to complete the work, selling a slightly modified program to Charlie for $10,000. In essence, it cost Ace $2000 for the resale: $1500 in additional development costs plus $500 in sales expenses. Therefore, in this instance Ace could recover

$ 10,000	contract price to Baker
− 10,000	contract price to Charlie
+ 2,000	additional resale expenses
2,000	recovery

Applying the formula

recovery = resale price − original price + incidental expenses

does not seem to do justice in this case, however, for two reasons. First, Ace has lost the profit it would have made in connection with the sale to Baker. The $2,000 is the additional development cost, an expense to Ace; and Ace then actually makes no profit on its sale to Charlie even though it does not lose money on the deal if it manages to get the $2,000 from Baker. In point of fact, however, Ace may lose money because of unrecovered attorney's fees, which probably would not be part of an award in a court suit for breach of contract. In addition to the fact that Ace has lost its profit with Baker, it still might have sold the program anyway to Charlie, even if Baker had not breached. Vendors of software services generally want to make as many sales as possible of the same package. Therefore Baker's breach is, in a genuine sense, a lost sale, one that is not at all replaced or recompensed by selling the package to Charlie. The software is not unique, like a particular house that a realtor can only sell to one customer. The package can be sold to as many customers as will pay for it.

It seems then that Ace cannot really be adequately compensated through use of the standard formula. In such an instance, Ace is permitted to sue for lost profits. Because the profit expected in this particular deal was $2,000, Ace can seek that amount from Baker. But that is the same amount that Ace received using the resale formula. That is true, but no one told Ace to sell the revised package to Charlie for $10,000. Baker is not responsible for that. Moreover, now that Charlie has paid for the major development costs of the package,

Ace's profits will be much higher on subsequent sales. In this latter case, can Ace recover the $500 sales expenses as well? Probably not, because its recovery of the lost profit was based on the assumption that the product would be sold again and again, and that its market was potentially unlimited. In the law, as elsewhere, you cannot have your cake and eat it too.

Can a seller sue under more than one theory, for example, that there is possibility of many resales, as well as that the product is unique? The answer oddly enough is yes. A plaintiff can sue, even under mutually inconsistent theories and let the court decide which theory, if any, should prevail.

Multiple theories of recovery

Remedies—the buyer's view

The buyer's situation is, in many ways, far more complex than the seller's. For one thing, the buyer may be confronted with an array of the vendor protective clauses in the contract. In the event of a breach of contract or warranty, the buyer may have to find a way around some of the clauses before he or she can have an adequate recovery.

One type of breach occurs when the seller simply fails to deliver the goods or services contracted for, or only makes partial delivery. If there has been no delivery of anything by the seller, then the buyer may cancel the contract and demand back any advances already made, and may also recover damages in one of two ways. First, the buyer may "cover." Covering is the purchase of substitute goods or services to replace those that the vendor refuses to deliver. Such substitutes usually will cost more than the original contract price. The buyer is entitled to recovery of the difference between the cover price and that contract price. If Ace refuses to deliver a package which is contracted to sell for $10,000, and Baker is able to cover by buying a similar package elsewhere for $12,000, she is entitled to a $2,000 recovery. Consequential damages are permitted and will be discussed later. Second, the buyer may choose to recover the difference between the market price of the goods in question at the time he or she learned of the breach and the contract price, together with appropriate incidental damages. If Baker ordered a computer system from Ace at a contractual price of $10,000, Ace defaults, and the market price of that system when Baker learns of Ace's repudiation of the contract is actually $15,000, then Baker may choose to recover the $5,000 difference, even if he decides not to buy another computer.

If the goods are quite unique, but do not involve personal service, then the buyer may even have a case for what is known as specific performance. In very special circumstances, a court will order a breaching party to go through with the contract, that is, specifically to per-

Failure to deliver

Cover

Other measures of damages

Specific performance

form its terms. Courts will almost never order specific performance in the case of a contract involving personal services, such as writing a particular program, because these are so hard to enforce and because the court runs the risk of violating prohibitions against "involuntary servitude." But if the breaching party has some piece of equipment that is rather unique or hard to obtain, which that party has contracted to sell to the injured party, and the equipment is such that its loss would create great harm, then the court may order the party with the equipment to sell it as promised to the other party. Specific performance is a remedy available only when money damages alone will not suffice as a suitable compensation for the nonbreaching party.

<small>Partial delivery</small>

If the seller has partially delivered, then there is the question whether there has been a material breach enabling the buyer to completely avoid the contract, or substantial performance, in which case the buyer must pay at least something for what has already been received, even though he or she may also sue for damages based on the breach. If what has been received is useless without what has not been delivered, then it is likely that there has been a material breach. The buyer may then sue for damages as if there had been no delivery at all, but has the added advantage of keeping the merchandise as security for any damages owed. If, in fact, the buyer intends to use that portion of the goods delivered, then he or she will have to pay for them, even though he or she may sue for breach on the undelivered portion and may withhold some of the payment due on what has been delivered to cover damages. If Baker contracts with Ace for a computer system costing $50,000, and Ace delivers disc drives worth $10,000, but nothing else; then, if the drives are useless to Baker because they are incompatible with the machine he later acquires, or even if he elects not to buy a machine at all, he need not pay for them, and can even retain them as security for losses suffered. If Baker elects to use the drives with a replacement machine, then he must pay for them and can recover damages only on the equipment that was not delivered. If the buyer uses the goods as security for unpaid damages with the intent of allowing the seller to reclaim them, then he must take reasonable care of the goods, but can charge the seller for such care and storage as well as shipping expenses to send them back to the seller.

<small>Conformity to contract</small>

When a seller tenders goods or services to a buyer, the buyer has a right to expect that these will conform to the terms of the contract. If they do not, then generally the buyer does not have to accept them. The matter, however, is not nearly that simple. As a general rule, a buyer should give a seller some chance to correct relatively minor defects, particularly if they are the kind of defects that would usually be expected to occur. Programs generally have bugs in them, and the software vendor should be given a reasonable opportunity to debug the product and to get it up and running properly on the buyer's hardware. If nonconforming goods are tendered, then the buyer has the option of rejecting them all, accepting them all (and retaining the right, however, to sue for damages because of the nonconformity), or accepting any commercial unit or units and rejecting the rest. For example, if a computer and disk drive are shipped under one contract, and the disk drive conforms to the contract but the computer does not, the buyer may generally reject the computer while accepting the disk drive. This is because the drive and the computer would each form commercial units and could reasonably be treated separately. If the buyer rejects, he must notify the seller within a reasonable time and hold the goods for the seller's instructions. If the buyer rejects the goods with a justifiable reason, it is essentially the same as if the seller was in total breach of the contract, at least as regards those goods that are rightfully rejected.

The problems of a buyer who accepts goods or services are somewhat compounded if he or she later finds that they are unsatisfactory. According to the Uniform Commerical Code (Section 2-606):

Acceptance of nonconforming goods

1. Acceptance of goods occurs when the buyer
   a) after a reasonable opportunity to inspect the goods signifies to the seller that the goods are conforming or that he will take and retain them in spite of their non-conformity; or
   b) fails to make an effective rejection [by not notifying the seller of the rejection in a timely fashion], but such acceptance does not occur until the buyer has had a reasonable opportunity to inspect them; or
   c) does any act inconsistent with the seller's ownership; but if such act is wrongful as against the seller it is an acceptance only if ratified by him.
2. Acceptance of a part of any commercial unit is acceptance of that entire unit.

Buyers should be especially careful about accepting goods, because once the goods are accepted, the buyer assumes certain obligations, among them:

1. he or she must pay for the goods at the contract rate;
2. he or she assumes the burden of proving any breach with respect to those goods accepted;
3. he or she must notify the seller within a reasonable time after he or she discovers *(or should have discovered)* any breach of contract or be precluded from seeking *any* remedy;
4. if part of a commercial whole is accepted, then the whole item is also.

Acceptance of the goods by the buyer precludes rejection of the goods accepted and if made with knowledge of a non-conformity cannot be revoked because of it unless the acceptance was on the reasonable assump-

tion that the non-conformity would be seasonably cured but acceptance does not preclude any other remedy provided by this Article [Article 2 of the Uniform Commercial Code] for non-conformity.
Uniform Commercial Code, Section 2-607(2).

Note several important facts. First, the buyer can accept goods by simply keeping them without notifying the seller that anything is wrong. Even if the goods are totally nonconforming, it does the buyer no good as far as rejection if he or she fails to tell the seller. Second, the buyer who uses the goods or treats them as his or her own will usually be found to have accepted them. Third, if the buyer knows of defects in the goods delivered, but accepts them anyway, he or she will not be able later to reject the goods unless he or she had good reason to believe that the defects would be corrected in a reasonable length of time. Fourth, acceptance of the goods means that the buyer must pay for them, but he or she still retains the right to sue for breach of contract if the goods have defects. Fifth, the buyer generally has a duty to inspect goods tendered under a contract to see if they conform; if he or she merely takes them without examining them for at least obvious faults, the buyer will probably be held to have accepted them even if blatant faults are later discovered. Moreover, even if obvious faults are later discovered, if the buyer has waited an unreasonable length of time in notifying the seller, or in discovering them, he or she may have no recourse at all against the seller.

The phrase "reasonable time" has been used over and over again. What does it mean? As is the case whenever "reasonable" is used in the law, what is reasonable must be judged in the light of all the circumstances. Whether something is, or is not, reasonable is often a matter of dispute to be decided at a trial. If a failure of the equipment, for example, is one which is likely to occur only under rather rare circumstances and could not otherwise be detected, a rather lengthy time to discovery might be considered reasonable. A fire extinguishing system is not rigorously tested until it has to put out a fire. If it fails during a fire, it has a serious defect, and the buyer may have a case for recovery of damages even if the fire occurs long after the extinguisher was delivered. On the other hand, it should be rather immediately evident if a computer component is delivered with a large bash in one side.

The buyer who rejects a tender of the seller unjustifiably leaves him- or herself open to a suit by the seller for remedies such as those listed in the section giving the seller's remedies in case of breach.

Once the buyer actually accepts goods, then he or she can no longer reject them except in the case where he or she reasonably believed the seller would correct the problems in a reasonable length of time. If the goods then prove unsatisfactory after acceptance, there are still avenues open to the buyer. These will be discussed shortly. We digress briefly to note that the buyer can recover some incidental and consequential damages when the seller is in breach, regardless of whether he or she has accepted or rejected the goods. According to Section 2-715 of the Uniform Commercial Code:

1. Incidental damages resulting from the seller's breach include expenses reasonably incurred in inspection, receipt, transportation and care and custody of goods rightfully rejected, any commercially reasonable charges, expenses or commissions in connection with effecting cover and any other reasonable expense incident to the delay or other breach.
2. Consequential damages resulting from the seller's breach include
    a) any loss resulting from general or particular requirements and needs of which the seller at the time of contracting had reason to know and which could not reasonably be prevented by cover or otherwise; and
    b) injury to person or property proximately resulting from any breach of warranty.

The UCC formula regarding consequential damages is more liberal than the classic law on the subject, which required that the seller be aware of the possibility of the consequential damages before the buyer might be able to collect for them if they came to pass. Regardless of the UCC provisions, or what the classic law on the subject might be, the typical computer contract specifically disclaims all responsibility whatsoever for any consequential damages, even if the buyer spelled out in great detail precisely what would happen if the seller's product did not work as the contract said it should. It should be noted though that under the UCC as well as under classic law, the buyer has a duty to "mitigate" damages, by trying to protect him- or herself as best as possible, by cover or other reasonable measures, to prevent more damage than is necessary after the breach occurred. In other words, the buyer is not free simply to sit back, let tides of misfortune stemming from the seller's breach sweep over him or her, and then hold the seller responsible for all of the damage. The buyer must take reasonable steps to protect his or her interests, because at most the seller will only have to pay for damages up to that point at which further damage could reasonably have been averted by the buyer.

Mitigation of damages

The seller's position after acceptance

Before acceptance, the buyer is in something of a favorable position. If the seller tenders no goods, or nonconforming goods that the buyer rejects, then the seller has not performed his or her part of the contract; hence the buyer is under no obligation to perform his or hers, that is, pay for the goods. If the seller is in total breach, as he or she would be in this instance, the buyer may treat the contract as void. The obvious advantage of this is that the buyer is not then bound by the oppressive terms that a vendor may have built into the contract.

Defective goods

The buyer who has accepted goods that are defective, but notified the seller of the defects, is entitled to recover "as damages for any non-conformity of tender the loss resulting in the ordinary course of events from the seller's breach as determined in any manner which is reasonable," according to Section 2-714(a) of the UCC. If the item in issue needs repair, then the cost of repair might be a reasonable measure of damages if the seller will not, or is not able to, fix the item in a reasonable length of time. Another measure of damages would be the value of the item as tendered subtracted from the contract price of the item. If a tape drive as delivered would have a fair market value of $1,500 due to defects, but the contract called for a payment of $6,000, then the buyer would be entitled to a recovery of $4,500. In point of fact, he or she can simply withhold this amount from the seller. If the seller then sued for the purchase price, the buyer could counter-claim for the damages, that is, use the defect as a defense to the seller's claim.

In essence, however, the failure to work properly is virtually the same as a breach of the Warranty of Merchantability which says that the goods must be fit for the ordinary purposes for which such goods are used. If the computer ordered doesn't work, there is certainly a breach of the implied Warranty of Merchantability as well as a direct breach of contract. The problem is that the Warranty of Merchantability is disclaimed in vendor contracts so that for the purchaser it is usually an action based on breach of contract or no action at all. Nevertheless, there is probably no court anywhere in the United States that will permit even a computer vendor to include a clause in a contract that absolves him or her of all liability for breach of contract, even if such a court is willing to have warranties disclaimed. If the computer simply does not work, then there is clearly a breach of contract. If the computer "works," but it does not do those things that the buyer thought it would do, or perhaps even was told it would do, then the only recourse may be on a warranty, in particular the Warranty of Fitness for a Particular Purpose, which the vendor has taken special pains to declare is not applicable. We return to this dilemma later.

Warranty damages

If damages for breach of warranty are appropriate, then the usual measure of such damages is the difference between the value of the goods or services if they had been warranted and their actual value as delivered. If a vendor promises that his or her computer will be every bit as good as an IBM 370/168, then the value of the IBM 370/168 may well be used as a measure of the value of the goods as warranted. The market price of the vendor's computer would be an apt measure of the value of the goods delivered. The purchaser is still entitled to incidental, and possibly some consequential, damages caused by a breach of warranty.

Even though the buyer is not able to reject any goods that have been accepted, he or she is able to revoke acceptance under special circumstances. The basic rules in this matter are set forth in Section 2-608 of the UCC:

Revocation of acceptance

1. The buyer may revoke his acceptance of a lot or commercial unit whose non-conformity substantially impairs its value to him if he has accepted it
   a) on the reasonable assumption that its non-conformity would be cured and it has not been seasonably cured; or
   b) without discovery of such non-conformity if his acceptance was reasonably induced either by the difficulty of discovery before acceptance or by the seller's assurances.
2. Revocation of acceptance must occur within a reasonable time after the buyer discovers or should have discovered the ground for it and before any substantial change in condition of the goods which is not caused by their own defects. It is not effective until the buyer notifies the seller of it.
3. A buyer who so revokes has the same rights and duties with regard to the goods involved as if he had rejected them.

One of the most important phrases in this section is "substantially impairs its value to him." The product may be quite valuable to another person and may even be in working order. There must, however, be something about the product that does not conform to the contract, such that the non-conformity makes the product far less useful to the buyer. If a contract calls for dress shoes, and the seller sends army boots, the army boots may be excellent for hiking and protecting the feet, but they are not at all valuable for business dress or party wear. It is doubtful that anyone would mistake dress shoes for army boots, but a business man or woman, particularly one not well-versed in computers, might mistake a machine designed primarily for batch processing, which he or she does not want, for one which has a very forgiving time-sharing operating system, which he or she does. Such a defect, or really mismatch, of machine and needs, would most likely only become apparent after acceptance. If the contract does not specify that time-sharing is an important capability the machine must have to a high degree, then the buyer will be hard put to revoke acceptance based on Section 2-608.

If someone knows that an item is defective and accepts it based on assurances that the defect will be corrected, and these assurances are not fulfilled, the buyer is free to revoke. The assurances are usually made *after* the contract has been signed, and as a consequence they are not covered by any integration clause in the contract, nor does the

Acceptance with knowledge of defect

34   LAW AND THE COMPUTER

<small>Waiver</small>

<small>Later agreements</small>

<small>Circumventing protective clauses</small>

<small>Unconscionability</small>

Parol Evidence Rule exclude evidence concerning the assurances. Courts in such an instance are very likely to find a modification of, or addition to, the existing contract. This is true even if the changes or promises are made orally but the contract expressly states that any changes must be made in writing, Courts, to do justice, will often find that the parties have simply waived the requirement of the writing. If a vendor and buyer conclude a contract for a computer system, but the contract makes no reference to the provision of software, or it is later agreed that the vendor will provide software as well as hardware, then if the system later fails consistently due to software problems, the various protective provisions in the hardware contract may be of little benefit to the vendor if sued for breach of contract. The contract sued upon would be that for provisions of software, a contract that snuck in through the back door after the formal and vendor protective contract for the hardware had been signed, and the vendor thought he or she was safe. The moral would be to get additional promises from the vendor after the initial contract has been signed, but get them without the rigid clauses of the initial contract. Sometimes merely the remarks of a salesperson while the system is being installed suffice to create such a contract. There has been more than one case where a hardware vendor has found itself open to successful suit on the basis of a salesperson's remarks and promises, which the court could and did consider to be outside the integration clause the vendor had used to try to shield itself from just such an eventuality. There have also been a number of instances where a dissatisfied buyer successfully revoked acceptance and canceled the contract, even recovering damages, when the vendor was unable to correct serious defects that continued for a long period of time.

Is there any way for a buyer to undo the severe effects of the various protective devices that vendors place in contracts other than to try to prevent their presence in the contract in the first place, or to use rejection or revocation? Yes, although the Uniform Commercial Code permits such protective clauses and courts have often upheld them, particularly in contracts between businesses of more or less equal bargaining power, courts have not been slow to either circumvent the clauses through some legal artifice, or even strike them down altogether when it seemed necessary for a fair result.

In the first place, it has been traditional for courts to void contracts or clauses of contracts which they find to be unconscionable. The Uniform Commercial Code phrases it this way in Section 2-302:

> 1. If the court as a matter of law finds the contract or any clause of the contract to have been unconscionable at the time it was made the court may refuse to enforce the contract, or it may enforce the remainder of the contract without the unconscionable clause, or it may

so limit the application of any unconscionable clause as to avoid any unconscionable result.
2. When it is claimed or appears to the court that the contract or any clause thereof may be unconscionable, the parties shall be afforded a reasonable opportunity to present evidence as to its commercial setting, purpose and effect to aid the court in making its determination.

Courts have been especially suspicious of so-called "contracts of adhesion," form contracts containing clauses highly favorable to the party that prepared them, which are presented to the other party (often unsophisticated as regards the law or subject matter of the contract) on a take-it-or-leave-it basis. Most vendor contracts could reasonably be considered contracts of adhesion because they essentially all contain the same protective clauses, and it is all but impossible for anyone seeking computers or computer services to negotiate the clauses out. A small business man or woman in need of computing services is especially vulnerable because of a lack of understanding concerning what he or she is buying and a very unequal bargaining position relative to the vendor.

Although warranties can be disclaimed or modified, the UCC also provides that

Conflicting warranty terms

> Words or conduct relevant to the creation of an express warranty and words or conduct tending to negate or limit warranty shall be construed as consistent with each other

but there is something of a presumption that the interpretation that favors excluding where doubt exists is unreasonable, that is, ambiguities or seeming contradictions are likely to be resolved in favor of including the warranties.

Any clause in a contract that attempts to disclaim the Warranty of Merchantability must be "conspicuous," and it is for the courts to determine, if need be, what conspicuous means. Courts can find a clause to be inconspicuous if they wish to strike it. Generally, a clause on the back of a standard order form in a pad of order forms will not be sufficiently conspicuous. At a minimum, such a disclaimer must be in type that is moderately larger than the rest of the type used in the contract, or be carefully set off in some clear manner, and it should not be lost in a jungle of pages and paragraphs. The vendor who attempts to cleverly conceal such a disclaimer is very likely to find him- or herself totally without its benefit.

Conspicuousness of disclaimer

Another "out" from oppressive limitation of remedy clauses is found in the Uniform Commercial Code Section 2-719. Two key sentences from that section are:

Minimum remedies required

> Where circumstances cause an exclusive or limited remedy to fail of its essential purpose, remedy may be had as provided in this Act.

> Consequential damages may be limited or excluded unless the limitation or exclusion is unconscionable.

Part of Official Comment 1 to this section helps explain the meaning of these provisions:

> Under this section parties are left free to shape their remedies to their particular requirements and reasonable agreements limiting or modifying remedies are to be given effect.
>
> However, it is of the very essence of a sales contract that at least minimum adequate remedies be available. If the parties intend to conclude a sale within this Article they must accept the legal consequence that there be at least a fair quantum of remedy for breach of the obligations or duties outlined in the contract.

It should be kept in mind that leases and contracts for services are not covered by the Uniform Commercial Code; hence the section and comment quoted above do not necessarily apply to those instruments. But, as has been noted earlier, many courts are willing to apply UCC principles to situations that are not, strictly speaking, transactions in goods, and many times, too, the UCC is a good guide to what the general law of contracts says about a particular situation.

The next section of this chapter delves into other protective devices that buyers should be aware of.

MISREPRESENTATION, FRAUD, AND OTHER SHIELDS AND WEAPONS

A buyer who is terribly dissatisfied with his or her treatment at the hands of the seller may, of course, find the avenues of escape or recovery of damages blocked by the written contract. Very often in such instances, the buyer will also believe that he or she has been "had" by the seller who the buyer feels made promises orally or by implication in advertisements, which the seller will not only refuse to honor once the contract is signed, but which cannot even be introduced in evidence in a court because the contract proclaims that it alone represents the agreement between the parties. How then can the aggrieved party get a court to consider his or her claims?

General principles — Unfortunately, there is no hard and fast answer to the question just posed, nor is there necessarily any satisfactory answer. The arguments to which a court is willing to listen, and how the court is likely to rule on those arguments depends upon the court and the jurisdiction the court represents. Some states have been extraordinarily sympathetic to claims of unconscionability or to striking clauses limiting remedies. Other states have been reluctant to interfere with virtually any contracts negotiated between businesses. What is covered here are some possibilities that might or might not work to get around an oppressive contract. The reader should be warned though that it is unjust and improper to attempt to avoid a contract merely because it turns out to be disappointing or brings about some loss. Risk is inherent in any business and not all contracts can be expected to be profitable. The law is intended to be a protection against injustice and not as an escape from a bad bargain. A mistaken notion of what the contract promises when it is drawn up is different by far from knowing what the contract really says and recognizing later that entering into it was a mistake. The first may enable a party to avoid or reform the contract; the second is just part of life.

Courts do not look kindly at outright fraud. Fraud is a deliberate misrepresentation made to a party to the contract, upon which the party relies and which is a major factor in his or her entering into the contract. If the fraudulent misrepresentation leads to injury to the defrauded party, a court will generally grant some form of relief, such as damages or cancellation of the contract. If there is true fraud, as in a deliberate and knowing misrepresentation, the injured party may even be able to get punitive damages in addition to actual damages. Punitive damages are not meant to compensate for an injury, but are meant to punish a party guilty of some especially serious intentional wrongdoing. A buyer who believes he or she has been induced to enter a contract by fraud may not only have an action in court to cancel the contract and recover damages, but may also have an action in tort. A tort is a "civil wrong." More will be said about torts in the next chapter. Suing in tort does have the advantage that it avoids the contract and its protective clauses, and the aggrieved party is free to introduce evidence about statements and promises that he or she believes to be fraudulent but that were never integrated into the contract. Some courts will, and some courts will not, permit evidence of fraud in a contract dispute where the contract contains an integration clause. The better rule by far is to permit evidence of fraud to be introduced in any suit whether in tort or on the contract, although those who oppose such admission argue that allowing such evidence will encourage anyone who is disappointed in a contract to cry fraud and go to court even when there has really been no fraud present at all.

<small>Fraud</small>

Akin to fraud, but of a little better character, is misrepresentation. Misrepresentation is simply fraud without the knowing intent. If a salesperson states, "This car has eight cylinders," honestly believing that it does have eight cylinders, but the car really has only six cylinders, then there is a misrepresentation, but no fraud. Some courts will permit evidence of misrepresentation to be introduced, even in the

<small>Misrepresentation</small>

face of an integration clause. It is more than a little harsh to permit someone to persuade another to enter into a contract on the basis of a claim that turns out to be false and then hold the injured party to the agreement anyway. If a salesperson claims that all of a computer user's existing library is immediately transportable to the machine being sold, and the user considers that transportability a major factor in the decision to purchase, then the buyer may be able to rescind, or **Rescission** void, the contract. If a court is willing to grant rescission based on either fraud or misrepresentation, then the court might also be willing **Restitution** to grant restitution, which is payment of money to place the parties in the position they would have been in had there been no contract in the first place. In the case involving the misrepresentation about the transportability of the software, restitution might involve a refund of any purchase price of the new computer plus an allowance for reconverting to the previous hardware, or perhaps if it seemed more reasonable, the cost of converting the old software for use on the new machine, in which instance, the buyer would, of course, still be bound to pay for the machine. The more serious the misrepresentation, the more likely a court is to grant rescission if the injured party reasonably relied on it. In the case of fraud, there does not have to be reasonable reliance, only reliance.

Good faith Courts also expect parties to deal in good faith. A vendor who promises that a computer will have certain capabilities when "pitching" it to a prospect, and then attempts to exclude any remedies for damages caused by the absence of the promised capabilities, may find that a court might also use the good faith requirements, as well as a theory of fraud or misrepresentation, to void the contract and order restitution.

Mistake Similarly, if there is a mistake in the contract, or a mistaken belief on the part of one of the parties as to the provisions of the contract, a court might be willing to rescind or modify the contract, particularly if the mistake were somehow brought about deliberately by one of the parties, or one party knew of the mistake but failed to properly clarify the matter for the other party. Because a mistake is so easy to claim, courts are more reluctant to grant rescission or modification for mistake than for fraud, or even misrepresentation. If there has been a mutual mistake of some substance, that is, both parties were in error as to the content of the contract, then there may not have been a contract at all because of the lack of agreement. A court might well be willing to admit evidence even against the terms of an integration clause, not to add or modify terms of the contract on some major point, but to see if there was a contract in the first place. Unilateral mistake, that is, a mistake of only one of the parties, is harder to deal with. However, if the mistake goes to the heart of the contract, and enforcement of the contract would cause serious hardship to the mistaken party, a court might be willing to grant rescission. Courts would generally not countenance deliberate withholding of information that permitted a party to continue in a grossly mistaken belief. For example, if A says to a computer vendor, "These computers are wonderful; all you have to do is talk to them and they will do what you tell them," and the saleswoman responds, "Yes, they are wonderful," then the saleswomen's failure to disabuse the buyer of his foolish ideas about the power of computers to understand spoken language would essentially amount to fraud, and it is quite possible that a court would treat it that way.

In addition to the arguments above that a buyer (or even a vendor in some instances) may use to try to circumvent the protective clauses in a contract, there are also certain defenses that a party can use if sued on the contract. A defense, as the name implies, is a claim which, if true, shields a party against liability in a suit brought by the other party to the contract. There are a great many defenses, and it would be impractical to discuss many of them here. Also, defenses should not be thought of as an aid only to the buyer. For example, a buyer may bring suit to rescind a contract for computer services on grounds that the nature of the services and how much they would do for his or her business were misrepresented. If the buyer waits too long, the seller can raise the defense of "laches," a technical term meaning simply that the buyer unduly delayed in raising his or her claim. If you want your rights under the law, you must assert them in a timely fashion.

Defenses

A defense must be distinguished from a counter-claim. A defense is a shield against a suit; a counter-claim is essentially a counter-attack. The party against whom a suit is brought is called the defendent, while the one bringing a civil suit is known as the plaintiff. The plaintiff files a complaint to institute a suit, supposedly asserting the basic elements of his or her action against the defendent as well as the specific relief that the plaintiff wants the court to grant him or her, usually a certain sum of money. The defendent, in turn, files an answer asserting defenses and raising counter-claims. Counter-claims stemming from the same transaction that brought about the initial suit usually have to be asserted in the answer, or the defendent risks losing them. As a rule, such counter-claims cannot be litigated in a later separate lawsuit.

Counter-claims

An example may help clarify these matters. Ace leases a computer to Baker. Baker makes two payments and refuses to make any further payments; in fact, Baker tells Ace, "Come get this piece of junk off my property or I will call the garbage collectors to take it away." Ace then files a complaint in the Superior Court of Qumquat County. The complaint states that there is a valid contract between Ace and Baker for the lease of a computer; a copy of the contract will probably be appended to the complaint. It will also state that Baker has not paid the rent for the last three months, and that she has repudiated the contract without justification. It will then ask the court for a judgment of the rent that is owed as well as any other damages that may be authorized by the contract, such as full payment of all rent under the contract accelerated to the present under a penalty late payment clause.

Once Baker is served with a copy of the complaint, she will respond. She may first deny any facts alleged in Ace's complaint with which she disagrees. If she fails to deny an allegation of Ace's complaint, or says that she does not have enough information to know if it is true, she will be deemed to have admitted that allegation and be bound by it in the sense that it will be accepted as a fact by the court. If Baker does not deny that there is a valid contract concerning the leased computer between herself and Ace (or at least state that she doesn't know if there is such a valid contract), then the court will assume that a valid lease contract does in fact exist. Baker can begin by alleging that she is not bound by the contract, assuming one exists, because of the failure of a constructive condition precedent to her obligation to pay rent, namely, Ace's furnishing her a satisfactory machine. By alleging that Ace did not fulfill his part of the bargain, thus excusing her from keeping her part, Baker is raising a defense. Baker can also counter-claim for breach of contract and can ask for storage costs for the defective computer (which, of course, she claims is useless to her), costs for replacement computer services obtained elsewhere, and anything else she can think of that might be incidental or consequential damages related to Ace's alleged breach of contract.

Once Ace and Baker have exchanged their initial shots, they may wish to amend their complaint and answer to add new facts or theories of recovery or defense. Later, as the proceedings go forward, Ace can claim that Baker never informed him of her dissatisfaction with the machine, that the machine was in perfect working order, the contract demands that all disputes of this sort go to arbitration but that the rent cannot be stopped, and so on. Baker can expand upon what she has to say as well. There are some perilous pitfalls in this, though, in that the plaintiff is not free to raise new theories of recovery at will throughout the legal process and may be bound only to those theories of recovery raised in the complaint. The defendent too is not able to roam all over the landscape in his or her defense or counter-claims and may lose some perfectly good defenses by not asserting them in a timely fashion. Matters such as these are best left to lawyers, but get a good one. More than one case has been lost by a poorly drafted complaint or answer.

Thus far, we have taken a brief, indeed all too brief, tour through the often foggy world of contract law. An attempt has been made to touch on those points which might be of most interest to computer professionals, but no one should believe that the material here has done any more than scratch the surface of the surface. What follows now are some specific suggestions concerning computer-related contracts.

SOME SUGGESTIONS CONCERNING COMPUTER CONTRACTS

1) Analyze your needs carefully before you negotiate a contract or select a vendor. Make your specifications and measures of performance as exact as possible, and let vendors bid competitively for your business. Not only are you more likely to get a satisfactory system, but you may have some leverage to get concessions from a bidder in order to get your business. Be sure that all your specifications and measures of performance are written into the contract.

There are two ways to go when you enter into a contract: the way of ignorance and the way of knowledge. If you have to rely on the vendor to pick out a product for you that will fulfill the needs you describe to him or her, you almost assuredly have a fine Warranty of Fitness for a Particular Purpose. Courts sometimes look unkindly toward merchants who take advantage of fools. But don't count on it. Courts also are not always well disposed toward commercial enterprises who should know better but who get suckered. And there is always the fearsome disclaimer of any Warranty of Fitness for a Particular Purpose to contend with. Know what you want ahead of time, even if an outside expert needs to be consulted, and then demand that what you want is carefully described in the contract. If what you purchase turns out to be a lemon, you may have a good suit on breach of contract despite the disclaimers of warranty and the limitations on remedy. And the contract will be as complete as you want so the integration clause may even work in your favor. And what about that outside consultant you hired who gave you bum advice? You may have an action against him or her independently of any you may have against the vendor. We will take a much closer look at this type of question in the next chapter.

2) Try to get rid of any disclaimers, limitations, and integration clauses the vendor wants to stick in. Good luck! If your leverage is in-

sufficient to effect this, point out that you believe such clauses are unconscionable and the contract itself is a contract of adhesion. If all else fails, try to get the vendor or his or her salesperson to make some rash claim or promise after the contract has been signed. Perhaps you can get the written contract to cover only part of the purchase, such as the hardware and try to get a less formal agreement concerning, say, the software. Software and hardware problems are often closely related, and you may be able successfully to litigate concerning the software to which the vendor protective clauses would not apply.

3) Be represented in the contract negotiations by a skilled attorney. Most amateurs simply do not understand the vagaries of contract law. Vendors have spent almost as much time and money designing their contracts as their equipment and software, so you are at a severe disadvantage if you try to go it alone. Your attorney's familiarity with the vendor's contract will also give him or her good ideas on how to advise you if or when something goes wrong. Your attorney can make a challenge out of outwitting the high-priced vendor lawyers.

4) Try to insert some protective clauses of your own. These might include some of the following:

a) Provide yourself an option to return the equipment for a full or partial refund, or a release of all obligations under the lease, if the system does not perform according to specifications and the vendor is unable to correct the problem within a specified length of time. Or include a provision for specific tests that the system must pass before you will have any obligations at all under the contract.

b) Leave yourself an out in case you have unexpected financial difficulties, labor problems, or whatever. Some severe difficulties will excuse you from the contract anyway, but it is better to agree ahead of time that certain specified difficulties will release you from your obligations.

c) Specify that any risk of loss of leased equipment in your possession must be borne by the lessor.

There are undoubtedly other protective clauses you would like to see in any contract for computer services you purchase. You may get some and not get others, but you won't get any if you don't try. Do not be intimidated by impressive form contracts. A contract does not have to be printed, and many do not have to be in writing.

5) Keep careful records of the negotiations leading up the contract, all promises, warranties, and so forth, that might be made after the contract is signed, and of all complaints you have about the goods delivered or services rendered. If you can get a vendor's representative to put a promise or substantial claim about the product's capabilities in

writing, do so. Otherwise, try to have other people around who hear such statements too. If the statements are made before the contract is signed, they might be able to be used as evidence of misrepresentation or fraud. If they are made after the contract is signed, they may be binding on the vendor either as separate contracts or as modifications of the original contract. A steady succession of small problems with a piece of equipment which the vendor cannot seem to correct properly may be adequate grounds for revocation of acceptance; you do not necessarily need something spectacular to show that the value to you of the product is substantially impaired by its poor performance. But in all instances, you do need records that will support your case. If you are always prepared for litigation, you may never have to litigate. If a party recognizes you have a good case, they may well be willing and anxious to settle favorably with you without going to trial.

6) Read the contract carefully before signing it. Understand its terms and the implications of its various clauses. Try to change what you don't like. A little money spent on an attorney at this time may save you a lot of money later on. The attorney can help you understand the terminology and law that puzzles you, draft clauses more to your satisfaction, and talk "turkey" directly with the vendor's attorney. Because attorneys understand the issues and the law, they can usually resolve problems of contract language much faster and more reliably than professionals.

These are but a few general suggestions: analyze and know your special needs; try to strike out the most oppressive of the vendor protective clauses; let an attorney help you negotiate; draft and try to insert in the contract clauses that will protect you; keep careful records before and after the contract is signed and concerning the performance of what you contracted for; understand the contract, and use an attorney to help you understand and write it.

Many of these suggestions are just common sense. The law is not totally irrational. Some historical anachronisms are yet found in modern contract law, but the Uniform Commercial Code has been a giant step toward updating and clarifying the law of commerce. One point the Code stresses heavily is the necessity of good faith between parties. Act in good faith and may the law be with you.

SUGGESTED ADDITIONAL READINGS ON CONTRACTS

Alan Taylor writes a column for *Computerworld* that regularly deals with various issues of computer-related law. Some of his columns that might prove helpful with regard to contracts, and the date and page of the issue of *Computerworld* in which they appear are: "Unreasonable Contracts: Lawyers Can Help," May 12, 1980, p. 32; "Lawyers Addressing Noncontractual Rights," May 26, 1980, p. 67; "How to Handle Unreasonable Contracts," April 7, 1980, p. 25.

For a recent article dealing with attempts to avoid liability, see R. Raysman, "Warranty Disclaimer in the Data Processing Contract, *Rutgers Journal of Computers, Technology & the Law*, Vol. 6, No. 2(1978), pp. 265-276.

For a thorough checklist of items to be considered in any computer-related contract, see: R. Freed, *Computers and Law* (5th Ed.), privately published by Roy N. Freed, Esq., c/o Powers and Hall, 30 Federal St., Boston, MA 02110, 1976, pp. 143-49.

In addition to the case found in Appendix II, IBM *v.* Catamore Enterprises, Inc., the following cases are worth reading for insights into computer-related contract disputes: *Chatlos Systems, Inc. v. National Cash Register Corp.*, 497 F.Supp. 738 (D.N.J. 1979); *OJ & C Co. v. General Hospital Leasing, Inc.*, 578 S.W. 2d 877 (Civ. App. Tex. 1979); *W. R. Weaver Co. v. Burroughs Corp.*, 580 S.W. 2d 76 (Ct. of Civ. Appeals of Texas 1979); *Triangle Underwriters, Inc., v. Honeywell, Inc.*, 457 F.Supp. 765 (E.D.N.Y. 1978); as well as 7 Computer Law Service Reporter 224, *604* F.2d 737 (2d cir. 1979); and *Investors Premium Corp. v. Burroughs Corp.*, 389 F.Supp. 39 (D.S.C. 1974).

TORTS

NEGLIGENCE AND MALPRACTICE

Because French was once the language of England's royal court, and, therefore, the language spoken in the highest legal court, a great many old French words and phrases are part of a lawyer's vocabulary. One of these words is "tort," which translates as "wrong" or "injury." A tort is, roughly speaking, an act which causes harm in such a way that the law will make the person responsible for the act pay money to the injured party or parties to compensate them for the injury. The mere fact that an act other than a breach of contract causes harm does not make it a tort. Lightning striking a house and causing it to burn down is an act which causes harm, but the law does not hold the weather forecaster, or anyone else, liable for damage. An insurance company may have to pay for the loss, but that is not because the insurance company is responsible for the lightning strike, but rather because there is a contract between the insurer and the homeowner to pay for the damage. Even human acts do not necessarily lead to liability in tort. If a guest in your house accidentally falls and breaks a leg, the chances are very high that the law will *not* make you pay for the medical expenses, lost wages, or whatever. Why? Because except under rather special and relatively rare circumstances, you are not held responsible for injuries to your guests, unless you have done something intentionally to harm them. A tort should also be distinguished from a crime, which is a certain type of act to which the law attaches penalties other than merely having to repay the victim for harm suffered on account of the act. Crimes will be studied in Chapter 5.

Obviously, computers have the capability of causing a great deal of harm. Computer malfunctions, including errors caused by faulty software, can result in airplane crashes, failure of a nuclear power plant, and even a false warning of a Russian missile attack, and thus a risk of a retaliatory strike that could lead to destruction beyond our ability to comprehend. In addition to truly spectacular "foul-ups," there are the many minor annoyances such as lost records, double billings, misdirected phone calls, etc., etc., etc. It, therefore, behooves a computer owner, operator, manufacturer, or software developer to know which computer malfunctions that cause injury are torts, that is, which could lead to an obligation to pay for the injury caused by the malfunction.

As is the case throughout the law, there are no hard and fast rules concerning "computer torts." Much of the law in this area is still unsettled. The number, and even the nature, of torts is not fixed, and computer technology will unquestionably lead to several new torts or a rethinking of some old ones. In this chapter, we will examine some of the torts of which those who work with computers should be aware. We will also examine some concepts closely akin to torts that also involve liability for injuries. We begin by looking at the most common and perhaps most complex of all torts, negligence.

Negligence

Duty of care

Negligence occurs when

1. Person A owes some duty or obligation of care to Person B;
2. Person A neglects that obligation or breaches the duty of care;
3. Person B suffers injury or harm, and
4. The harm is caused by that lack of care.

This definition requires a good deal of explanation.

There are many ways in which we can owe others some duty of care. One of the ways is through contract. We can agree to do something for another, and thereby bind ourselves to act with care in that regard. But we can owe many obligations to be careful even without any contract at all. We are not permitted to drive recklessly, because we have a duty to watch out for the welfare of others when we are behind the wheel. We are not supposed to serve food we know to be spoiled, because we have a duty not to furnish food we know is dangerous. But the extent of our duty to others is not always clear. Do we have a duty to inspect any trees on our property on a regular basis to prevent a limb from falling on someone? Do we have to check our home carefully before a visitor comes to be sure that there are no conditions present, such as a loose stair carpet, that might cause that visitor injury?

Even if we owe someone a duty of care, we are not negligent unless we somehow breach that duty. We owe others a duty to drive carefully, but if we are driving carefully and someone is injured, we are not negligent. We may, or may not, be liable for the injuries anyway, but, if we are liable, it would not be because we were negligent drivers. If a property owner really does have a duty to inspect all his trees every day for limbs that are about to fall, but on the one day he neglects the inspection, a limb falls and a passerby is injured, then there is negligence because there is a duty (to inspect for loose limbs) and a breach of that duty (failure to inspect on that occasion).

Even if we are negligent by breaching a duty of care, the law will not hold us liable, that is, make us pay for injuries suffered, unless our negligence somehow caused that injury. Obviously too, the law will not make us pay for injuries if there were no injuries. If the limb falls and doesn't hit anyone, we may have been negligent, but we are also lucky—no injury, no liability. Likewise, if we fail to inspect for loose limbs and someone is injured on our property, not by a falling limb, but by tripping on the sidewalk because she was not looking where she was going, our negligence is not the cause of the injury—it is not even related to it at all—thus, again, our negligence could not be used to make us liable for injuries suffered for an entirely different reason.

"Cause," however, is one of the most difficult of all legal notions. Cause, as the term is used in the law of negligence, has two aspects: cause-in-fact and proximate cause. A particular act was the, or at least a, cause-in-fact of an injury if the injury would not have occurred *but for* the act; or, if several different acts contributed to the injury, the act in question was a *substantial factor* in bringing about the injury. John drives his car into Jane who is crossing a street. John's car hitting Jane is certainly the cause-in-fact of any injuries she suffers from the mishap. Likewise, if John's car hits Jane at the very moment a limb falls from a tree and strikes her on the head, then the blow from the car can still be a cause-in-fact of Jane's injuries if it contributed substantially to them, even if injuries were also sustained because of the falling limb. The fact that other acts or events may have contributed to harm suffered does not prevent an act from being a cause-in-fact of that harm if it helped bring about the harm in a significant way.

Cause-in-fact

"Proximate cause" is one of the most slippery notions in law. In essence, it is a device to limit liability by deciding that in certain instances the harm that results from an act is so remote from that act that the person or persons responsible for the act should not have to pay for the harm. Consider the following: John crashes his car into a gas pump. The crash causes a fire, which destroys the station. So far there seems to be no problem saying that the crash was the cause-in-

Proximate cause

fact of the fire, and, hence, was the cause-in-fact of the destruction of the station. Suppose the fire now spreads to a house next to the station; the relationship between the crash and the house fire is a bit more remote. Suppose that gasoline spills from the damaged pump, flows into a sewer, and is carried in the sewer lines for several blocks. The fumes then ignite, blowing a hole in a street, causing a car to swerve out of control and to strike a ladder on which Jane is standing, painting her house. Jane is injured in the fall from her ladder. Now the causal relationship between the car hitting the pump and Jane's injury is stretched so thin that a court might think twice about letting Jane recover from John. And, of course, John might not have even been negligent in the first place. He may have been driving his car with proper caution, but he lost control near the pump because a station attendant had spilled a can of oil on the ground and that caused John's car to slide. If we stretch causes back far enough, then we might find that a seemingly trivial negligent act might subject the person responsible to billions of dollars in liability. The courts have, therefore, said, "At some point we must draw the line and say, 'Beyond this line there is no further liability.' " But where to draw the line? The question has not been answered uniformly by all courts; but the answer, as we shall see, may be vitally important for computer operators facing possibly immense damage claims for a computer malfunction.

Before exploring how the general concept of negligence might particularly apply in the computer industry, two observations should be made. First, negligence does not require an intentional act. John does not have to intend to hit Jane with his car to be responsible for paying for Jane's injuries if he does hit her. Negligence may involve a careless act, but it need not involve a willful act. A programmer may make a negligent mistake without meaning to make any mistake at all. Second, parties to a contract cannot generally disclaim liability to one another in tort. It is doubtful a court would uphold a clause in the contract which states that a party will not be responsible for any negligent acts that cause injury to the other party, because such a clause would, in essence, be an excuse in advance to do a sloppy job, a full pardon before committing the crime. This is true even if warranties are successfully disclaimed. A disclaimer of warranty on a product simply indicates that no guarantee is made that the product will perform satisfactorily. There is no excuse granted thereby not to use proper care in manufacturing the product, or to furnish a product so hazardous that it ought never to have been offered for sale at all. A computer services vendor may still be found liable in the proper circumstances in a suit based on tort, even if his or her contract has every protective device known to the industry.

There is no dispute that a vendor of products or services owes a duty of care to the consumer. The real question is the degree of care required, that is, the standard of care to which the law will hold the vendor. The usual standard in negligence law is that of the "reasonable person." Did the person accused of the negligent act behave as a reasonable and prudent person would have under similar circumstances? The "reasonable and prudent person" is something of a mythical creature in the law, a legal "everyman." Such a test may make some sense in such matters as traffic accidents, but it does not do the job very well as it stands in instances of computer malfunctions. In the first place, someone who claims to have special expertise in an area will be held by the law to the standards applicable to that level of expertise. The standard of care owed by a programmer, acting as a programmer, will not be judged according to what a reasonable person who knows nothing about computers would have done because such a reasonable person would necessarily have done nothing at all. Furthermore, the more serious the harm that might come about from a mistake, the higher will be the duty of care to avoid mistakes. A programmer responsible for a routine that will automatically monitor the vital signs of patients in an intensive care unit will be held to a higher standard of care than someone programming a home computer to play "Star Trek." In other words, the expert will also be held to the standard of care appropriate to intended use. The person engaged in the dangerous task will be expected to exercise a proper degree of caution.

"Reasonable person" test

Susan Nycum, one of the nation's foremost computer attorneys, believes that programmers might be held to a professional's standard of care, instead of merely the standard of care that might be expected of an expert nonprofessional. Professionals, and others who undertake work calling for very special skill, are required to have a standard minimum of related knowledge and competence. How much knowledge and competence is enough? To a large extent that depends on practices common throughout the profession.

There are obviously severe difficulties in applying the professional standard of care to software developers and computer personnel. The first difficulty arises from the fact that although a programmer may hold him- or herself out as an expert in programming, programming is but a small part of software development and computer usage. An expert in FORTRAN, for example, may have little or no knowledge concerning the principles involved in generating the flowchart or algorithm which he or she translates into the source program. A programmer who knows little accounting may work with an accountant who knows little programming to try to develop a software system to keep the financial records of a complex business. Both are experts in their own ways, but neither is really an expert relative to the final product.

A second difficulty is that it is as yet impossible to speak of a "standard minimum of related knowledge and competence" in the field of computing. There is no licensing of programmers, and no uniform test in any state that anyone has to pass in order to be able to set up "practice" as a programmer. The demand for programmers is so high that students are snapped up to do programming before they even have a bachelor's degree, and sometimes before they have even had a formal course in any programming language whatsoever. Perhaps the best an injured purchaser of software services could do is pursue relief based on a claim that the provider of the services warranted that he or she could, in fact, provide services which were beyond his or her abilities. Nor are there any industry standards by which a vendor might be judged.

The conclusion must be drawn, therefore, that the standard of care that applies to computer personnel is not settled. But it is also likely that someone who purports to have special expertise will be judged as if he or she had that expertise. If you claim to know certain facts, you will be treated by the law as if you did know them if someone relied upon your purported knowledge and was injured thereby. What difference does it make if the law assumes that you knew what you said you knew? If there is no assumption that you know FORTRAN, then the law will not generally find you responsible for not writing a FORTRAN program correctly. The law might find you liable for trying to do something you had no business doing in the first place, but your actions will be judged according to what the mythical "reasonable person" would have done. On the other hand, if you are assumed to have the knowledge, and you make a blatant error, then you will almost certainly be found to be negligent. You will have breached a duty to use your presumed knowledge with at least reasonable care.

Not only is there a significant question concerning the standard of care that applies in computer negligence cases, but there is also a problem concerning to whom the standard of care is owed. A software developer certainly owes whatever standard of care applies at least to the client. Suppose, however, that that client is a hospital? Does the duty to exercise that standard of care (whatever it may be) extend to the patients of the hospital? Does it extend to the families of the patients in the hospital? Does it extend to the friends of the families of the patients in the hospital? How far is the obligation of the vendor going to run before it stops? This is largely a question of public policy, and it is one that cannot be long ignored. Computers have become so prevalent and are used in so many ways of critical importance to society that a truly major computer failure could have consequences as dangerous and costly as the failure of a nuclear power plant. Congress has seen fit to pass legislation, the Price-Anderson Act, which limits liability in the case of a catastrophe at a nuclear power plant. Similar legislation might well be called for in the case of computers, or at least those computers that are used in ways that pose substantial hazards.

Please, dear reader, do not throw up your hands in disgust quite yet. If the standard of care is unclear and it is not settled to whom that standard of care is owed, it is also difficult to prove any breach in that standard of care. Gross incompetence might be easily identified, but, given the inherent difficulties in producing correct software and getting it to run properly, not to mention the various vagaries that one finds in any large computer, proof of breach of duty might be intolerably difficult. "I did the very best that anyone anywhere could have done under the circumstances," is a defense that courts are often willing to accept. Because most software must be tailored to each particular user, perhaps the only way to show breach of duty of care is to produce an expert witness who was able to do what the allegedly negligent vendor failed to do in exactly the circumstances in which the vendor failed. This would at least show that the job was technically feasible, and that an expert should have been able to do it properly. But the courts have never taken it to be clear evidence of malpractice if one doctor was able to cure a given patient while another doctor was not. And if the task was technically impractical from the beginning given the present state of the art, particularly if that impracticality was unknowable, it is hard to see how a claim of negligence could prevail.

Proof of breach

But if there is no way to guarantee that a particular program or machine will not fail, then there may well be a duty to warn the user of the possibility of failure. The warning must be fairly specific and clear, or it has little value. The proposed Model Uniform Product Liability Act, of which more later, states that a warning that merely proclaims that some accident may occur is entirely inadequate as a matter of law. Yet it is hard to see how such a warning could be too explicit, because a vendor who knew precisely how the product was going to fail could take action to prevent the failure in the first place. Unlike the possible adverse side effects that drug manufacturers must warn against, such as blindness, nausea, dizziness, or whatever, which can usually be pinpointed with some particularity, computer problems must be left somewhat vague and uncertain.

Duty to warn

Perhaps more realistically, a vendor should be expected to supply test data and corresponding output with the product. The user would be expected to run the test data periodically and compare the output thus obtained with the vendor supplied output. Discrepancies would, of course, indicate that some part of the program or machine was not functioning properly; and, if the test were appropriately designed, it would even indicate what portions of the product had gone awry. Directions could also be given concerning possible corrective measures.

Causation revisited

We must still touch on cause-in-fact and proximate cause. We will assume that harm is relatively easy to prove; someone knows if he or she has been injured in some way, even if the injury is economic rather than physical. We also assume that the measure of damages, which must be proved to the court, does not present drastic difficulties, although some care may be required to demonstrate the value of what was lost when many valuable business records were destroyed by an errant computer, or a business went under because a service bureau was negligent in billing its accounts. Causation, however, is not so easily disposed of.

First, as has already been pointed out, it is not clear how far the duty of care extends. A reason for placing some limitation upon the reach of the duty of care is that it is simply unwise and even silly to make even a negligent person responsible for all of the consequences of his or her negligent act, no matter how far they reach in time and space. Another means of carrying out the same policy of keeping liability within "reasonable" bounds is to decide that only effects within some specified degree of "proximity" to the act, close either in space or some other manner, are caused by the negligent act. Some courts have used a test of "foreseeability" to set the bounds. Was it reasonably foreseeable that such and such an injury would flow from the negligent act? If it was not reasonably foreseeable, then there would be no liability. Other courts have used a "zone of risk" test. Was the person injured within the zone of risk one might associate with the negligent act? If someone was injured outside that zone, then the negligent person would not be liable. In some cases, courts have considered the effect of holding the negligent person responsible. For example, courts have simply carved out an exception to negligence liability by holding that public water companies will not be liable if a building burns down because the water company does not supply the fire department with adequate water to put the fire out. Are workers who lose their jobs, because the company they work for folds due to negligent computing, able to collect damages from the computer vendor? Probably not, but it is generally the courts who make such decisions, and it is the computer industry who must be aware that they run more than the risk of a dissatisfied client if they render negligent service.

Foreseeability

Cause-in-fact

As to cause-in-fact, the cause of a computer failure can often be identified with some certainty after the fact. An automobile is usually "totaled" only once, and an airplane rarely crashes a second time. Experts must sift through tangled wreckage trying to figure out whether there was mechanical failure, driver or pilot error, or some other cause. A program which crashes can be run again with identical data. The planes that collided due to the faulty software in the air control computer cannot be resurrected, but the software can be analyzed and the hardware checked out after the disaster. The reason for the failure can thus be determined in many instances. If the reason for the harm was a defect in the design of the hardware, or a software error, or an error in the input data, then there may be liability if that error was a negligent one. But if the error arose despite the exercise of all due care, then there will be no liability, at least in negligence.

Defenses to negligence

Someone may have a duty of care, breach that duty of care, cause injury by that breach to a person to whom care is owed, yet still not have to pay one penny in damages. Why? The reason is that there are defenses that even someone who has been negligent can assert that will protect that person against liability. The three defenses we will consider that may be of special interest in a computer-related case are contributory negligence, assumption of the risk, and a state-of-the-art defense. This latter "defense" is not really a true defense, because it is not related to a statement of the form, "Yes, I was negligent and harm resulted from my negligence but I should not be made to pay because . . . " What it says instead is "I did the best I could with what anyone knew at the time, and, therefore, I did not breach a duty of care; hence I wasn't really negligent in the first place."

Recall that in a suit for negligence there will be a plaintiff, who seeks recovery for harm he or she asserts is due to the negligence of the defendant, the party to the suit whom the plaintiff accuses of committing a wrong against him or her. The defendant who claims a defense of contributory negligence is saying that even if he or she was negligent, the plaintiff was also negligent, *and* that the plaintiff's negligence was at least partially responsible for the plaintiff's own injury. It is not enough that the plaintiff has been negligent in some manner. His or her negligence must contribute in some substantial way to the harm he or she suffers. For example, Sam and Alice each run a four-way stop sign and plow into one another in the middle of the intersection. Both are probably negligent because they each ran a stop sign. The negligence of both contributed to the collision; hence it is unlikely that either will be able to receive anything from the other. On the other hand, if Sam knew he had a problem with his brakes, but stopped at the intersection anyway and then proceeded carefully, only to be struck by Alice, who ran the stop sign, then Sam may have been negli-

Contributory negligence

gent in not having his brakes in proper working order, but he would not be found to have been contributorily negligent because his faulty brakes did not cause the collision. This is a fairly straightforward example, but rarely does one find such clear-cut situations arising in litigation.

The mere fact that there is litigation to begin with indicates that two parties feel strongly about their respective and opposing points of view. If you are involved in a tort suit, you should not be surprised if your opponent does not see matters the way that you do. How might contributory negligence arise in a computer-related case? The following are some examples:

1) The plaintiff claims that the defendant's software (or hardware) was negligently designed and caused substantial errors in data output, which resulted in billing errors and a loss of business. The defendant claims that the plaintiff was contributorily negligent by supplying defective input data, by giving the defendant misleading and false information concerning the needs and nature of the business, and in not informing the defendant in a timely manner about the problems so they could be corrected.

2) A ground control computer "loses" a plane from the screen shortly after it takes off and the plane crashes into another plane. The problem is traced to faulty operating systems software supplied by a commercial vendor. The plaintiff is the family of a passenger killed in the disaster, and suit is filed against both the airport authority and the software vendor. The plaintiff charges that the airport authority was negligent in not paying proper attention to its radar when it lost track of the plane, was negligent in buying software from an incompetent vendor, and was negligent in not testing the software properly itself before using it in such a hazardous operation, and had inadequate back-up hardware and files. The plaintiff charges the vendor with not using proper care in the production of software it knew was to be used in a mode in which failure could endanger human life, and with selling the software without adequate on-site testing. Note that if the plaintiff's charges are true, then both the airport authority and the software vendor are contributorily negligent in the sense that the negligence of each was a substantial factor in the loss that the plaintiff suffered. In this case, contributory negligence is not a defense against the plaintiff because the plaintiff was not negligent. The defendants may have both been negligent, but only the plaintiff's contributory negligence may be used as a defense. If the plaintiff first sued the airport authority and won a judgment, then the airport authority might attempt to bring suit against the vendor to recover the money it had to pay the plaintiff. But the vendor could then interpose a defense of contributory negligence because the authority's own negligence contributed to its own losses. The situation is actually a bit more complex than this, so if

you are ever unfortunate enough to be a defendant in a case such as this one, get yourself the best lawyer you can find.

A second defense which a defendant can try to use in a negligence suit is assumption of the risk. As its name implies, this defense says, "Yes, I was negligent, but you knew of the danger and decided to go ahead anyway. Now you can't come back and make me pay for what happened." For example, if Sam notices that a mechanic who repaired his brakes did not adjust them properly but, nevertheless, continues to drive without getting them fixed, then he may be found to have assumed the risk of driving with bad brakes. If Sam later has an accident due to the faulty brakes and tries to collect damages from the negligent mechanic, the mechanic can defend on the grounds that Sam had assumed the risk. The mechanic could also maintain that Sam was contributorily negligent because he deliberately drove with brakes he knew were not working properly. Assumption of risk and contributory negligence are closely related, and some legal scholars would say that assumption of the risk is merely one form of contributory negligence and not really a separate defense.

Assumption of risk

Given the rapidly changing technology and the widespread knowledge that computers can fail, it might be argued that anyone who uses computers has assumed the risk of their use. This would be particularly true if the buyer had been warned in advance by the vendor of the possible hazards of overreliance upon computers. Likewise, loss of valuable records may be attributed in part to negligence, contributory negligence, of failing to provide adequate back-up files. A buyer may be contributorily negligent by failing to educate him- or herself to an appropriate extent on what a given machine can, or cannot do, or how to operate it properly, or even by hiring computer personnel who are incompetent. As will be seen later, there may be the possibility of pursuing a successful claim against the vendor on other grounds than negligence, but if contributory negligence is established, it will completely bar recovery on a negligence theory in most states and in the federal courts, just as will successfully proving assumption of risk.

Some states have adopted a comparative negligence rule which provides a formula to assessing damages according to the degree of fault of each party. For example, if one party is 90 percent responsible for the damage, and the negligence of the other party accounted for only 10 percent of the injury, then the 10 percent party can get 90 percent of his or her damages from the other. In most states, it is still the rule that the 10 percent party should get nothing because he or she was at least partly to blame. This, of course, is a harsh rule and it is not surprising that legislatures and courts have tried to find ways around it. Even in states where contributory negligence remains an absolute defense, one will find "compromise verdicts" on the part of jurors, which are a form of comparative negligence damage recovery.

Comparative negligence

A defendant sued in negligence could also argue that the immense complexity of computers and software, and, indeed, even the mathematical impossibility of finding an algorithm to check the correctness of every program, mean that no duty of care is breached unless there is truly gross malfeasance on the part of a computer manufacturer, vendor, or operator. The situation might be compared to having a new medicine that seems to cure a great many previously incurable ailments, but that has side effects that are not as yet completely understood. In such a case, a doctor would generally not be negligent in prescribing the drug for those patients, at least, for whom it would seem to be worth the risk, those for whom it is likely to do more good than harm. Computers can do wonderful things, but they also have some potentially dangerous side effects. Harm can come from not using a computer in an appropriate instance just as harm can come from a computer failure. One question to which a court may seek an answer is, "Was the risk in this case worth the benefits?" Computers are not for everyone, and any vendor, if there be any such, who attempts to sell computers in situations where they are uncalled-for may wind up paying for his or her greed should anything go wrong, as it almost certainly will.

STRICT LIABILITY

The American Law Institute is a prestigious body of legal scholars that, among other activities, publishes what are known as "Restatements" of law. The Restatements, each covering some specific area of the law, are attempts to summarize and clarify the law. Because of the caliber of scholarship that has gone into each Restatement, many of them have helped to shape law instead of merely to say what the law is. Perhaps no section of any of the Restatements has been more influential that Section 402A of the Restatement 2d of Torts:

Section 402A—
statement
on strict
liability

1. One who sells any product in a defective condition unreasonably dangerous to the user or consumer or to his property is subject to liability for physical harm thereby caused to the ultimate user or consumer, or to his property, if
    a) the seller is engaged in the business of selling such a product, and
    b) it is expected to and does reach the user or consumer without substantial change in the condition in which it is sold.
2. The rule stated in subsection (1) applies although
    a) the seller has exercised all possible care in the preparation and sale of his product, and
    b) the user or consumer has not bought the product from or entered into any contractual relation with the seller.

The more one analyzes this section, the more amazing, yet the more reasonable it may seem. Note some of its key aspects: The liability for the harm involved is absolute. That liability does not depend on any lack of care by the seller; indeed, the seller can exercise all possible care and still be liable. The user or consumer who is injured by the product need not be the one to whom the seller initially sold the product. It used to be the law that a seller was liable for any breach of Warranty of Merchantability only to that party to whom the warranty was made directly, that is, the party to whom he or she personally sold the goods involved. If Sam sold a car to Linda, a car dealer, and Linda later sold the car to Oscar, a consumer, and the car had a dangerous defect which caused an accident while Oscar owned the car, Oscar could only sue Linda, but he could not sue Sam because Oscar did not buy the car directly from Sam. This would be true even if Sam had negligently manufactured the car and the defect that caused Oscar's accident was actually there when Sam sold the car to Linda. The law simply said that there was no "privity" between Sam and Oscar, so Oscar was free to sue Linda alone. Fortunately and quite reasonably, the barriers of privity have been tumbling rapidly in recent years, and manufacturers, for example, have been found to make warranties of merchantability to the consumer, even though the consumer buys the goods through a retailer. In any event, Section 402A strips away any defense of lack of privity. The manufacturer who sells a "defective product unreasonably dangerous," will be liable all the way down the line of purchasers of the product, provided the product does not undergo some substantial modification after it leaves the manufacturer. *[margin: Traditional view—privity required]* *[margin: Modern view—no privity needed]*

There are other observations that must be made about Section 402A, but we might first pause and ask, "Why have so many states and courts been quick to adopt this section? What policies are served by the rule of 402A?" Here are some of the more important answers to this question.

[margin: Policies behind strict liability]

1. Section 402A often shifts liability to a large manufacturer, who is much better able to pay for any injuries caused by a defect in the product than is a small retailer. It is reasonable too that a manufacturer who put the defect into the product, even while exercising all due care, ought to be the one to pay for the harm the defect causes. The manufacturer is also more likely to have insurance, or be able to afford insurance, to cover such liability.
2. Recognizing that liability may follow from a defective product, even if no negligence is proved, the manufacturer may become more careful in production, or in putting new untested products in the marketplace.

3. Given the complexity of many products and the difficulty any consumer faces in proving negligence of a manufacturer, it is best to simply let the consumer be compensated for injuries caused by a defective product without having to go to the expense and trouble of establishing negligence.
4. Given certain kinds of socially desirable products, such as cars, it is a virtual certainty that some of these will contain dangerous defects, and that some consumers will be injured by the presence of these defects. Rather than letting the entire burden of the risk of injury fall upon those unlucky few who happen to get the dangerously defective products, the risk should be shared equally by all who use the product, that is, some provision for compensating the victims should be built into the price of the product itself. This, in turn, can be done through a system of strict liability outlined in Section 402A.

Personal injury usually required

Courts have generally restricted recovery under Section 402A to cases involving actual bodily injuries, although a few courts have permitted recovery of purely economic losses. Also, this section applies to products, which have usually been interpreted to be tangible manufactured goods such as cars and appliances, rather than services. Although a few courts have been willing to extend Section 402A to cover services, most have not. Most of the courts which have considered the question seem willing to classify software as "goods" for purposes of including it under the Uniform Commercial Code for contract and warranty purposes, but it is not at all clear that courts will be willing to consider software a product for purposes of liability under 402A.

If software is not a product, then hardware certainly ought to be. But here other problems are present. In the first place, not only must a product be defective under the terms of 402A, but it must also be unreasonably dangerous because of the defect. Is a computer with a faulty memory chip or a defective vendor-supplied operating system inherently dangerous? It may be hard to convince a court that it is, at least in the same sense that an automobile or power mower is dangerous to the user if it has some problem that is likely to cause it to blow up or veer wildly out of control. A computer becomes inherently dangerous only if the purpose to which it is put is inherently dangerous. One would have to convince a court that a defective computer was inherently dangerous to hold its seller strictly liable under 402A.

There is, moreover, another hurdle to clear on the way to 402A liability. A computer is useless unless programmed, and an applications program can be considered to be a substantial change in the condition of the machine from that in which it was sold. For that matter, there is almost a "Catch 22" here, for a program cannot be entered into a machine without a substantial change either. Therefore both the computer and the software are substantially modified from the form in which they left the vendor's hands. This may take both hardware and software outside the scope of Section 402A. All of these possibilities are as yet quite conjectural because there are so few cases on this subject. It is hard to know what the courts will do with a very new and complex area of the law until they actually go ahead and do it. Nevertheless, those who deal with computers in situations where physical injury at least *may* result from a defect in the hardware or software should be mindful of Section 402A. The definition of "defect" is broad enough to cover a lack of adequate instructions for proper and safe operation, as well as inadequate warnings of potential dangers. A vendor who dumps a computer on a naive buyer without making sure that the buyer is trained to use the computer "safely" may incur 402A liability on that basis alone, if the defect in instruction leads to harm.

It should almost go without saying that the harm spoken of in relation to 402A must flow from the defective condition. The defective condition must cause the harm in essentially the same sense that a breach of duty must cause the harm in a negligence case in order for liability to be found. A car may have seriously defective brakes, but this will not lead to manufacturer's having to pay for an accident that was caused by drunken driving in which the bad brakes played no part. The problems in causation under Section 402A are similar to those encountered in relation to negligence.

_{Cause of harm}

Is strict liability so strict that no defenses can be raised against it? No, among the defenses which a defendant can plead are the following:

1. The danger involved is sufficiently obvious that the plaintiff was unreasonable in exposing him- or herself to it. If a television set emits clouds of smoke every time it is turned on, yet the owner insists on using it anyway, that continued use in the face of a clearly dangerous condition could be used as a defense by the manufacturer if the set causes a fire. Computers rarely involve obviously dangerous defects. The use to which a computer may be put may be dangerous, but this is more a question of the degree of care that must be exercised with that use. It does not involve a defective condition that poses a threat which should have been obvious to the user.

2. The danger may be such that it is inevitable given the current "state of the art." Medicine may have a harmful side effect, but there may also be no known way to either get rid of the side effect, or substitute a safer medicine which is equally effective. The "state of the art" defense is apt to be critical in many computer product liability cases because of the advanced technology involved in computing and the virtual impossibility of completely

debugging complex programs and safeguarding against all possible causes of failure.
3. The product in question may have been misused. One who is injured trying to trim a hedge using a power mower is not likely to find much sympathy with a court. If a user attempts to use a program written for one machine on another machine without taking adequate precautions for the transition, then misuse might be found. Likewise, because computer programs must be maintained, the use of a program for some time without rechecking its correctness may constitute misuse.
4. The consumer may have assumed the risk of the use of the product because anyone using a machine as sophisticated and complex as a computer must realize that errors may creep in in many diverse ways, the mere use of a complicated system may be held to include an implied assumption of risk.

Computer foul-ups are sufficiently commonplace that anyone who uses computers should be aware of the risk of failure. If there is indeed a high risk of failure, then strict liability would impose an intolerable burden on computer manufacturers; but, more to the point, this high risk of failure, if properly advertised, like the health warning on a cigarette package, should insulate software and hardware vendors from strict liability for malfunctions.

Ultrahazardous activity

There is another form of strict liability of which computer operators should be aware. If injury occurs because of a mischance associated with carrying out some ultrahazardous activity, such as blasting, then the person who carries out the activity will be held strictly liable for the injury. Again, because this is strict liability, it does not matter if that person took every reasonable precaution in what he or she was doing. The policy behind this rule is not hard to find: There are certain very useful activities that are at the same time extremely dangerous. Because of their utility to society they should be permitted, but because of the high risk of harm they pose, those who suffer injury on account of them should be compensated for the injury. Is computing truly in the category of such highly dangerous enterprises? Section 520 of the Restatement of Torts provides some tests for the answer:

> In determining whether an activity is abnormally dangerous, the following factors are to be considered:
> a) existence of a high degree of risk of some harm to the person, land or [personal property] of others;
> b) likelihood that the harm that results from it will be great;
> c) inability to eliminate the risk by the exercise of reasonable care;
> d) extent to which the activity is not a matter of common usage;
> e) inappropriateness of the activity to the place where it is carried out; and

f) extent to which its value to the community is outweighed by its dangerous attributes.

Is dependency on a computer, at least in certain situations, an ultrahazardous activity? The question at least presents food for thought. Perhaps to those tests listed in Section 520 might be added the following: Is there really a safer means of achieving the same end?

ADDITIONAL TOPICS IN PRODUCT LIABILITY

Third parties

The buyer and the seller are the principal parties in any sale, but the sale, particularly if what is sold is defective or dangerous, may have serious consequences for others. If a car veers out of control because a pin falls out of the steering mechanism, the driver-owner may be the one who is hurt, but a pedestrian, a driver of another vehicle, or a house the car crashes into may suffer damage as well. The driver of the car may not even be the one who bought it, but someone to whom the car has been loaned. If a computer monitoring vital signs "crashes," it is the hospital patient, not the vendor or the hospital, who is most likely to suffer direct injury. Persons other than the principals in a contract and/or sale are known as "third parties." What are the rights of third parties when injured through negligence or by a defective product?

Third parties

With regard to negligence, the notion of third party is not entirely appropriate. Some injury is either sufficiently closely related to a negligent act that recovery can be had from the negligent party or it is not. Someone who is negligent will be held responsible for all of the consequences of his or her negligence, at least as far as the policy of the law deems fit.

More complex questions arise with respect to breach of warranty and strict liability. State law concerning breach of warranty varies widely, so much so that the drafters of the Uniform Commercial Code supplied three distinct options so that states could have their pick. These options are found in Section 2-318. Under the most restrictive alternative, the seller is liable for breach of warranty only for personal injuries, not for damage to property, and only to the buyer, members of the buyer's household, and guests in the buyer's home. The second alternative is more inclusive and provides for recovery by any person who could be expected to use, consume, or be affected by the goods if they are personally injured (that is, suffer personal bodily harm) by the breach. The third alternative covers the same group of people as does the second alternative, but also provides for recovery for damage to property, even if there is no bodily injury. The first alternative is the most widely enacted, but courts have sometimes tended to be more liberal than the statutes, using the statute as the bare minimum for recovery rather than the maximum. Because computer vendors try so hard to disclaim warranties anyway, these sections of the Uniform Commercial Code may not be all that important. But it should also be noted that any attempt to disclaim liability for personal injuries due to a defective product is likely to be treated with extreme disfavor by almost any court. Note too that privity of contract is not required for recovery under breach of an express warranty that accompanies the product.

Given the wide variation in the way that warranty law treats third parties, the conclusion might be drawn that a new approach that yields more uniform results is needed with regard to third parties injured by a defective product. Despite the differences in the way that breach of warranty covers third parties, courts have been more or less consistent in permitting third parties to recover in strict liability, if the injury the party suffered was reasonably foreseeable. Again, there is the policy question of how much liability is too much. No manufacturer can afford to pay for every conceivable consequence of an accident involving one of his or her defective products. But "by-standers" have a better chance of recovery from a manufacturer under Section 402A than under breach of warranty, at least in most states. The reader may gain some comfort from the fact that courts have as yet been unwilling to extend Section 402A liability to professional services such as those provided by engineers and architects, although such persons may be held to a high standard of expert care for purposes of negligence. A programmer who makes an error that causes physical injury is, therefore, not likely to be held personally strictly liable for the defective product. But if a program is a product for Section 402A purposes—it is not clear that it is—then a seller of the program might be strictly liable.

The Model Uniform Product Liability Act

In late 1979, the Department of Commerce published "The Model Uniform Product Liability Act" as a guide for states in drafting product liability legislation. Reasons given for suggesting this legislation include:

1. to insure that parties injured by defective and dangerous products will be adequately compensated,
2. to stabilize product liability insurance rates,
3. to bring some uniformity to product liability law throughout the nation as is required by commercial considerations,
4. to place incentives on appropriate parties to prevent injuries,

5. to expedite the claim process and minimize costs all around, and
6. to try to express product liability law in language that is readily understood.

The Model Act is, in fact, a fairly clear piece of legislation and is well worth reading to gain an overview of current product liability law. The draft Model Act and commentary is found in the October 31, 1979, issue of the *Federal Register*. If the Model Act is passed, it will answer some of the more pressing questions concerning product liability and computing. It should be understood that the Model Act is not yet law, but only suggested legislation. It is up to each state and Congress if they wish to pass it as proposed, modify it, or reject it entirely.

For example, providers of professional services are specifically excluded from the group of "product sellers," as are nonprofessional providers of services unless the provider supplies the sale or use of a product as a principal part of the transaction, "and the essence of the relationship between the seller and purchaser is not the furnishing of judgment, skill, or services." This provision would seem to exclude programmers from persons subject to product liability. It is not clear whether a program is itself a product, but it would seem that it would not be. The Model Act at least provides a definition of product, whereas previous discussion of product liability had assumed that everyone knew what a product was to begin with. The Model Act also specifically excludes direct and consequential economic harm from those injuries that are compensable under product liability. Thus, a computer foul-up that causes the bankruptcy of a business would not involve a product liability claim, even though liability might be found under some other theory such as breach of contract, breach of warranty, or negligence.

The Model Act neatly categorizes various grounds for liability, various defenses, basic standards of responsibility for manufacturers, and numerous other important concepts. The comments accompanying each section of the Model Act are especially useful in understanding the intent and philosophy of the Act, as well as why various possible alternatives were not selected for inclusion. There is a wealth of references to books and articles on virtually every aspect of product liability. If the Act is adopted it will be a giant step toward bringing order into a currently chaotic area of law.

Saying too much or too little

Vendors of any goods or services should always be careful what they say. You can say so much that you are then bound by many express warranties that you had no intention of making, or so little that negligence may be found for failure to instruct properly or warn. Two more statements in the Restatement of Torts are worth mentioning in this regard. The first is Section 402B of the Restatement Second:

> One engaged in the business of selling chattels who, by advertising, labels, or otherwise, makes to the public a misrepresentation of a material fact concerning the character or quality of a chattel sold by him is subject to liability for physical harm to a consumer of the chattel caused by justifiable reliance upon the misrepresentation, even though
>
>   a) it is not made fraudulently or negligently, and
>
>   b) the consumer has not bought the chattel from or entered into any contractual relation with the seller.

Chattels, goods, products

Thus, if a product is conspicuously labeled *Completely Safe for Children*, the manufacturer may be liable under 402B if a child is injured by the product. This section uses the word "chattel." The reader may be confused by the distinctions between goods (Uniform Commercial Code), products (Section 402A), and chattels (402B). The fact is that the distinctions are not always clear, and there is a great deal of overlap. The situation is clouded still further by the fact that many transactions involve combinations of goods and services, or products and professional advice, etc. In its broadest sense, a chattel includes any form of property except real property and ideas. "Real" property, of course, is not the opposite of "imaginary" property (there is no such thing except in the imagination), but consists rather of various interests in land and buildings.

Mere "puffing" will generally not be accepted as a misrepresentation. Puffery is expected in advertising, and each manufacturer is allowed some license in maintaining that his or her product is the "the best," or is "new and improved." But the more specific the claim, the more likely it is to lead to 402B liability in case of harm. Computer programs, at least in tangible form, might well be classified as chattels even though they might not qualify as products. If a software vendor advertises that his or her program will save lives in a cardiac care unit, and it fails and causes the death of a patient, liability may well follow under 402B. Note that 402B does refer expressly to physical harm, so that mere economic loss would not be covered.

Negligent misrepresentation

Negligent misrepresentation is another hazard of talking too much. Section 552 of the Restatement of Torts declares:

> One who in the course of his business . . . supplies information for the guidance of others in their business transaction is subject to liability for harm caused to them by their reliance . . . if
>
>   a) he fails to exercise the care and competence in obtaining or communicating which its recipient is justified in expecting, and
>
>   b) the harm is suffered
>
>   (i) by the person or one of the class of persons for whose guidance the information was supplied, and

(ii) because of his justifiable reliance upon it in a transaction in which it was intended to influence his conduct or in a transaction substantially identical therewith.

This section does not exclude recovery for economic losses and is grounded in negligence rather than strict liability. Some of the ways in which this section might come into play are:

1. An instruction manual for a system is inadequate or erroneous, or the documentation for software is inaccurate or misleading.
2. Professional advice is given concerning the selection of hardware or software, but that advice turns out to be misguided.
3. A salesperson makes recommendations or representations concerning the product and what it can do for the client's business, statements which later turn out to be wrong.

In addition to saying too much, if one says too little, then that lack of information may be found to be a defect in the product for purposes of product liability, either in negligence, or even strict liability. For example, manufacturers of highly flammable materials have been held strictly liable for burns suffered by persons using their products if the packaging failed to display a conspicuous warning of the flammability or clear instructions for safe use.

OTHER TORTS

Strict liability in tort is not contained solely within the confines of tort law, but slops over into contract and just plain social policy. Breach of warranty is really contract law, the breaking of an express or implied agreement. The one real pedigree tort we have considered thus far has been negligence. But there are other torts of which the computer professional should be aware. We consider some of them in this section.

Trespass to chattels and conversion

Trespass to chattels is a fairly straightforward tort with a strange name rooted deep in legal history. Property is more or less divided into real property, meaning the ownership of land, and chattels, meaning just about everything else. Trespass generally involves interference with someone's right to possession of property. Trespass to chattels, therefore, involves interference with one's right to possession of chattels. Trespass in one of the so-called "intentional" torts, which means that the act involved must be willful. The breach of duty in

<small>Trespass to chattels</small>

negligence may, or may not, be willful, although the law tends to deal more harshly with intentional wrongdoers than with those who simply make a careless slip. If the act involved is not intentional, however, it will not be trespass, although it may still subject the person responsible to some form of liability.

What then is trespass to chattels? The elements of this tort are

1. an intention to interfere
2. coupled with an act by the defendant
3. which actually does interfere with, or invades, the plaintiff's possessory interest, and
4. which causes real injury or damage.

The most obvious example of this tort is taking something that belongs to another without permission. Theft is both a criminal act and also a tort. We will consider theft from the viewpoint of the criminal law later. A thief may be liable for civil damages for the tort of trespass to chattels as well as criminal penalties.

Interference with rights

Someone does not have to deprive someone completely of possession to be guilty of this tort. One may simply interfere with some right normally associated with possession, such as exclusive use or use for profit. A computer program reduced to tangible form is a chattel. If someone takes a copy of a computer program that does not belong to him and uses it without permission of the owner, he is exercising a type of control over the property that interferes with the owner's right of exclusive use. If a student at a university causes the system to crash as a lark—just to see if she could do it—she is committing the tort of trespass to chattels because her irresponsible action prevents those who have the right to use and "possess" the system from fully exercising that right. Someone who inadvertently crashes the system does not commit trespass to chattels because the act was inadvertent and not intentional. If someone believes that some act may crash the system but goes ahead anyway, and if the system then crashes, there may or may not be the equivalent of an intentional act, depending on how irresponsible the action really was. One cannot drive a car 80 miles an hour on the wrong side of the road and then claim no intention of having an accident when an accident does occur.

The defendant must perform some act—mere wishing is never enough—and that act must cause measurable damage. If a chattel is actually lost, then the measure of damages is the value of the chattel. If there is simply interference, then some value for the damage caused will have to be proved. The proof of value can be a special problem in computer-related products. Because magnetic impulses have no intrinsic worth and electricity is cheap, the best hope is to try to get a court to accept the cost of producing a stolen program, or the cost of reconstructing a damaged file as the value in question.

Conversion

Related to, but distinct from, trespass to chattels is the tort of conversion. Conversion is a tort that is described concisely in Section 222A of the Restatement Second of Torts:

1. Conversion is an intentional exercise of dominion or control over a chattel which so seriously interferes with the right of another to control it that the actor may justly be required to pay the other the full value of the chattel.
2. In determining the seriousness of the interference and the justice of requiring the actor to pay the full value the following factors are important:
   a) the extent and duration of the actor's exercise of dominion or control;
   b) the actor's intent to assert a right in fact inconsistent with the other's right of control;
   c) the actor's good faith;
   d) the extent and duration of the resulting interference with the other's right of control;
   e) the harm done to the chattel;
   f) the inconvenience and expense caused to the other.

Note that conversion, like trespass, is an intentional tort. Note too that with conversion, the person responsible is forced to "buy" the converted chattel at its full value. Computer professionals might keep this tort in the back of their minds for use when someone intentionally destroys files or misappropriates a program. Value still remains a problem. The following might be argued as possible values that a converter should be ordered to pay: the commercial value of what is taken, the cost of development of what is taken, the intrinsic value of what is taken. Naturally, you would want to use the highest value that a court would be willing to accept if you were the plaintiff, and the lowest value if you were the defendant. In most cases, the intrinsic value of say a card deck or tape would be negligible in comparison with the value of the information stored on it.

Taking of copies

A more serious question is presented in the case in which only a copy of a program or file is taken. Taking a copy is not necessarily inconsistent with the owner's right of control of the originals since he or she still has control of those. But the owner does lose control over the copy, which may well contain material that belongs to him or her. Whether the material taken in such an instance is just an idea (in which case it probably would not be held to be a chattel) or the fact that the owner does not lose complete control of the chattel would defeat a claim of conversion is yet to be fully tested in the courts.

Consequential damages

A plaintiff in a suit in trespass or conversion may seek damages for harm that is caused directly by the defendant's tort. For example, if the defendant has misappropriated a trade secret, and through his or her actions the material taken has lost its secret character, the plaintiff may seek damages not only for the value of a license to use the secret, but for any lost profits that he or she can actually prove if the loss was caused by the misappropriation. This may be harder than it sounds because the defendant can rightly maintain that the length of time the trade secret would have remained secret without the tortious disclosure is nothing more than a matter of conjecture; hence the lost profits are merely a matter of idle speculation. But courts are not all that sympathetic to those who willfully commit torts.

Defamation

The often indiscriminate capacity of a computer for compiling and storing, and then, of course, retrieving, vast amounts of material about virtually any human being on earth has been a source of substantial analysis, criticism, and legislation. Before analyzing the special character of computer-related torts concerning privacy and reputation, we first take a general look at defamation and invasion of privacy.

Defamation traditionally has consisted of two distinct torts, libel and slander. Slander is defamation by speech; libel is defamation by the written word. Because computers are likely to do whatever damage they do in this regard through "hard copy," and because libel alone is sufficiently complicated, we will restrict our attention to libel.

Libel "Written communication" needed for libel, however, need not be taken too literally. Almost any embodiment of the defamatory statement can be taken as sufficient to constitute a libel, and, if the statement is given sufficiently wide dissemination, such as in a radio or television broadcast, that alone may be held enough to invoke the more severe rules that apply in cases of libel.

Defamatory statements But what is a defamatory statement? One rather narrow view held by some courts is that it is a statement which exposes the plaintiff to "public hatred, contempt, or ridicule." But there are very few things one can say about virtually anyone nowadays that will expose that person to public hatred, ridicule, or contempt, and some of those things that could be said that provoke such a reaction may well not even be defamatory. A defamatory statement is more generally held to be a statement that injures one's reputation, lessens the respect of the individual in the eyes of the public, or brings about adverse or hostile feelings toward him or her. Such a statement must carry some implication of bad character or lack of virtue, since almost any statement about anyone will diminish that person in someone's eyes. Even declaring that someone is an "intellectual" will undoubtedly bring some disrepute among anti-intellectuals, but such a declaration is not libelous because there is supposedly no disgrace in being an intellectual. If the group in which a person's reputation would be diminished by a statement is negligibly small, or not "respectable," then it is likely that the statement is not defamatory. A statement to the effect that Sam is a policeman who does not take bribes may diminish Sam's reputation among the criminal element and among the few dishonest policemen, but it would not be defamatory because it would be expected to add to Sam's esteem within the general community.

Who is to decide whether a statement is, or is not, defamatory? The Supreme Court of the United States has said that this is a question for both the judge and the jury:

> A publication claimed to be defamatory must be read and construed in the sense in which the readers to whom it is addressed would ordinarily understand it. . . . When thus read, if its meaning is so unambiguous as to reasonably bear but one interpretation, it is for the judge to say whether that signification is defamatory or not. If, upon the other hand, it is capable of two meanings, one of which would be libelous and actionable and the other not, it is for the jury to say, under all the circumstances surrounding its publication, including extraneous facts admissible in evidence, which of the two meanings would be attributed to it by those to whom it is addressed or by whom it may be read.

A defamatory thought itself is, of course, no grounds for a law suit. We have all had nasty thoughts about a great number of people; many of these thoughts could have led to defamation suits had they been published, but we had the good sense to keep them to ourselves or within a small circle of friends. A plaintiff does not have a "cause of action" for defamation unless and until the defamatory statement is published to third persons and his or her reputation is actually injured. Note that you may call someone defamatory names to his or her face and not publish the statement to a third person if no one else hears it. Plaintiffs themselves are not third persons. Moreover, if the plaintiff has been the one who published the statement, then you would still not be liable for defamation. For example, if you call Sheila a thief to her face when no one else hears your accusation, and she then repeats to others that you called her a thief, this is not the type of publication that will lead to liability. If, however, you repeat to others, "Sheila is a thief," or others are present when you accuse her of being a thief, then Sheila may file a complaint against you in court for defaming her. *Publication needed*

In order for a defamatory statement to be published, it is necessary that the one to whom it is communicated actually understands it. If the statement is encoded, for example, such that no one but its author can read it, then there is no publication even if it is printed in the daily paper. Moreover, if a plaintiff is to win a defamation action, the defamatory statement must be shown actually to refer to him or her. *Understanding required*

Sam cannot sue Agnes for defamation if Agnes called Joe, another person altogether from Sam, a thief. If Sam could somehow prove that everybody who heard the statement, "Joe is a thief," understood that Agnes was really referring to Sam, then there might well be defamation.

Intention not required

Is defamation an intentional tort, that is, does it require that the defendant willfully make the defamatory statement, or might it be sufficient, for example, for someone to leave a note to herself containing a defamatory statement on her desk which happens to be read by an office worker and is published in this inadvertent and unintentional manner? There is no requirement at all that anyone have an intention to defame to be liable for defamation. Someone may make a defamatory statement who believes that it is not defamatory, or that the statement is perfectly true and the person about whom it is made will not mind, or that the statement will not injure the plaintiff in any way. At one time there did not even have to be even negligence in making the statement or in causing it to be published or in not checking carefully as to its truth. In many situations now, perhaps all situations, at least some degree of negligence or intention is required on the part of a defendant in an action for defamation before liability can be found. We will discuss this issue at greater length below because it may well be an important one for computer operators.

Damages

In some torts, such as trespass to chattels, actual damages must be proved, that is, the plaintiff must prove some specific dollar loss in order to gain monetary recovery. It is virtually impossible in most instances to prove precisely what profits one lost, or to assign a dollar value to a drop in esteem in the community, caused by a defamatory statement. Many courts, therefore, allow at least some recovery without proof of special damages in cases involving libel. The majority of courts, probably still distinguish between "libel on its face" and "libel *per quod.*" Libel on its face exists when no additional facts need to be known by the person who reads the statement to understand its defamatory character. For example, "Joseph Smith of 45 Aardvark Place is a thief," is a statement which does not require additional information to be defamatory. No extrinsic facts need to known to understand that this accuses Joseph Smith of being a thief. Libel *per quod*, on the other hand, concerns statements that are defamatory only if one knows further unstated facts. An example of possible libel *per quod* is "Joe and Mary had a lovely baby girl," the extrinsic fact being that Joe and Mary are not married to each other. In cases of libel *per quod*, many courts insist that actual damage be proved before a recovery can be had, unless the libelous statement falls into one of the four categories:

1. statements accusing a woman of lack of chastity (equal rights and changing ideas of morality may make this category obsolete or even unconstitutional);

2. statements that the plaintiff has some "loathsome disease" (most commonly interpreted as some form of venereal disease);
3. accusations of criminal activity; and
4. statements that adversely reflect upon the plaintiff's business ability, solvency, or anything else that might have special significance to his or her business or profession.

Surely by this time the reader is thinking, "You mean I can never say or print anything bad about someone without being sued for it?" One must first remember that one can scarcely do anything without some risk of a lawsuit. Remember that lawsuits do not have to be particularly meritorious, and the mere fact that a plaintiff files a suit does not mean that he or she wins. Lawyers are not supposed to file suits they do not believe have a good foundation, but some lawyers are rather loose in their interpretations of what constitutes adequate basis for a suit. Obviously too, we all say nasty things about many people and are never sued for them. The statements are not that important in what they say or in the impact they have, to cause anyone to want to go to the bother of suing us for making them. Finally, there are times when we can make defamatory statements and "get away with it" because we have defenses that will prevent the plaintiff (person to whom the statements refer) from recovering one thin dime. We consider these defenses now.

The first defense in a defamation action is truth. In most states, if the statement at issue is actually true, then the defendant is not liable, at least in defamation. Be warned, however, that there may be liability under one or more categories of invasion of privacy; this tort will be discussed later. The plaintiff is not responsible for proving that the defamatory statement is false. The court will assume that the statement is false and the burden will be on the defendant to show that it is true if the defendant is claiming truth as a defense. If Sam says, "Paula is a thief," and Paula hauls him into court for defaming her, then Sam will have to prove that Paula is a thief, either by proving that Paula stole something, or furnishing a record of a conviction for theft. Mere arrests will not do since Paula is presumed innocent until proven guilty. But if Paula were arrested on suspicion of theft and all Sam said was, "Paula was arrested on suspicion of theft," then the statement is true and Sam would generally not be liable for defaming Paula.

<!-- margin: Defenses -->

In addition to the defense of truth, there are various immunities and privileges which can be invoked relative to defamation. An immunity, as it name implies, is a bar to suit for defamation if the statement at issue was made under certain circumstances. A judge, for example, is absolutely immune from liability for defamation for any statements made while acting in his or her judicial capacity. Likewise, most persons involved in a "judicial proceeding," such as lawyers, jurors, witnesses, investigators, have immunity as long as what they say relates

<!-- margin: Immunity -->

to the proceeding. This, of course, is another reason why some defamation suits do not go to trial. If what was published was bad, what might be said at trial could well be worse. It also may be better to let people think you have risen above a false statement by not making a big issue of it than to risk having the statement proved true in open court, or to be accused of even worse things from the witness stand. Other immunities are granted for statements made in legislative hearings and various administrative proceedings, communications of high government officials acting within the scope of their offices, statements made with the consent of the plaintiff, and certain others of unlikely benefit to those who may be in a position to combine defamation with computing.

Qualified privilege

An immunity is also known as an absolute privilege. There are certain instances where a person has a qualified privilege to make defamatory statements. Because a qualified privilege by its very nature is not absolute, there are times when a plaintiff may defeat the privileges and recover from a defendant who does have such a privilege. The complexity of this area of the law is staggering, and much of the law regarding qualified privilege has been made in the last few years. Nevertheless, qualified privilege is likely to be a much used defense in computer-related defamation suits. We must therefore review, at least briefly, some of the various kinds of qualified privilege and the grounds on which they can be defeated.

Public v. private communications

Statements generally may be divided into public statements, such as those printed in a newspaper, and private statements, such as those that might be made in a confidential letter of recommendation or to a limited circle of contacts. The rules governing the two forms of statement are somewhat different because public statements may come at least partially under the protection of the First Amendment right to free speech, while strictly private communications are not thus protected.

Private statements may be made with a qualified privilege if they are made

1. to defend some legitimate interest of the defendant, for example, to deny some charge made against him or her, or to try to recover stolen property;
2. in the interest of some third party, for example, to prevent harm from befalling a friend, or made in response to a bona fide request for a recommendation concerning a job applicant;
3. in the interest of both the defendant and a third party, such as a report that might be made by a credit rating service, or the report of a psychologist who has been asked to evaluate a candidate for employment;

4. concerning a matter which is in some way a matter of public interest, such as a complaint about an official whom the statement alleges is not performing his or her work properly, or a warning to a police agency that a crime is going to be committed.

The qualified privilege in a private communication can be lost if the information given goes beyond what is needed to protect the plaintiff's, the third party's, or the public's interests. For example, if Agnes has told Oscar that Sally is a thief, then Sally has a qualified privilege to tell Oscar that Agnes is lying, this in order to protect her good reputation; but if Sally goes beyond this and accuses Agnes of being a thief, then Sally may be liable to Agnes for defamation because it was not necessary to accuse Agnes of a crime to defend herself. A qualified privilege may also be lost in this case if the defendant has acted "maliciously." Malice may be found if the defendant has deliberately lied, or has recklessly made an incorrect assertion, or made the statement with a motive of vengeance or ill will toward the plaintiff. If Joe, Sam's former employer, writes a letter of reference to Alma, who is thinking of hiring Sam, and states that Sam stole materials from the storeroom, then Joe's qualified privilege will be defeated if Sam did not steal any materials and Joe should have known this if he had bothered to check, or Joe made the statement knowing that it was false, or with the deliberate intention of hurting Sam whom he hates because Sam ran off with his daughter.

Malice

With regard to public statements, the law wallows in a morass of fine distinctions. There are public actions of public figures, and private actions of public figures, and figures who are public with regard to some particular event because they have interjected themselves into it, and so on and on. Generally, and perhaps too simplistically, recent law has tended to favor public speech, although there are some indications that the pendulum has begun to swing back. As the law now stands, public media at least must have a virtually reckless and complete disregard for the truth to be liable for defamation, and not necessarily always even then. The reader should be warned that this is a terribly confusing area of law. More importantly, for our purposes, it should not be one that computer personnel will encounter very frequently. Information gleaned from a computer file is virtually always a private communication, so we will not take the time or space to develop the free speech aspects of defamation. We will, however, now return to the theme of this text and explore the implications of the law of defamation to the computer industry.

Whenever data is collected about any living person and is stored in a computer file, there is some danger of defamation. Production of information from that file would almost certainly be publication and

Defamation and data files

also satisfy the condition of a writing necessary for libel, even if the information were merely displayed on a CRT to a single operator. If there were inadequate safeguards on the system to prevent unauthorized access to the file, or if proper care were not exercised when material was entered in the file, or if the file were not checked for accuracy on a periodic basis, a court might be willing to find the negligence demanded in a defamation action. One might argue successfully, however, that retrieval of material already in the file was not really a new publication of the material, but merely a recall of information that was actually published when it was given to the company operating the computer.

A computer, of course, not only stores information, but processes it. Errors may be made in entering data or in drawing conclusions from it. For example, data intended for one file may inadvertently be entered in another, or a false conclusion that a company is in financial trouble may be drawn. Publishing an erroneous credit report, e.g., a credit bureau's notifying its clients that XYZ Corporation is bankrupt when it is not, is grounds for an action in libel, and it is doubtful that such a report would ever be eligible for First Amendment protection. One court in ruling that First Amendment standards do not apply to protection of credit rating reports gave as reasons that the reports are not public communications, but are confidential statements between private parties; moreover, the reports are intended to represent facts and not merely the opinions or thoughts of the one who sends them. Because of the high credibility that much of the public associates with computer-generated analyses, courts may even hold credit bureaus and others who provide such analyses to a higher standard of care than an economist or financial expert who is merely providing what amounts to his or her personal opinion on a matter. It should also be noted that a mistake in a credit rating or business report may be particularly dangerous because defaming someone with regard to his or her business is libel on its face and subjects the defendant to damages even if no special losses can be proved.

Improper security

If improper security is maintained and unauthorized persons gain access to confidential and defamatory information, liability may also be found. Although the theory has not yet been tested in the courts, negligence in securing a computer system may be tantamount to publication if the lack of adequate security results in dissemination of defamatory material. One way a computer service might protect itself to some degree is to encode its information and only furnish subscribers with a key. For example, corporations reported on could be identified only by a number so that anyone but a client would be unable to associate the information with any particular company. Clients would be contractually bound to keep their codes confidential or risk liability if defamatory material became public through their negligence or breach of contract. A plaintiff could still prove that defamatory statements in the credit service's reports applied to him or her because the code could be "discovered" as part of the pretrial process, but liability might be sharply limited. Generally, the smaller the circle within which the defamatory material is circulated, the less the damage and the less evident the negligence of the company that spread the false report, and, perhaps most important, the easier it is to correct the false report by specifically notifying all of those who received it in the first place. Correcting the error is considered favorably by courts in assessing damages. If a defamatory statement is retracted and a correction made, in many circumstances it tends to lessen damages to a substantial degree.

Although much of what has been said has been cast in terms of credit bureaus, it should not be assumed that these are the only computer users who have to be careful about what information they generate from their computer files and how they use it. Computerized personnel files pose special risks and hard copy back-ups should always be available to check entries, as well as the source of the information. Hard copy files may even be required by law, and it is not clear that computer files alone are satisfactory "records" for all legal purposes. Computerized files concerning alleged criminal activity can also bring litigation. For example, if a state trooper uses the state central data processing to determine if a driver arrested for a minor traffic violation is wanted on more serious charges, and is told that the driver is so wanted due to a mistaken entry in a file or a case of confusing different individuals with similar names, there could well be a cause of action against the state for defamation. The matter might be aggravated if a crowd has gathered and the incident becomes known to members of the public who then spread the false report. Be warned, however, that suits against the state raise special problems that must be addressed on a state-by-state and case-by-case basis.

Files of personal data

Even a relatively minor item such as the format of output can cause problems. This writer once made an inquiry concerning his Blue Cross account and was sent a photocopy of a print-out that not only included the information requested but a substantial amount of information about other people as well. As it turned out, I did not care about that other information and, to my recollection, it was not libelous, but it might have been considered an invasion of privacy by those others listed on the print-out if they had found out about it. It made me wonder too what information about me was carelessly being released to others in response to legitimate requests that had nothing to do with me.

Other possible sources of defamation

There are, of course, still other problems. If a computer is responsible for monitoring delinquent accounts and erroneously decides that some account is delinquent, the notice of delinquency and an attempt to collect the account might be considered a form of defamation, an accusation that the person whose account it is does not pay his or her bills.

The computer professional must be aware that false information stored in, and particularly that published to others by a computer may result in liability for defamation. There is no way to entirely circumvent this problem. Certainly, care must be taken to avoid dissemination of any information in a computer beyond those who have a right to that information. This can, and should, be done by operating systems security devices, encoding the information so that persons without a proper key cannot read it, contractual provisions, and the like. Liability for defamation can also be avoided by making certain that all information stored is accurate and true. Even this, however, is not a sure protection.

Invasion of privacy

Americans have always attached a high value to privacy; hence, the ability of a computer to enable government and industry to gather vast amounts of data about even the most obscure people is very troubling. However, even before computers came upon the scene, the law recognized four separate torts under the heading of "invasion of privacy." Two of these, physical intrusion and misappropriation of personality, are of little import to the computer industry. The other two, public disclosure of private information and "false light" privacy, are serious potential areas of liability.

True privacy

Public disclosure of private facts, sometimes known as "true privacy," involves publicizing private facts of an objectionable or offensive nature. The publication must be more than merely a private communication, and this would work in favor of the computer industry as a rule, but, on the other hand, the facts involved need not be false; truth is not a defense to this tort. The mere revelation of some fact about an individual is not grounds for liability. The fact revealed must be such as might offend a reasonable person of "ordinary sensibilities." Liability would almost certainly not be found if a computer-generated print-out of property taxes paid in a certain community were published in the local paper. It is quite probable that this information is public anyway and would not involve private facts about anyone. If, however, a list of people who were seriously delinquent in their tax payments were so published, then there might be some grounds for liability. One of the earliest cases involving this tort concerned a merchant who advertised in a window of his store that one of his customers owed him money. Perhaps the area of greatest danger is saving damaging files too long. If someone was arrested for drunken driving ten years ago, and the arrest was dredged up in a long-stored computer file to be used to hurt the individual, a tort might be found. Beware of revealing private sins, particularly stale ones, even if they are true. It would be best to be selective of what goes in a file to begin with. It is also important that a file be kept up-to-date and that material that ought to be purged is.

False light privacy occurs when a person is portrayed in a misleading way in the public eye. The tort is rather hard to define more specifically. It can be committed though when someone's name appears in a context that is damaging without any basis in fact. For example, a person whose name is included on a list of "welfare cheats" may have a cause of action for this tort if, in fact, he or she is not on welfare, or is on welfare legitimately. Similarly, an innocent bystander may have a cause of action if a newspaper runs a picture identifying the bystander as one of a group of looters.

<small>False light privacy</small>

Obviously, false light privacy and true privacy have much overlap with defamation. One distinction, however, is that the facts involved in invasion of privacy may be true. This may happen even in false light privacy. Certain facts may be publicized from which one can draw a completely erroneous conclusion about a person's character. In such a case, a half-truth is worse from the viewpoint of liability than the whole truth. Almost all of what was said earlier about immunities and privileges applies equally well to the two forms of invasion of privacy we have touched upon in this summary.

<small>Privacy v. defamation</small>

When compiling files on people, if such files must be compiled, in addition to taking the precautions already alluded to, be sure that the file portrays a balanced and generally accurate picture of the person. If you keep just a record of unpaid bills, then it may convey an unfair picture of the person as a deadbeat. If only records of arrests are kept, but records do not indicate if charges were dismissed or the person exonerated, the record may portray the individual in a false light as a criminal. In computing, the best defense against tort liability are much what they are outside of computing: honesty, fairness, common sense, and proper care.

<small>Precautionary measures</small>

SUGGESTED ADDITIONAL READINGS ON TORTS

The following are but a sample of page-one stories in *Computerworld* dealing with real or potential disasters in which a computer malfunction played a significant role: "CPU Fails, Two Jets Nearly Collide," November 12, 1979; "Norad System Goofs, Calls Missile Alert," November 19, 1979; "NASA Jumbles Skylab Data," July 9, 1979.

For surveys of the law of product liability, see P. Rheingold, "The Expanding Liability of the Product Supplier: A Primer," *Hofstra Law Review*, Vol. 2 (1974), pp. 521–59, and "Model Uniform Product Liability Act," *Federal Register*, Vol. 44 (Oct. 31, 1979), beginning at p. 62714. This latter presentation (the text of the Model Act with extensive commentary) is also a rich source of other materials dealing with various aspects of product liability.

The following articles deal more specifically with computer-related product liability or torts: D. Petras and S. Scarpelli, "Computers, Medical Malpractice, and the Ghost of *The T. J. Hooper*," *Rutgers Journal of Computers and Law*, Vol. 5 (1975), pp. 15–49 (The *T. J. Hooper* was a tugboat whose operators were found liable in negligence for damage caused by a storm because they had failed to install a radio on their boat, which would have alerted them to the danger. The article addresses the question of liability for failure to employ computers.); S. Nycum, "Liability for Malfunction of a Computer Program," *Rutgers Journal of Computers, Technology and the Law* (note the name change), Vol. 7 (1979), pp. 1–22; and G. Stevens and H. Hoffman, "Tort Liability for Defamation by Computer," *Rutgers Journal of Computers and Law*, Vol. 6 (1977), pp. 91–102.

For an actual defamation case involving a computer, see *Wortham v. Dun & Bradstreet, Inc.* 399 F.Supp. 633 (S.D. Tex. 1975).

For an extensive discussion of the potential liability of the computer professional, see D. Jordan, "The Tortious Computer—When Does EDP Become Errant Data Processing?" *Computer Law Service*, Section 5-1, Article 2(1972).

LEGAL PROTECTION OF SOFTWARE

THE NATURE OF THE PROBLEM

No one wants to spend a great deal of time and money developing an idea only to have others appropriate the idea free to their own advantage. Even young children acquire a sense of ownership of personal property and a sense that it is wrong to steal the property of another. But the property that most people associate with the Commandment, "Thou shalt not steal," is tangible property, property you can feel and hold and see. Intellectual property presents a different question, "If you have a good idea, why am I not free to use it as I please?" The next chapter will deal with the subject of criminal acts. This chapter concerns the protection of intellectual property in a civil sense, even though in some instances a criminal act may also have been committed.

Intellectual property

The law recognizes that, at least in certain instances, it is in the best interests of society to accord some degree of protection to ideas as well as tangible objects. The Constitution of the United States states that Congress can enact certain forms of protection "to promote the progress of science and useful arts." In keeping with the mandate of the Constitution, Congress has established a complex body of legislation and an elaborate administrative structure to handle patents and copyrights. This legislation provides severe penalties for those who infringe upon the protection granted by copyrights or patents, but the penalties are not in the form of jail sentences, but of monetary compensation to the injured party; infringement has the nature of a civil wrong, a tort, rather than a criminal act in most instances. Likewise, all states have some form of statutory or case law to protect trade secrets. There

Applicable law

79

is also the law of contracts that applies where one party agrees with another party not to reveal secret processes or use the ideas of the other party without compensation. All of these devices—copyright, patent, trade secrecy, and contract—as well as other means, are used to insure that certain forms of ideas are accorded safety from use without the proper permission of the one who owns the rights to those ideas. The Constitution declares, in fact, that Congress has the power to pass laws which secure "for limited times to authors and inventors the exclusive right to their respective writings and discoveries." Buried within this brief phrase are a host of thorny legal questions: What is a limited time? Who is an author? Who is an inventor? What is a writing and what is a discovery? Is there a distinction to be made between the protection that may be accorded a writing and that which may be accorded a discovery?

Special software problem

The rapid evolution of computer technology has presented problems undreamt of in prior law. One of the most troublesome areas has been the forms of protection that might be appropriate for computer software. To understand why this is a problem, one should consider the variety of forms that software can take. To avoid controversies about potential differences between systems and applications programs, we assume software refers to an applications program.

Evolution of program

An applications program really begins with a problem to be solved or some job to be done. Once the problem is clearly defined, an algorithm must be developed to solve it. The algorithm, in turn, may be expressed in terms of a flow chart. The flow chart may be translated into a program design using some appropriate mechanism, schemata, or program design language. The general program design, whether in the form of an algorithm or something a bit closer to the source program, then becomes the source program through coding in some higher level language such as FORTRAN or COBOL. The source program may then be transferred to some medium, such as cards or paper tape, for entry into the computer, or it may be entered directly through a terminal. The program is compiled and becomes the object program, the program in machine language. The object program sets the switches, so to speak, within the computer, and the program becomes a pattern of magnetic impulses or electrical signals. These patterns themselves change as the program is run. Perhaps the nature of the patterns change as the program is swapped from disk to core memory to CPU and back again.

At what point then in the progression from problem to machine implementation of a method of solution do we have *the* program? What is it we are protecting if we invoke the law to protect a program we have written? The question is even more complicated, because, even if we restrict our attention to the program at one point in its existence, that program may be viewed in many different ways. We now direct our attention to that which most people are thinking about when they speak of the computer program, the source program.

A program can contain more than a million instructions and cost hundreds of thousands, or even millions of dollars to develop. For example, the SABRE program used by American Airlines in making flight reservations has more than one million instructions and cost more than $30 million to develop back in the early 1960s. More typically, the initial cost for a software product runs between $50,000 and $500,000, with an average of $200,000. As noted above, a program begins as a response to a problem, regardless of its size or cost. The source program is obtained by translating the algorithm for solving a problem (or doing a task) into a high level language. The program may thus be viewed merely as a specially formulated version of the algorithm itself.

Many different definitions of program can be found in legal and technical literature. Many of these definitions involve the phrase "set" or "series" of instructions. Two typical such definitions are:

> A program is a "series of instructions which controls or conditions the operation of a data processing machine [computer]." (Bender, "Computer Programs: Should They Be Patentable?," 68 *Columbia Law Review* 241 (1968).

> "[C]omputer program" means an instruction or statement or a series of instructions or statements, in a form acceptable to a computer, which permits the functioning of a computer system in a manner designed to provide appropriate products from such computer system . . . (Federal Computer Systems Protection Act of 1979).

What is a program?

In a technical sense, of course, a program is a set of instructions. "Instruction" in computerese is simply one line of computer code; a computer instruction, e.g., FORMAT (17), may be virtually meaningless as an instruction to a human being. Nevertheless, because this definition of a program occurs so often, it is worth examining in great detail.

Those who understand the computer language in which the program is written can, at least theoretically, carry out the procedure which the program embodies. You will no doubt get a chuckle out of even thinking about someone trying to execute manually the programs you deal with regularly. Nevertheless, a program might thus be viewed as a type of instruction manual. This view, however, has its weaknesses, even from a purely technical point of view. In the first place, although the process leading up to actually writing the program may be excellent training for dealing with the particular problem, the program itself is not designed as an instruction manual, and no one, to this writer's knowledge at least, has ever used one for this purpose. In addition, programs require documentation to explain how the program is to be used and what each part of it does. The documentation is more properly an instruction manual, and there is something unsatisfying about an instruction manual for another instruction manual.

If we do not like the idea that a computer program instructs humans, then is the idea that the program instructs a computer more palatable? The ability to learn and be instructed is an attribute that we normally reserve for higher forms of life. Some, including Professor Joseph Weizenbaum of M.I.T., seem to believe that "men and computers are merely two different species of a more abstract genus called 'information processing systems,'" that reason is equatable with logic, and life with "what is computable." The issue is complicated by the fact that the program often looks much the same as instructions humans are accustomed to giving and receiving. But, of course, the computer does not see what humans see. Although the word ADD in a program presents a clear command to a human eye, it appears to the computer as a string of 0's and 1's or a pattern of switch settings. In other words, the program is merely a means to manipulate various components of a machine. The program may thus be viewed as a process or means of bringing about a desired result within the computer.

The function of the program is sometimes defined in terms of "control" rather than "instruct." For example:

> A computer program is basically a plan that controls the activity of the computer, directing the calculations needed to solve a problem . . . (Banzhaff, "Copyright Protection for Computer Programs," 64 *Columbia Law Review* 1274 [1964]).

If a program controls a computer in the same way that a distributor controls the sequence of firing the sparkplugs in an internal combustion engine, then the program can be viewed as an integral part of the computer itself. This view is strengthened by the fact that a computer will not, and cannot, carry out its appointed task until it has been properly programmed. The programming sets the switches, in effect redesigning the internal structure of the machine and becoming an inseparable part of the machine. The program may thus be viewed as a machine part or as the completion of a previously incomplete machine.

The view, however, has its critics. Otho Ross points out that

1. the emphemeral electrical charges or magnetizations that represent the program inside the computer do not really modify the hardware;
2. the program itself can be modified by the user or the computer itself, even while the program is running; and

3. in time-sharing computers, programs of many different users are constantly being "swapped" in and out of the CPU.

He asks whether the computer really becomes a new machine every time its operation shifts to a new program.

A further objection to considering the program to be a machine part in some sense is that the source program, which is what we are primarily considering, lies outside the machine and apart from it; therefore, although it may result in the creation of a new machine or part of a machine, it itself is not a machine part. But just as a person who understands the language could use a program to reconstruct the algorithm, so too a person who has an adequate background in electrical engineering could use the program to build an electronic circuit that would carry out the program in conjunction with input and output devices. This is, of course, manifest in "firmware." The program could be used by a suitably trained engineer as a circuit diagram or the blueprint for building special purpose hardware. Even if it is not part of a machine, the program could be used to construct a machine of specific design, that design being contained implicitly in the program itself. The program thus stands midway between the abstract solution to a problem and a machine which actually carries out the solution.

There are other ways to describe a program. The Association for Computing Machinery defines a program as an "ordered set of data that are coded instructions or statements that when executed by a computer cause the computer to process data." This considers the program to be a special kind of data compilation. This makes even more sense when one remembers that the machine code in hard copy form appears as strings of 0's and 1's. If "code" is interpreted literally in its cryptologic sense, the ACM's definition might inspire a view of a program as a coded message, cryptic writing.

A program may also be thought of as bearing the same relationship to a computer as a phonograph record does to a record player. This analogy is used in the CONTU Report, of which much more later, although it might be more accurate to say that the program is the sheet music, and the program expressed in a form acceptable to the computer is the record. Nevertheless, there are highly significant differences between a record and record player on the one hand and a computer and computer program on the other. First, a record is specifically intended to communicate with human beings; the program is intended to communicate with a machine. Second, the record player's exclusive purpose is to reproduce a performance in audible form. The computer, on the other hand, uses the program to process data. The data processed by the computer acting in accordance with the instructions contained in the program is actually more analogous to the phonograph record. The purpose of the computer, however, is not to play back the data, but to transform it. People rate a record player according to the quality at which it reproduces the sound of the original performance. But a computer that merely plays back the data fed into it is of little use to anyone. Third, the record does not determine what the phonograph can do; the phonograph has the ability to play the record even before it does so. But a computer has the capacity to do very little until it is programmed. The record does not control the phonograph as a program does a computer.

Finally, a program may be described merely as a string of symbols, a nonsense writing, so to speak. Although this view is perhaps the most unsatisfactory from a technical point of view, it does have the advantage of avoiding the profound and sometimes troubling philosophical and psychological problems that stem from forcing ourselves to look deeply into a machine and seeing a reflection of the very workings of our minds.

A computer program, therefore, may be viewed as any one or more of the following:

> a particular form of expression of a flowchart or algorithm, an instruction manual for human beings,
> a process for controlling or bringing about a desired result inside a computer,
> a machine part or completion of an incomplete machine,
> a circuit diagram or blueprint for a circuit board,
> a data compilation,
> a code writing,
> a "phonograph record" or "sheet music," or
> a mere pattern of symbols or nonsense writing.

What a program is determines how the law can and will protect it.

COPYRIGHT

Copyrightability

At one time a good many words were written about whether programs are copyrightable. Remember that by "program" we are still referring to source program unless we explicitly state otherwise. There is really little doubt now that programs can be copyrighted; in particular; the new Copyright Act passed in 1976 and now in full effect clearly implies that programs are copyrightable as "literary works." This indeed is the official position of the Copyright Office, and these are the words of Marybeth Peters, Senior Attorney-Advisor for that Office:

> *Computer Programs.* Although they are not mentioned as copyrightable subject matter in Section 102(a) and they are not referred to explicitly in the definition of "literary works" in Section 101, a careful reading of the

new law with the legislative reports makes it clear that computer programs or "software" is within the subject matter of copyright. The definition of "literary works" refers to work expressed in "words, numbers, or other verbal or numerical symbols or indicia."

If then the matter is settled that programs are copyrightable, what then is the problem? Why not just copyright programs and be protected? Unfortunately, there are complex questions associated with copyright and programs:

1) What precisely does copyright protect if a program is copyrighted?
2) Is copyright an appropriate and practical form of protection for software even if it is available?

Tentative answers to these questions will be suggested later in this section. It must be noted, at least in passing, that the Copyright Office and Congress do not have the last word on what is proper subject matter for copyright. The Supreme Court can strike down copyrightability of programs on the grounds they are not writings of an author in the sense intended by the Constitution in the clause that grants Congress the power to protect certain writings and discoveries. Section 102(b) of the Copyright Law embodies much of what the Supreme Court has already said concerning what may not be copyrighted:

> In no case does copyright protection . . . extend to any idea, procedure, process, system, method of operation, concept, principle, or discovery, regardless of the form in which it is described, explained, illustrated, or embodied in such work.

Copyrights are reserved for a "writing." A program may be eligible for a patent, even if it is not eligible for a copyright, or it may not be proper subject matter for either a copyright or a patent under the Constitution. It may seem highly strange that a group of nine lawyers, none of whom have any special expertise in computer technology, can ultimately decide the nature of a computer program in the eyes of the law, but that is the way our judicial system works.

Section 102(a) of the Copyright Law states what can be copyrighted:

What can be copyrighted?

> Copyright protection subsists . . . in original works of authorship fixed in any tangible medium of expression, now known or later developed, from which they can be perceived, reproduced, or otherwise communicated, either directly or with the aid of a machine or device.

Programs certainly seem to fit this description, but if the Supreme Court decides that programs are really processes or methods of operation, they will not be copyrightable.

Even if an individual program copyright is found to be constitutional, the program must still satisfy the requirements set forth in Section 102(a) above; that is, it must be an original work of authorship fixed in a tangible medium of expression. The "author" of a program is simply the one who originates it. Origination implies some originality, but the degree of originality required to obtain a copyright is minimal. As one court put it:

> All that is needed to satisfy both the Constitution and the statute is that the "author" contributed something more than a "merely trivial" variation, something recognizably "his own." Originality in this context "means little more than a prohibition of actual copying."

The reader may guess that something which requires such a low standard of originality may be accorded a comparably low level of legal protection. If a program is recorded on paper, tape, cards, or whatever, in a manner that permits it to be perceived directly or by means of a computer print-out, then it would also seem to satisfy the requisite degree of "tangibility" or fixation required by the copyright law. It is more problematic whether a program that exists solely as electrical impulses or magnetic patterns is sufficiently tangible to meet the necessary conditions. It would seem here too that the transient nature of the program might also bring into question whether or not it is "fixed" in any medium of expression, tangible or not.

Little interest in program copyrights

But even if a program is granted a full, complete, and unassailably valid copyright, what does that copyright protect? Whatever it is, it has not induced programmers to line up outside the Copyright Office. The Register of Copyrights has, in fact, accepted programs for registration since 1964. As of January 1, 1977, only 1,205 programs had been registered; 971 of these came from two large hardware manufacturers, IBM and Burroughs. It is estimated that at least 1,000,000 programs are developed each year. These statistics seem to evidence very little interest in copyright of programs. Moreover, there has not been a single suit filed either challenging the validity of a program copyright or charging infringement of such a copyright. The closest any court has come to ruling on the protection accorded programs by copyright is a case in which a data input format was held to be an "idea expressed" rather than the "expression of an idea"; consequently, the format was not entitled to copyright protection because an idea in itself is not copyrightable. In this particular case, *Synercom Technology* v. *University Computing Company*, a competitor of the copyright holder wrote a preprocessor program that enabled users of the plaintiff's software service to convert to the competitor's service without changing the input format. The competitor constructed his preprocessor program from descriptions contained in the plaintiff's instruction manual. The court held in essence that the "order and sequence" of software formats are uncopyrightable ideas. The court suggested that the program itself might have been protectable by copyright. The court in this case was able to protect the developer of the special format by finding an infringement of the copyright on his instruction manual. The defendant had written his preprocessing program using the plaintiff's manual, which in itself is not an infringement. But the defendant still had to inform his clients how to use his new service and here he relied too heavily on the plaintiff's copyrighted material.

If a court is willing to uphold a program's copyright, what aspects of the program is it likely to find protected? Underlying any computer program is an algorithm or method for solving a problem or doing a task. The algorithm, even if highly unique and of great commercial value, will not be protected. But the algorithm is often the most important aspect of the program and that which its creator most wants to protect. A competitor who could gain knowledge of the underlying method by examining a program, could then design his or her own flow chart and write his or her own program, taking advantage of all the hard work and thought and ingenuity that went into the development of the algorithm without paying one cent for the privilege. What is protected?

How a court views a program will, of course, affect what protection the court will consider to be appropriate. If the court believes that the program is an instructional manual, then it will probably find no infringement if an unauthorized individual follows those instructions by running the program on a computer. One does not infringe the copyright on a book on how to play bridge by playing bridge, even if one learns how to play that game by reading the book. Court's view of program decisive

If the court views the program as a blueprint for a circuit board or a wiring diagram, then it will probably also not find any infringement if someone actually builds the circuit following the instructions contained in the program. This is analogous to building a house from copyrighted plans without the permission of the holder of the copyright. Most courts hold that there is no infringement in such an instance because one is not copying the plans, but merely using them to construct something quite distinct from them. Copying the plans themselves would constitute an infringement.

If the program is considered to be a data compilation, then a competitor is free to acquire a similar compilation, provided he or she contributes some of his or her own effort to the project. How much effort is needed to make the new compilation sufficiently original that there is no infringement is not clear and must be decided in each instance by the court. Authorities disagree, however, whether the competitor may use the original compilation after verifying its statements, or the original can be used for verification only after he or she has completed an independent compilation. But here, even having an opportunity to compare the independent program-compilation against a program that is known to work could be a significant aid in making sure that the program does what it is supposed to, as well as in finding and correcting bugs. Of course, if one is free to look at another's copyrighted program before even attempting to write his or her own, and uses that program as the model for his or her own compilation, "verifying" that compilation would consist of little more than trying the run the "new" compilation. The idea of a program as compilation does not appear to be very satisfactory from the viewpoint of protection afforded.

Infringement

But before any court will grant a plaintiff any remedy for an alleged infringement of copyright, before it will protect any aspect of the work the plaintiff alleges was infringed upon, the court must find that an infringement actually took place. Proving an infringement of a copyright of a computer program is a formidable task indeed, even without the added burden of defending the copyright against an attack on constitutional grounds.

The plaintiff in a copyright infringement suit must prove that the defendant has copied the protected work *and* that the copying was of such a nature as to constitute an improper appropriation. This latter requirement is sometimes expressed by saying that there must be a substantial similarity between the two works.

Copying is an essential element of the plaintiff's case. Since it is all but impossible for two programs of any length to be identical without copying, a court faced with identical programs could find the presence of the "striking similarities" that can form an adequate basis for a conclusion that copying has occurred. Striking similarities, that is, those that are plausibly explainable only by copying, suffice to establish copying; but that is only half the battle. The plaintiff must often also prove access. This may be done by showing that the defendant had a reasonable opportunity to see the plaintiff's program. Even if the defendant's computer program is in every way identical to the plaintiff's, there is no infringement if the defendant establishes that he or she independently produced that program without access to the plaintiff's. The defendant could also argue that the similarities come from coincidence or some common source used by both the plaintiff and him- or herself.

After proving that actual copying occurred, the plaintiff must still establish that the copying constituted improper appropriation. In deciding this issue, the court must first ascertain what part of the plaintiff's work is entitled to protection. Then the court must decide whether the appropriation of that protected part is improper. The taking of as few as three lines of text was found in one case to infringe, while in another case no infringement was found in the taking of an entire work.

The line between improper appropriation and fair use is not easily drawn. A court will consider such factors as the extent to which the defendant relied on the plaintiff's work, and the quantity and quality of the defendant's own independent contribution to the "copy" in determining whether there has been an infringement. Some courts have protected the labor expended by the plaintiff even though there was little in the plaintiff's work, other than the effort expended to bring it about, that was entitled to protection. Infringement may even be found where there is no identity of language between the original and the copy.

Fair use

Expert testimony can be introduced with regard to whether or not copying has occurred. Copying can exist without infringement since it takes both copying and improper appropriation to make an infringement. The test, however, for improper appropriation, and hence for the ultimate claim of infringement where copying is established or even admitted by the defendant, is the "response of the ordinary lay person," not the opinion of the specialist. This is to say that it does not depend on whether an expert in computer science believes that there is improper appropriation, but whether an average person, possibly with no background at all in computers, thinks the defendant has gone too far in using the work of another.

Test for improper appropriation

Special problems are encountered in a suit alleging infringement of a program copyright. First, showing access may prove troublesome. The mere fact that a competitor has a program similar to the plaintiff's program is insufficient to establish infringement. If the competitor developed the program independently, there is no infringement. If the competitor's access to information stored inside the computer goes undetected, the plaintiff may be unable to prove copying. The reader is no doubt aware that the contents of a computer's memory can be stolen over telephone lines from great distances, often without leaving a trace of the theft. Computers too emit electromagnetic signals while they are operating, and it is at least theoretically possible for someone to monitor this radiation. Of course, in some instances proof of access may be easy: the presence of a common employee, or a trial use by the accused of the program in question. But a computer specialist bent on misappropriating the work of another may use techniques that will make proof of access difficult, if not impossible. The defendant might have even used a computer to help disguise his or her copying by means of a program that automatically disguises the infringing copy through significant changes in the format, variable names, statement

Access and programs

numbers, or even the high level language in which the program is written. There is no need for the defendant to even make a hard copy of the program, since all he or she usually wants is its use, or the use of the idea expressed in it.

Striking similarities and programs

It is also difficult to prove that there are striking similarities. Most courts do not possess sufficient technical background to determine whether striking similarities exist between seemingly dissimilar programs. Therefore, expert witnesses are usually permitted to testify concerning the degree of similarity, or lack thereof, between the programs. Even experts, however, may find it extremely difficult to determine if one program has been copied from another. The same computer program can appear in a bewildering variety of forms including the flow chart, source program, and object program. Both the source and object programs can appear in a variety of media including tape, cards, and disk. The source program can be written in an increasing number of high level languages; and, of course, there are even "dialects" of each of these languages. Even two source programs that do exactly the same thing and are written in the same language can differ significantly in a number of ways: the order and manner in which data is to be entered, the variable names, the order of instructions, or the statement numbers. They could have different underlying algorithms (in which case copying is certainly highly unlikely) and use different input and output devices. All of these differences and more must be explained to a judge and possibly a jury as well, who have at best a minimal understanding of the terminology and the technology involved.

Improper appropriation and programs

Most of the problems encountered when trying to prove striking similarities are encountered as well in trying to prove improper appropriation. The algorithm underlying a program, perhaps its most valuable aspect, cannot be copyrighted at all. "Protection is given only to the expression of an idea—not the idea itself," said the United States Supreme Court in 1954. Given an uncopyrightable algorithm, a court may find that the range of ways in which the algorithm could be expressed as a program is so small, despite the seeming differences that programs can display, that no program using that algorithm is protected. It is part of copyright law that if some idea can be expressed only in a fairly restricted number of ways, then none of these ways may be pre-empted by copyright. Certainly the number of ways that a particular instruction can be expressed is limited. Many computing routines have a more or less standardized expression. The use of such expressions could, therefore, not be found to have the element of originality needed for protection against use by the general public. Alternatively, the court might hold that there is improper appropriation only if there is verbatim copying.

The broad wealth of common knowledge in the computer industry and the mobility of programmers presents additional problems. If Joe Programmer writes a program for Company A, then leaves to work for Company B at a higher salary, and Company B then asks him to write that same program for them—indeed, they may have hired him for precisely that reason—there might be no infringement of Company A's copyright if Joe relies solely on his memory and his personal skill. It should be noted in passing that Company A would be presumed to have the copyright on the program under the "works for hire" doctrine which states that when an employee's work is produced at the expense and request of his or her employer, the employer is presumed to have a copyright in the absence of any express contractual provisions to the contrary. There may be a breach of contract here or violation of trade secrecy in addition to any copyright infringement. But the question of whether Joe or Company B has infringed upon Company A's copyright is not yet subject to a clear answer, even though that answer may have sweeping implications for the entire software industry since programmers are often hired to do much the same work as they did for their former employers. In any event, this thorny question represents yet another issue that may have to be argued in a suit for infringement.

<small>Mobility of programmers</small>

Even this brief discussion should convince the reader of the awesome obstacles that confront the plaintiff in seeking compensation for infringement of a program copyright. Judges, juries, and most attorneys are ignorant of the terms and practices of the computer industry; the law is still very unsettled, and, because so few cases involving computer programs have been decided, arguments must be still very much by analogy. Courts have not even come to an agreement on the nature of a computer program, a question which, if decided in certain ways, could preclude copyright of programs altogether.

<small>Serious copyright problems</small>

The problems of the plaintiff begin even before any complaint is filed. Because a program can be copied from a great distance and without leaving a trace, and because someone who misappropriates a program will usually use it inside his or her own computer operation rather than distribute it, the detection of any infringement may be extraordinarily difficult. A program is not performed publicly like a musical composition, nor does it necessarily depend on wide distribution to be of great commercial value to its owner. Moreover, a program can be read from one computer to another at almost the speed of light, even when the program being "copied" is actually being run. Simply transmitting the pattern of switch settings from one computer to another may not even be copying in the eyes of the law. It would not have been copying under the old copyright law; it does appear that it would constitute copying under the new, *if* that new law were to be applied to computer programs.

If an infringement is detected, then the copyright owner must determine if the economics of the situation justify the risk and expense of a suit. If the copyright owner wins, he or she may recoup both damages and attorney's fees, and may obtain a court order forbidding the infringer any further use of the program. If he or she loses, the copyright owner may not only be forced to pay the defendant's attorney's fees as well as his or her own, but may also lose the copyright if the court decides that it is invalid. Furthermore, the owner may update and modify his or her own program and redesign it to meet the needs of individual licensees. Unless every version of the program has been copyrighted, the owner is faced with the question of what the copyright actually covers. A book that has entered the stream of commerce is unlikely to be altered by its author; this is not the case with computer programs that are subject to constant revision.

Constant modification

The new copyright law, however, protects any program having the requisite degree of originality as soon as it becomes "fixed in any tangible medium of expression . . . from which [it] can be perceived, reproduced, or otherwise communicated" directly or with the aid of a computer. Because a limited distribution of such a program under a contract not to disclose would not be a publication, the program owner does not have to put a copyright notice on this program to maintain this protection if the contract is the sole means by which the program is made available. He or she does not even have to register the program with the Copyright Office.

Copyright registration not required

It may come as a surprise that copyright protection can exist without even applying for a copyright. It should come as no surprise, though, that copyright protection for an unregistered work is limited and can easily be lost altogether. The reader who still wants copyright protection for a program, despite the shortcomings that such protection might have, should know the following:

Term of copyright

1. Copyright in a work created on or after January 1, 1978, subsists from its creation and generally continues for the lifetime of the author plus fifty years after his or her death.

Notice needed

2. Whenever a copyrighted work is published by authority of the owner of the copyright, a proper notice of copyright must be placed on all publicly distributed copies from which the work can be visually perceived, either directly or with the aid of a machine or device. This notice generally has the format

© XXXX Name of copyright owner

where XXXX is the year of first publication. The notice must be displayed in some manner that those using the work are reasonably likely to get notice of the claim of copyright.

3. If the copyright notice described above is missing from copies of the work which are distributed by the authority of the copyright owner, the copyright protection as well as the copyright itself may be lost. The rules about this are somewhat complex and the safest course of action is to make sure that the copyright notice in proper format occurs conspicuously on all copies sent out or published. The copyright owner, of course, is not responsible for policing what appears on unauthorized copies of the work. *Consequences of missing notice*

4. If the work is not registered with the Copyright Office, then in many instances the copyright owner will risk losing an award of damages for misappropriation of the work. Copyright registration is a simple and inexpensive procedure. A copy of Form TX, that form most likely to be used to register a program, is reproduced on pages 94-98. The Copyright Office does not check to see if the work is really original, only that it is proper matter for copyright. Having a certificate of copyright does give the holder some advantages in a trial in a suit for infringement, but these advantages are in no sense decisive of the outcome of the suit. *Registration desirable*

If anyone wants copyright protection for programs, then, as has been pointed out earlier, it is probably available. Nevertheless, given whatever protection copyright will afford, and the ease of registration, the software industry generally has not found copyright protection to be adequate, at least in its present form. Later on, we will look at proposed extended copyright protection designed especially for programs to see if that is any better. As of now, only an infinitesimal fraction of existing programs have been registered, and no case involving direct infringement of any computer program has yet been reported. The reason for this apathy is not hard to understand. It is not clear what copyright protects in programs, or even if it protects anything at all. The risk and expense of litigation is high, and the courts are generally not well equipped to hear such highly technical cases. It is patent protection for which the software industry has lobbied most actively, and it is to an examination of that method of protection that we now turn. *Industry apathetic to copyright*

PATENTS

Although the power of Congress to legislate both copyright and patent protection is conferred in the same brief sentence in the Constitution, these two forms of protection are vastly different. Obtaining copyright registration is a trivial matter; obtaining a patent is an arduous and expensive process. The scope of copyright protection is very limited, while patent protection confers a virtual monopoly on *Patent v. copyright*

94   LAW AND THE COMPUTER

APPLICATION FOR COPYRIGHT REGISTRATION
for a Nondramatic Literary Work

FORM TX
UNITED STATES COPYRIGHT OFFICE
LIBRARY OF CONGRESS
WASHINGTON, D.C. 20559

HOW TO APPLY FOR COPYRIGHT REGISTRATION:

- *First:* Read the information on this page to make sure Form TX is the correct application for your work.
- *Second:* Open out the form by pulling this page to the left. Read through the detailed instructions before starting to complete the form.
- *Third:* Complete spaces 1-4 of the application, then turn the entire form over and, after reading the instructions for spaces 5-11, complete the rest of your application. Use typewriter or print in dark ink. Be sure to sign the form at space 10.
- *Fourth:* Detach your completed application from these instructions and send it with the necessary deposit of the work (see below) to: Register of Copyrights, Library of Congress, Washington, D.C. 20559. Unless you have a Deposit Account in the Copyright Office, your application and deposit must be accompanied by a check or money order for $10, payable to: *Register of Copyrights.*

WHEN TO USE FORM TX: Form TX is the appropriate application to use for copyright registration covering nondramatic literary works, whether published or unpublished.

WHAT IS A "NONDRAMATIC LITERARY WORK"? The category of "nondramatic literary works" (Class TX) is very broad. Except for dramatic works and certain kinds of audiovisual works, Class TX includes all types of works written in words (or other verbal or numerical symbols). A few of the many examples of "nondramatic literary works" include fiction, nonfiction, poetry, periodicals, textbooks, reference works, directories, catalogs, advertising copy, and compilations of information.

DEPOSIT TO ACCOMPANY APPLICATION: An application for copyright registration must be accompanied by a deposit representing the entire work for which registration is to be made. The following are the general deposit requirements as set forth in the statute:

   Unpublished work: Deposit one complete copy (or phonorecord).

   Published work: Deposit two complete copies (or phonorecords) of the best edition.

   Work first published outside the United States: Deposit one complete copy (or phonorecord) of the first foreign edition.

   Contribution to a collective work: Deposit one complete copy (or phonorecord) of the best edition of the collective work.

These general deposit requirements may vary in particular situations. For further information about copyright deposit, write to the Copyright Office.

THE COPYRIGHT NOTICE: For published works, the law provides that a copyright notice in a specified form "shall be placed on all publicly distributed copies from which the work can be visually perceived." Use of the copyright notice is the responsibility of the copyright owner and does not require advance permission from the Copyright Office. The required form of the notice for copies generally consists of three elements: (1) the symbol "©", or the word "Copyright", or the abbreviation "Copr."; (2) the year of first publication; and (3) the name of the owner of copyright. For example: "© 1978 Constance Porter". The notice is to be affixed to the copies "in such manner and location as to give reasonable notice of the claim of copyright." Unlike the law in effect before 1978, the new copyright statute provides procedures for correcting errors in the copyright notice, and even for curing the omission of the notice. However, a failure to comply with the notice requirements may still result in the loss of some copyright protection and, unless corrected within five years, in the complete loss of copyright. For further information about the copyright notice and the procedures for correcting errors or omissions, write to the Copyright Office.

DURATION OF COPYRIGHT: For works that were created after the effective date of the new statute (January 1, 1978), the basic copyright term will be the life of the author and fifty years after the author's death. For works made for hire, and for certain anonymous and pseudonymous works, the duration of copyright will be 75 years from publication or 100 years from creation, whichever is shorter. These same terms of copyright will generally apply to works that had been created before 1978 but had not been published or copyrighted before that date. For further information about the duration of copyright, including the terms of copyrights already in existence before 1978, write for Circular R15a.

FORM TX

UNITED STATES COPYRIGHT OFFICE

REGISTRATION NUMBER

TX   TXU

EFFECTIVE DATE OF REGISTRATION

....
(Month)   (Day)   (Year)

DO NOT WRITE ABOVE THIS LINE. IF YOU NEED MORE SPACE, USE CONTINUATION SHEET (FORM TX/CON)

① Title

TITLE OF THIS WORK: **PREVIOUS OR ALTERNATIVE TITLES:**

If a periodical or serial give: Vol....... No....... Issue Date ....

PUBLICATION AS A CONTRIBUTION: (If this work was published as a contribution to a periodical, serial, or collection, give information about the collective work in which the contribution appeared.)
Title of Collective Work: .... Vol...... No...... Date .... Pages............

② Author(s)

IMPORTANT: Under the law, the "author" of a "work made for hire" is generally the employer, not the employee (see instructions). If any part of this work was "made for hire" check "Yes" in the space provided, give the employer (or other person for whom the work was prepared) as "Author" of that part, and leave the space for dates blank.

1
NAME OF AUTHOR: **DATES OF BIRTH AND DEATH:** Born......... Died......... (Year) (Year)
Was this author's contribution to the work a "work made for hire"? Yes...... No......
AUTHOR'S NATIONALITY OR DOMICILE: Citizen of .... (Name of Country) or Domiciled in .... (Name of Country)
WAS THIS AUTHOR'S CONTRIBUTION TO THE WORK: Anonymous? Yes...... No...... Pseudonymous? Yes...... No......
AUTHOR OF: (Briefly describe nature of this author's contribution)
If the answer to either of these questions is "Yes," see detailed instructions attached.

2
NAME OF AUTHOR: **DATES OF BIRTH AND DEATH:** Born......... Died......... (Year) (Year)
Was this author's contribution to the work a "work made for hire"? Yes...... No......
AUTHOR'S NATIONALITY OR DOMICILE: Citizen of .... (Name of Country) or Domiciled in .... (Name of Country)
WAS THIS AUTHOR'S CONTRIBUTION TO THE WORK: Anonymous? Yes...... No...... Pseudonymous? Yes...... No......
AUTHOR OF: (Briefly describe nature of this author's contribution)
If the answer to either of these questions is "Yes," see detailed instructions attached.

3
NAME OF AUTHOR: **DATES OF BIRTH AND DEATH:** Born......... Died......... (Year) (Year)
Was this author's contribution to the work a "work made for hire"? Yes...... No......
AUTHOR'S NATIONALITY OR DOMICILE: Citizen of .... (Name of Country) or Domiciled in .... (Name of Country)
WAS THIS AUTHOR'S CONTRIBUTION TO THE WORK: Anonymous? Yes...... No...... Pseudonymous? Yes...... No......
AUTHOR OF: (Briefly describe nature of this author's contribution)
If the answer to either of these questions is "Yes," see detailed instructions attached.

③ Creation and Publication

YEAR IN WHICH CREATION OF THIS WORK WAS COMPLETED: **DATE AND NATION OF FIRST PUBLICATION:**

Year...........   Date .... (Month) (Day) (Year)
     Nation .... (Name of Country)

(This information must be given in all cases.)   (Complete this block ONLY if this work has been published.)

④ Claimant(s)

NAME(S) AND ADDRESS(ES) OF COPYRIGHT CLAIMANT(S):

TRANSFER: (If the copyright claimant(s) named here in space 4 are different from the author(s) named in space 2, give a brief statement of how the claimant(s) obtained ownership of the copyright.)

- Complete all applicable spaces (numbers 5-11) on the reverse side of this page
- Follow detailed instructions attached   • Sign the form at line 10

DO NOT WRITE HERE
Page 1 of .... pages

HOW TO FILL OUT FORM TX
Specific Instructions for Spaces 1-4

- The line-by-line instructions on this page are keyed to the spaces on the first page of Form TX, printed opposite.
- Please read through these instructions before you start filling out your application, and refer to the specific instructions for each space as you go along.

SPACE 1: TITLE

- **Title of this Work:** Every work submitted for copyright registration must be given a title that is capable of identifying that particular work. If the copies or phonorecords of the work bear a title (or an identifying phrase that could serve as a title), transcribe its wording completely and exactly on the application. Remember that indexing of the registration and future identification of the work will depend on the information you give here.

- **Periodical or Serial Issue:** Periodicals and other serials are publications issued at intervals under a general title, such as newspapers, magazines, journals, newsletters, and annuals. If the work being registered is an entire issue of a periodical or serial, give the over-all title of the periodical or serial in the space headed "Title of this Work," and add the specific information about the issue in the spaces provided. If the work being registered is a contribution to a periodical or serial issue, follow the instructions for "Publication as a Contribution."

- **Previous or Alternative Titles:** Complete this space if there are any additional titles for the work under which someone searching for the registration might be likely to look, or under which a document pertaining to the work might be recorded.

- **Publication as a Contribution:** If the work being registered has been published as a contribution to a periodical, serial, or collection, give the title of the contribution in the space headed "Title of this Work." Then, in the line headed "Publication as a Contribution," give information about the larger work in which the contribution appeared.

SPACE 2: AUTHORS

- **General Instructions:** First decide, after reading these instructions, who are the "authors" of this work for copyright purposes. Then, unless the work is a "collective work" (see below), give the requested information about every "author" who contributed any appreciable amount of copyrightable matter to this version of the work. If you need further space, use the attached Continuation Sheet and, if necessary, request additional Continuation Sheets (Form TX/CON).

- **Who is the "Author"?** Unless the work was "made for hire," the individual who actually created the work is its "author." In the case of a work made for hire, the statute provides that "the employer or other person for whom the work was prepared is considered the author."

- **What is a "Work Made for Hire"?** A "work made for hire" is defined as: (1) "a work prepared by an employee within the scope of his or her employment"; or (2) "a work specially ordered or commissioned" for certain uses specified in the statute, but only if there is a written agreement to consider it a "work made for hire."

- **Collective Work:** In the case of a collective work, such as a periodical issue, anthology, collection of essays, or encyclopedia, it is sufficient to give information about the author of the collective work as a whole.

- **Author's Identity Not Revealed:** If an author's contribution is "anonymous" or "pseudonymous," it is not necessary to give the name and dates for that author. However, the citizenship or domicile of the author **must** be given in all cases, and information about the nature of that author's contribution to the work should be included.

- **Name of Author:** The fullest form of the author's name should be given. If you have checked "Yes" to indicate that the work was "made for hire," give the full legal name of the employer (or other person for whom the work was prepared). You may also include the name of the employee (for example, "Elster Publishing Co., employer for hire of John Ferguson"). If the work is "anonymous" you may: (1) leave the line blank, or (2) state "Anonymous" in the line, or (3) reveal the author's identity. If the work is "pseudonymous" you may (1) leave the line blank, or (2) give the pseudonym and identify it as such (for example: "Huntley Haverstock, pseudonym"), or (3) reveal the author's name, making clear which is the real name and which is the pseudonym (for example, "Judith Barton, whose pseudonym is Madeleine Elster").

- **Dates of Birth and Death:** If the author is dead, the statute requires that the year of death be included in the application unless the work is anonymous or pseudonymous. The author's birth date is optional, but is useful as a form of identification. Leave this space blank if the author's contribution was a "work made for hire."

- **"Anonymous" or "Pseudonymous" Work:** An author's contribution to a work is "anonymous" if that author is not identified on the copies or phonorecords of the work. An author's contribution to a work is "pseudonymous" if that author is identified on the copies or phonorecords under a fictitious name.

- **Author's Nationality or Domicile:** Give the country of which the author is a citizen, or the country in which the author is domiciled. The statute requires that either nationality or domicile be given in all cases.

- **Nature of Authorship:** After the words "Author of" give a brief general statement of the nature of this particular author's contribution to the work. Examples: "Entire text"; "Co-author of entire text"; "Chapters 11-14"; "Editorial revisions"; "Compilation and English translation"; "Illustrations."

SPACE 3: CREATION AND PUBLICATION

- **General Instructions:** Do not confuse "creation" with "publication." Every application for copyright registration must state "the year in which creation of the work was completed." Give the date and nation of first publication only if the work has been published.

- **Creation:** Under the statute, a work is "created" when it is fixed in a copy or phonorecord for the first time. Where a work has been prepared over a period of time, the part of the work existing in fixed form on a particular date constitutes the created work on that date. The date you give here should be the year in which the author completed the particular version for which registration is now being sought, even if other versions exist or if further changes or additions are planned.

- **Publication:** The statute defines "publication" as "the distribution of copies or phonorecords of a work to the public by sale or other transfer of ownership, or by rental, lease, or lending"; a work is also "published" if there has been an "offering to distribute copies or phonorecords to a group of persons for purposes of further distribution, public performance, or public display." Give the full date (month, day, year) when, and the country where, publication first occurred. If first publication took place simultaneously in the United States and other countries, it is sufficient to state "U.S.A."

SPACE 4: CLAIMANT(S)

- **Name(s) and Address(es) of Copyright Claimant(s):** Give the name(s) and address(es) of the copyright claimant(s) in this work. The statute provides that copyright in a work belongs initially to the author of the work (including, in the case of a work made for hire, the employer or other person for whom the work was prepared). The copyright claimant is either the author of the work or a person or organization that has obtained ownership of the copyright initially belonging to the author.

- **Transfer:** The statute provides that, if the copyright claimant is not the author, the application for registration must contain "a brief statement of how the claimant obtained ownership of the copyright." If any copyright claimant named in space 4 is not an author named in space 2, give a brief, general statement summarizing the means by which that claimant obtained ownership of the copyright.

LEGAL PROTECTION OF SOFTWARE 97

	EXAMINED BY:	APPLICATION RECEIVED:	
	CHECKED BY:		FOR COPYRIGHT OFFICE USE ONLY
	CORRESPONDENCE: ☐ Yes	DEPOSIT RECEIVED:	
	DEPOSIT ACCOUNT FUNDS USED: ☐	REMITTANCE NUMBER AND DATE:	

DO NOT WRITE ABOVE THIS LINE. IF YOU NEED ADDITIONAL SPACE, USE CONTINUATION SHEET (FORM TX/CON)

PREVIOUS REGISTRATION:

- Has registration for this work, or for an earlier version of this work, already been made in the Copyright Office?   Yes ....   No ....
- If your answer is "Yes," why is another registration being sought? (Check appropriate box)
  - ☐ This is the first published edition of a work previously registered in unpublished form.
  - ☐ This is the first application submitted by this author as copyright claimant.
  - ☐ This is a changed version of the work, as shown by line 6 of this application.
- If your answer is "Yes," give: Previous Registration Number .... Year of Registration ....

⑤ Previous Registration

COMPILATION OR DERIVATIVE WORK: (See instructions)

PREEXISTING MATERIAL: (Identify any preexisting work or works that this work is based on or incorporates.)
....

MATERIAL ADDED TO THIS WORK: (Give a brief, general statement of the material that has been added to this work and in which copyright is claimed.)
....

⑥ Compilation or Derivative Work

MANUFACTURERS AND LOCATIONS: (If this is a published work consisting preponderantly of nondramatic literary material in English, the law may require that the copies be manufactured in the United States or Canada for full protection. If so, the names of the manufacturers who performed certain processes, and the places where these processes were performed *must* be given. See instructions for details.)

NAMES OF MANUFACTURERS	PLACES OF MANUFACTURE
....	....
....	....
....	....

⑦ Manufacturing

REPRODUCTION FOR USE OF BLIND OR PHYSICALLY-HANDICAPPED PERSONS: (See instructions)

- Signature of this form at space 10, and a check in one of the boxes here in space 8, constitutes a non-exclusive grant of permission to the Library of Congress to reproduce and distribute solely for the blind and physically handicapped and under the conditions and limitations prescribed by the regulations of the Copyright Office: (1) copies of the work identified in space 1 of this application in Braille (or similar tactile symbols); or (2) phonorecords embodying a fixation of a reading of that work; or (3) both.

  a ☐ Copies and phonorecords   b ☐ Copies Only   c ☐ Phonorecords Only

⑧ License For Handicapped

DEPOSIT ACCOUNT: (If the registration fee is to be charged to a Deposit Account established in the Copyright Office, give name and number of Account.)

Name: ....
Account Number: ....

CORRESPONDENCE: (Give name and address to which correspondence about this application should be sent.)
Name: ....
Address: ....
.... (Apt.)
....
(City)   (State)   (ZIP)

⑨ Fee and Correspondence

CERTIFICATION: ✱ I, the undersigned, hereby certify that I am the: (Check one)
☐ author ☐ other copyright claimant ☐ owner of exclusive right(s) ☐ authorized agent of: ....
(Name of author or other copyright claimant, or owner of exclusive right(s))
of the work identified in this application and that the statements made by me in this application are correct to the best of my knowledge.

Handwritten signature: (X) ....

Typed or printed name: ....   Date ....

⑩ Certification (Application must be signed)

MAIL CERTIFICATE TO

....
(Name)
....
(Number, Street and Apartment Number)
....
(City)   (State)   (ZIP code)

(Certificate will be mailed in window envelope)

⑪ Address For Return of Certificate

✱ 17 U.S.C. § 506(e): Any person who knowingly makes a false representation of a material fact in the application for copyright registration provided for by section 409, or in any written statement filed in connection with the application, shall be fined not more than $2,500.
☆ U.S. GOVERNMENT PRINTING OFFICE: 1978-261-022/16

April 1978—500,000

98 LAW AND THE COMPUTER

PRIVACY ACT ADVISORY STATEMENT
Required by the Privacy Act of 1974 (Public Law 93-579)

AUTHORITY FOR REQUESTING THIS INFORMATION:
• Title 17, U.S.C., Secs. 409 and 410

FURNISHING THE REQUESTED INFORMATION IS:
• Voluntary

BUT IF THE INFORMATION IS NOT FURNISHED:
• It may be necessary to delay or refuse registration
• You may not be entitled to certain relief, remedies, and benefits provided in chapters 4 and 5 of title 17, U.S.C.

PRINCIPAL USES OF REQUESTED INFORMATION:
• Establishment and maintenance of a public record
• Examination of the application for compliance with legal requirements

OTHER ROUTINE USES:
• Public inspection and copying
• Preparation of public indexes

• Preparation of public catalogs of copyright registrations
• Preparation of search reports upon request

NOTE:
• No other advisory statement will be given you in connection with this application
• Please retain this statement and refer to it if we communicate with you regarding this application

---

INSTRUCTIONS FOR FILLING OUT SPACES 5-11 OF FORM TX

SPACE 5: PREVIOUS REGISTRATION

• **General Instructions:** The questions in space 5 are intended to find out whether an earlier registration has been made for this work and, if so, whether there is any basis for a new registration. As a general rule, only one basic copyright registration can be made for the same version of a particular work.

• **Same Version:** If this version is substantially the same as the work covered by a previous registration, a second registration is not generally possible unless: (1) the work has been registered in unpublished form and a second registration is now being sought to cover the first published edition, or (2) someone other than the author is identified as copyright claimant in the earlier registration, and the author is now seeking registration in his or her own name. If either of these two exceptions apply, check the appropriate box and give the earlier registration number and date. Otherwise, do not submit Form TX; instead, write the Copyright Office for information about supplementary registration or recordation of transfers of copyright ownership.

• **Changed Version:** If the work has been changed, and you are now seeking registration to cover the additions or revisions, check the third box in space 5, give the earlier registration number and date, and complete both parts of space 6.

• **Previous Registration Number and Date:** If more than one previous registration has been made for the work, give the number and date of the latest registration.

SPACE 6: COMPILATION OR DERIVATIVE WORK

• **General Instructions:** Complete both parts of space 6 if this work is a "compilation," or "derivative work," or both, and if it incorporates one or more earlier works that have already been published or registered for copyright, or that have fallen into the public domain. A "compilation" is defined as "a work formed by the collection and assembling of preexisting materials or of data that are selected, coordinated, or arranged in such a way that the resulting work as a whole constitutes an original work of authorship." A "derivative work" is "a work based on one or more preexisting works." Examples of derivative works include translations, fictionalizations, arrangements, abridgments, condensations, or "any other form in which a work may be recast, transformed, or adapted." Derivative works also include works "consisting of editorial revisions, annotations, elaborations, or other modifications" if these changes, as a whole, represent an original work of authorship.

• **Preexisting Material:** If the work is a compilation, give a brief, general statement describing the nature of the material that has been compiled. Example: "Compilation of all published 1917 speeches of Woodrow Wilson." In the case of a derivative work, identify the preexisting work that has been recast, transformed, or adapted. Example: "Russian version of Goncharov's 'Oblomov'."

• **Material Added to this Work:** The statute requires a "brief, general statement of the additional material covered by the copyright claim being registered." This statement should describe all of the material in this particular version of the work that: (1) represents an original work of authorship; and (2) has not fallen into the public domain; and (3) has not been previously published; and (4) has not been previously registered for copyright in unpublished form. Examples: "Foreword, selection, arrangement, editing, critical annotations"; "Revisions throughout; chapters 11-17 entirely new".

SPACE 7: MANUFACTURING PROVISIONS

• **General Instructions:** The copyright statute currently provides, as a general rule, and with a number of exceptions, that the copies of a published work "consisting preponderantly of nondramatic literary material that is in the English language" be manufactured in the United States or Canada in order to be lawfully imported and publicly distributed in the United States. At the present time, applications for copyright registration covering published works that consist mainly of nondramatic text matter in English *must*, in most cases, identify those who performed certain processes in manufacturing the copies, together with the places where those processes were performed. *Please note:* The information must be given even if the copies were manufactured outside the United States or Canada; registration will be made regardless of the places of manufacture identified in space 7. In general, the processes covered by this provision are: (1) typesetting and plate-making (where a typographic process preceded the actual printing); (2) the making of plates by a lithographic or photoengraving process (where this was a final or intermediate step before printing); and (3) the final printing and binding processes (in all cases). Leave space 7 blank if your work is unpublished or is not in English.

• **Import Statement:** As an exception to the manufacturing provisions, the statute prescribes that, where manufacture has taken place outside the United States or Canada, a maximum of 2000 copies of the foreign edition can be imported into the United States without affecting the copyright owner's rights. For this purpose, the Copyright Office will issue an import statement upon request and payment of a fee of $3 at the time of registration or at any later time. For further information about import statements, ask for Form IS.

SPACE 8: REPRODUCTION FOR USE OF BLIND OR PHYSICALLY-HANDICAPPED PERSONS

• **General Instructions:** One of the major programs of the Library of Congress is to provide Braille editions and special recordings of works for the exclusive use of the blind and physically handicapped. In an effort to simplify and speed up the copyright licensing procedures that are a necessary part of this program, section 710 of the copyright statute provides for the establishment of a voluntary licensing system to be tied in with copyright registration. Under this system, the owner of copyright in a nondramatic literary work has the option, at the time of registration on Form TX, to grant to the Library of Congress a license to reproduce and distribute Braille editions and "talking books" or "talking magazines" of the work being registered. The Copyright Office regulations provide that, under the license, the reproduction and distribution must be solely for the use of persons who are certified by competent authority as unable to read normal printed material as a result of physical limitations. The license is nonexclusive, and may be terminated upon 90 days notice. For further information, write for Circular R63.

• **How to Grant the License:** The license is entirely voluntary. If you wish to grant it, check one of the three boxes in space 8. Your check in one of these boxes, together with your signature in space 10, will mean that the Library of Congress can proceed to reproduce and distribute under the license without further paperwork.

SPACES 9, 10, 11: FEE, CORRESPONDENCE, CERTIFICATION, RETURN ADDRESS

• **Deposit Account and Mailing Instructions (Space 9):** If you maintain a Deposit Account in the Copyright Office, identify it in space 9. Otherwise you will need to send the registration fee of $10 with your application. The space headed "Correspondence" should contain the name and address of the person to be consulted if correspondence about this application becomes necessary.

• **Certification (Space 10):** The application is not acceptable unless it bears the handwritten signature of the author or other copyright claimant, or of the owner of exclusive right(s), or of the duly authorized agent of such author, claimant, or owner.

• **Address for Return of Certificate (Space 11):** The address box must be completed legibly, since the certificate will be returned in a window envelope.

the use of the invention. Almost no tax advantages flow to the holder of a copyright, but huge tax advantages can accrue to an inventor who is lucky enough to obtain a patent. I point out at once, however, that tax questions are not going to be covered in this text. One would almost guess that Congress has preferred inventors over writers and artists from the type of legal protection accorded the works of each.

But if the state of program copyrights is confused, the state of program patents is altogether chaotic. The plot has all of the elements of a comic opera with four principal characters: First, there is the Patent Office, which has made a practice of turning down virtually every application for a program patent. Second, there is the Court of Customs and Patent Appeals, which, as its name implies, is a court to which a disappointed patent seeker can apply after the Patent Office has turned down his or her application. The Court of Customs and Patent Appeals, perhaps the closest thing to a scientific or technical court of law in this country, has fought rather bravely for program patents in the face of increasing opposition from the Supreme Court, and has been one of the only courts to try to answer some of the difficult and troubling questions concerning the nature of a computer program. Next, there is the United States Supreme Court, which one author, Harold Davis, describes as trying to apply "nineteenth century legal notions to computer technology without understanding the technology," which keeps reversing the Court of Customs and Patent Appeals, but without ever directly confronting the issue of program patentability. Finally, there is Congress, which the Constitution has charged with legislating in this area, and which the Supreme Court has implored to act to clarify the questions of program patents, but which, as of this writing, has steadfastly refused to do anything in this area.

Program patent law chaotic

Software manufacturers seem, at least in their public statements, to be genuinely interested in patents, in contrast to their indifference toward copyrights. This is because the protection provided by a patent is immensely greater than the protection conferred by a copyright. As one federal judge put it:

Protection accorded by patent

> A patent is a grant of the right to exclude others from making, using or selling one's invention, and includes the right to license others to make, use or sell it. It is a legitimate monopoly . . .

Because a patent grants a monopoly, someone who develops a program substantially the same as a patented program, but without any knowledge whatsoever of the existence of the protected program, still infringes, while that same independent developer could, if he or she wished, even obtain his or her own copyright on the new substantially identical program.

100 LAW AND THE COMPUTER

Rigid standards for patents

Because the protection accorded by a patent is so sweeping, it is granted only upon very rigid terms. Instead of the minimal originality that suffices to support a copyright, the attributes of utility, novelty, and unobviousness must all concur to support a patent. Utility is a property that most programs easily satisfy: the program must be able to perform at least one of the beneficial functions its inventor claims that it can. A "claim" is a special term used in patent law, but, as used here, it basically has its common meaning.

Novelty is a more difficult attribute to satisfy. A patent lacks novelty if all of the elements of the patent, or their equivalents, are found in a single prior structure or device where they do substantially the same work in substantially the same way.

Obviousness is the attribute that is likely to give applicants for program patents the most difficulty. The test for obviousness was set forth by the United States Supreme Court in the case of *Graham* v. *John Deere Company:*

> [T]he scope and content of the prior art are to be determined; differences between the prior art and the claims are to be ascertained; and the level of ordinary skill in the pertinent art resolved. Against this background, the obviousness or nonobviousness of the subject matter is determined.

Novelty and obviousness are related. An invention that lacks novelty is likely to be obvious as well. However, an invention that is novel may still be obvious. The mere fact that no one has previously built a certain machine, or written a certain program, is sufficient to confer novelty, but not unobviousness. What the prior art is and what the claimed invention is are both questions of fact, as opposed to questions of law. One may imagine the problems resolving this question of fact would pose for a judge or jury uneducated in the techniques and art of computing. Moreover, the test of obviousness is to be applied as of the time of the invention and not as of the time of the suit. One needs, in other words, to be able to discern what could or could not be done using prior art at the time the program to be patented was actually written.

Process for obtaining patent

The process of obtaining a patent is far more tedious and expensive than the process for obtaining a copyright. Although an author can register virtually any writing that he or she has independently created, an inventor seeking a patent is assumed to have complete knowledge of all prior art, even though he or she may be totally ignorant of it. And although the Register of Copyrights makes no check of prior copyrights before issuing a certificate of registration, the Patent Office requires a thorough search of all prior patents to determine if any invention submitted to it is truly novel enough to warrant a patent. As one Supreme Court Justice once stated it, "He who seeks to build a better mousetrap has a long path to tread before reaching the Patent Office." The average length of time it takes to tread that path is more than two years.

Despite the strict scrutiny given patent applications and the length and expense of the procedure for obtaining a patent, nothing discussed thus far precludes program patentability. Indeed, software manufacturers at least claim to be willing to spend the time, effort, and treasure to gain patent protection. If a software package costs several hundred thousand dollars to develop, a few thousand dollars more for protection against unauthorized use is certainly a reasonable investment. There are things, however, which cannot be patented at all. Included among these are ideas, scientific principles, mathematical algorithms, phenomena of nature, and mental processes. These restrictions exist to prevent the pre-emption of entire fields of science and the establishment of a monopoly on human thought. One could well imagine the utter chaos that would result if someone could patent, say, the law of gravity or the sine function.

But even though an abstract idea or principle is not patentable, a device or process which utilizes it may be patentable. If a court determines that a program is identical with the algorithm it contains, then the court will necessarily hold against patentability. But if the program is merely a useful process that utilizes the algorithm without pre-empting it, and the program clears the hurdles of novelty and unobviousness as well, the court will find that it is patentable.

Idea v. device using idea

Patents and copyrights are divided into different categories. The classification (nature) of a copyrighted work determines the degree of protection for the copyright owner. In patent law, however, the classification determines whether there will be any patent protection at all. A patent sought under the wrong classification may be held invalid, even though the invention would be fully patentable if it had been classified correctly.

Classification of patents

Permissible classifications of claims include process, machine, manufacture, composition of matter, or any new and useful improvement thereof. There are also design patents, but these refer primarily to ornamental objects and are of no relevance to computer programs. Claims for program patentability by their nature must be concerned with either machines or processes, and both types of claims can appear on the same patent application. Machine patents cover devices that must be used in connection with an actual mechanism. On the other hand, a process is described as:

> [A] mode of treatment of certain materials to produce a given result. It is an act, or series of acts, performed upon the subject matter to be transformed and reduced to a different state or thing.

These are the words of the Supreme Court. A process patent does not require that the machine used in carrying out the process be itself new or patentable.

History of program patents

This brief look at the principles of patent law paves the way for a summary of the strange history of program patents in the courts. In 1964 the Patent Office itself did not believe programs to be patentable because they were "creations in the area of thought;" but the Board of Patent Appeals, one step lower than the Court of Customs and Patent Appeals, had not yet ruled on the patentability of programs. In 1965, the President's Commission on the Patent System was established to suggest revisions to the Patent Act; the Commission released its report at the end of 1966. With regard to computer programs, the Commission made this recommendation:

> A series of instructions which control or condition the operation of a data processing machine, generally referred to as a "program," shall not be considered patentable regardless of whether the program is claimed as: (a) an article, (b) a process described in terms of the operations performed by a machine pursuant to the program, or (c) one or more machine configurations established by a program.

Legislation was introduced in both houses of Congress to implement this recommendation, but it did not pass.

In 1968, the Patent Office officially declared that "computer programs per se . . . shall not be patentable." In 1969, the Court of Customs and Patent Appeals, in *In re Prater*, rejected this guideline. The court explicitly declared that it saw no reason based on the Constitution, statute, or case law, for denying program patents under either machine or process claims. The Patent Office, on the other hand, contended that Prater's process, which could be carried out with pencil and paper alone, was an idea or mental process and therefore was not proper matter for a patent, even though Prater had actually produced a machine to carry out the steps so that they would not have be done mentally. The Office rejected the machine claim because the novelty was in the process and not the machine, and the process, in its opinion, was simply an idea. Thus was born the so-called "mental steps" doctrine. In particular, the Patent Office stated that if an integral part of any process or machine consisted of a "mental step," that is, a function that was, or could be, carried out in one's head, then the invention was one that could not be patented.

The Court of Customs and Patent Appeals rejected the mental steps doctrine in *In re Musgrave* in 1970. The Court indicated that the doctrine might have validity only when some step in a process was "purely mental" and incapable of being performed by a machine. In *In re Bernhart*, decided in 1969, the Court declared that a computer that is programmed in a new and unobvious way is physically different from the computer without the program. Even if programming did not produce a new machine, it was a new and useful improvement and therefore statutory matter for a patent. Bernhart's invention was a method of illustrating a three-dimensional object by means of an already existing computer and plotter. There was little question that the real novelty of Bernhart's invention was a set of mathematical equations that the computer was programmed to solve. In 1971, the Court twice affirmed the principle that a process whose sole purpose was to enhance the internal operation of a computer was appropriate subject matter for a patent for that reason alone. It was in 1972 that the Supreme Court first spoke to the issue of program patentability.

Gary Benson and Arthur Talbott had developed a method of programming a computer automatically to convert the binary coded decimal notation for a number into the pure binary notation for the same number. The Supreme Court held that the process claimed by Benson was in reality an algorithm, and, as such, was not patentable. The Court considered programs as "specific applications" of an algorithm which, in turn, was, in the Court's words, a "procedure for solving a given type of mathematical problem." Benson's claim was so broad that it included not just one application, but all possible applications and, hence, gave Benson a monopoly on the algorithm itself. The principal concern of the Court was that a patent would give Benson a monopoly on a general method of solving a mathematical problem as well as all such uses to which the method of solution could be put. While the Court noted that the entire process could be carried out with existing computers, or even without the use of a computer, it did not pursue this theme, and therefore did not rule on the mental steps doctrine. The Court also specifically indicated that the decision did not hold that programs are not patentable, but it did request that Congress act in this area.

In the intervening years, the Court of Customs and Patent Appeals had continued the policy of finding statutory subject matter in inventions that included programs, provided that the claims combined machines and process.

The next Supreme Court decision regarding program patentability was *Dann* v. *Johnston* in 1976. Thomas Johnston had developed a "record-keeping machine system for financial accounts." The Board of Patent Appeals rejected Johnston's application in part because it felt that granting the patent would give him a monopoly on a method of banking. The Court of Customs and Patent Appeals reversed the Board of Patent Appeals, pointing out that Johnston's claim was in the form of an apparatus; hence a bank could conduct its business any way it wanted, provided that it did not use Johnston's particular machine. By contrast, the claims made by Benson in the application the Supreme Court struck down earlier related to a process rather than a machine. Judge Markey of the Court of Custom and Patent Appeals did not agree with the Court's opinion, on the grounds that the machine in question was obvious to those skilled in the art of recordkeeping machine systems. Judge Rich of the Court also dissented, stating that the Court could no longer maintain the fiction that a computer program changed a computer into a new machine in the light of what the Supreme Court had said about Benson's application. The Supreme Court reversed the decision of the Court of Customs and Patent Appeals on the grounds raised by Judge Markey (the machine was obvious) but chose not to address the questions that troubled Judge Rich. Johnston's application was denied, but the decision of the Supreme Court cast no new light on the increasingly complex question of program patentability.

As in its opinion in *Benson*, the Supreme Court indicated that the decision did not hold that programs were not patentable. Perhaps the Court's purpose was to delay in order to give Congress time to act. If so, the Court has been frustrated because Congress has consistently failed to provide guidance.

Program patents still awarded

Chastened, but still undaunted, the Court of Customs and Patent Appeals continued to reverse the Board of Patent Appeals, which likewise continued to reject applications involving computer programs. The Court of Customs and Patent Appeals upheld the Board whenever an applicant relied too heavily on merely using a computer to solve mathematical equations. It also reversed the Board and found the following patentable: a process using a computer to control and optimize the operation of a system of multi-plant units; a system for typesetting, using a computer-based control system in conjunction with a conventional typesetter; and a method of using a computer to carry out translations from one language to another.

The Court of Customs and Patent Appeals suggested a two-step analysis of program claims. It must be determined if a claim recites an algorithm in the *Benson* sense. If an algorithm is found, then the patent claim must be analyzed to determine if it pre-empts the algorithm. The court found no mathematical equations or algorithms in the typesetting and language translation applications referred to above. It did concede that there were algorithms in the control system application, but held that there was no pre-emption because the algorithms in question were freely available to be used for any purpose other than the control of plants. Even if mathematical equations were found, what the solutions of the equations were to be used for was the determinative factor in whether a patent should issue.

The Court of Customs and Patent Appeals also criticized the Supreme Court's definition of algorithm. It pointed out that using the dictionary's definition of algorithm leads to the conclusion that most processes are really algorithms. If the Court had pursued this line of reasoning further, it could have also pointed out that virtually all inventions rely on algorithms and mathematical equations, since all inventions depend on the laws of nature to make them work.

The Court of Customs and Patent Appeals stated that even if the only novel aspect of an invention is an algorithm, the invention may still be proper subject matter for a patent. However, in *Parker* v. *Flook*, decided in 1978, the Supreme Court disagreed. Flook had developed a method to update parameters, called "alarm limits," which were used to detect the presence of abnormal conditions in catalytic conversion. The method consisted of three steps: the measurement of the present value of the process variables used to compute the alarm limit, the calculation of an updated alarm limit value using a *Benson*-type algorithm, and the replacement of the previous alarm limit by the newly computed value. The only novelty in the process rested in the second step algorithm. The Court stated that Flook's invention was not patentable "because once that algorithm is assumed to be within prior art, the application, considered as a whole, contains no patentable invention." Novel algorithm not basis for patent

The Court's rule that the algorithm should be considered as within prior art stemmed from the Court's belief that an algorithm "reveals a relationship that has always existed." The philosophical perspective that a law of nature or mathematical algorithm has some real existence outside of the human mind that first conceived it is not shared by everyone. While the Court did admit that natural phenomena could be processes, it denied that they were the kind of processes that the patent law was intended to protect. In essence, the Court said that those inventions which have universal impact or are of sufficient importance to society ought not to be patentable. The Supreme Court in *Benson* had previously said, "Phenomena of nature, . . . mental processes, and abstract intellectual concepts are not patentable, as they are the basic tools of scientific and technological work." It is likely, however, that the safety pin and the bottle cap, both patentable, have been items of far greater impact on society and importance to the economy than Benson's algorithm. Critique of Supreme Court's views

But Flook did not even pre-empt one single algorithm. His use of the algorithm in his process was narrowly related to catalytic conversions. The entire world could have used the algorithm in any way whatsoever with the sole exception of computing alarm limits in catalytic conversions. The Court nevertheless held that a claim for "an improved method of calculation, even when tied to a specific end use, is unpatentable." Henceforth, a process may still be judged as a whole, but any algorithm it contains must be treated as prior art. Yet once again in *Flook*, the Court repeated that computer programs may yet be patentable, even though it gave no hint as to how this might come about if one had to assume that the underlying algorithm in any program, probably the only truly original thing about the program, could not be found patentable in any circumstances. And yet again the Court appealed to Congress to settle the difficult questions of policy.

Current state of law unclear

What is the current status of the law on program patents? No one dares say. The decision in *Flook* appears to clash head-on with a number of previous decisions of the Court of Customs and Patent Appeals. But some program patents still stand, and the Supreme Court reiterates that under the proper circumstances a program is patentable. Perhaps the matter will be decided by the Court in cases it has agreed to hear in its next term. These are *Diamond* v. *Diehr*, which concerns the patentability of a computer program that regulates the curing time of rubber products, and *Diamond* v. *Bradley*, which addresses the critical question of "firmware" patentability. What the Supreme Court will do with these cases is anyone's guess.

Despite the fact that there are more cases dealing with program patents than with program copyrights, the state of the law in both areas is essentially the same: uncertain. This uncertainty is a serious impediment to those who have programs for which they would like patent protection. It is, however, far from the only problem with program patents. On balance, a patent may afford no better protection for the software developer than a copyright. Even assuming that no additional legal or administrative problems existed for the software developer than for any other inventor seeking a patent, the software developer would find that patents are not a suitable protective device for the product.

Programs, of course, can be very long and complex. Drafting the claims for such programs would be an expensive, meticulous, and time-consuming task. Once the application is properly completed, it must be submitted to the Patent Office where it faces a delay of two to three years before the application is approved, assuming it is approved at all. The commercial lifetime of the program might be shorter in some instances than the time it takes to get a patent. If the patent is granted, its validity may still be challenged by an alleged infringer. The odds are quite high that some court of appeals will find the patent invalid, even if a trial court does not. According to one survey, the Supreme Court considered 403 patent cases between 1881 and 1945 and held 80 percent of those patents invalid. Of course, the Supreme hears but a small fraction of the requests for its review. The rate of invalidation in the Circuit Court of Appeals, the rung in the federal court ladder just below the Supreme Court, was 40 percent. These figures are for all patent cases, not just those bearing the special stigma of program patentability. If the commercial value of the program has not dwindled greatly by the time a patent is granted, it probably would by the time the validity of its patent was tested in the courts.

Even more important, patent protection and secrecy are incompatible. Although secrecy of an invention may be protected while the patent is being sought and during any appeal if the patent is denied, once the patent is obtained, the program is available for public inspection at the Patent Office, and anyone may obtain a copy of it. Detection of an infringement would be difficult because many users would run the program only on their own machines and could destroy their *legally* obtained photocopies once they had loaded the program on tape or other media in which it could not be seen.

Even once the patent holder has sufficient evidence to file suit for infringement, he or she faces difficulties as great, or greater than, those confronted in a suit for copyright infringement. First, there will undoubtedly be a challenge to the validity of the patent itself. Such a challenge might assert that the program lacked novelty. The defendant could show the court many programs that looked remarkably similar to the plaintiff's program. The court, lacking expertise in computer science, would be hard put to make an intelligent finding of fact.

The challenge might also attempt to establish the program's obviousness. The mere fact that a program is long, complicated, or commercially valuable, does not mean that a patent can be granted; indeed, if other programmers could have written the same program with the existing state of the art at the time the program was written, then the patent will fail. With many programmers involved in intricate and often similar projects, it would be easy to build a strong case that a programmer of ordinary skill, particularly one working in the same specialty as the plaintiff, could easily have written the plaintiff's program at the time the plaintiff did. Once again the technology would create confusion in the mind of the court and will work in the defendant's favor. About the only advantage a patent holder has in such a suit over a holder of a copyright is that an independently developed program defeats a copyright, but not a patent. The race to the Patent Office is far more decisive than a race to the Copyright Office. But the fact that several people were able to do the same thing at the same time might well be taken as evidence of obviousness, or lack of novelty.

Although the protection accorded a patent is broader than that accorded a copyright, that protection is by no means limitless. A

Infringement

patent holder, for example, who relies on the law of gravity to make an invention work, does not thereby gain a monopoly on the law of gravity. What then constitutes an infringement of a patent? Generally, the allegedly infringing device must have substantial identity of function, means, and results. Therefore, with regard to machines, an infringing machine must perform substantially the same function by substantially the same means, and the principle or mode of operation must be the same as that of the machine infringed upon. An infringing process must operate in substantially the same manner and under the same physical laws as the infringed process to produce the same result. It is not clear what these tests imply with respect to computer programs.

Underlying any program is an algorithm. It could reasonably be argued that a court should never consider that two programs use the "same principle of operation" or operate "under the same physical laws" unless they use essentially the same algorithm. The Supreme Court has made it clear, however, that it will not tolerate any patent that attempts to pre-empt any algorithm, that is, gain a monopoly on all uses to which an algorithm might be put. The claims for a program patent will, therefore, have to spell out precisely the particular result the patent holder is to obtain, and the patent will extend only to that result. Moreover, the algorithm, in any event, will be assumed to be a part of the art prior to the development of the program. Therefore it cannot follow that merely because another program used the same algorithm, it would infringe. Would there be an infringement if the same algorithm were used to achieve precisely the same result? Perhaps, since that seems to be the only thing left to consider. But it is rare that any program would be so straightforward as to use the same algorithm to get the same result. It is more likely that the allegedly infringing program would use but a portion of the plaintiff's program, perhaps a subroutine; combine the plaintiff's algorithm with another algorithm to produce another result; produce in hardware form what the plaintiff has expressed in software; or obtain a result which is arguably different from the plaintiff's. Many of these possibilities involve technical questions. Can any court reasonably be expected to cope with programs thousands of instructions long written in different languages and formats? Even if the plaintiff ultimately wins, the suit is likely to be long and expensive, although the plaintiff is permitted to recover the attorney's fees as part of the damages if he or she prevails. Defending a patent suit is much like a game of "double or nothing."

Industry slow to seek patents

Perhaps it would matter more whether programs are patentable if software developers were clamoring for patents in large numbers. They are not. If the figure cited by the Supreme Court is still valid today, some 100,000 patent applications are filed each year, but only approximately 450 of these are for program patents. The number seeking patent applications for programs might be much larger if the legal situation in this area were less muddied, but it does not seem that software developers are more interested in patents from a practical point of than they are copyrights.

TRADE SECRECY AND CONTRACTS

There is no doubt whatsoever that the principal means that the software industry has relied upon to protect its product are trade secrecy and contract law. The two methods are closely related, but not identical; moreover, trade secrecy in some states at least is governed in part by criminal law rather than being enclosed just within the law of torts, or civil wrongs which carry no criminal penalties. Because the criminal law will be considered in the next chapter, we will not touch on it here.

The contract aspect of software protection is easily summarized. An employer who wishes to prevent a prospective employee from revealing to others, even subsequent employers of that employee, information that the employer wants to keep from his or her competitors, will make a contract with the employee as part of the terms of employment that the employee will, among other things, not make unauthorized copies of, reveal to others, or perhaps even bring outside certain areas of the employer's property, any program of the employer, including those that the employee helps write. Similar nondisclosure clauses are usually included in contracts used by software developers in licensing to others use of their product. Contract

In point of fact, a contract is not even really absolutely necessary in this regard. An employee has what is known as a fiduciary duty to his or her employer, which is to say that an employee must refrain from acting against his or her employer's interests. An employee who intentionally harms his or her employer, for example, by giving away trade secrets to a competitor, is then liable to that employer for the damages caused by this breach of duty. It is less clear, however, that a licensee has a similar duty to refrain from sharing a program in the absence of a contractual obligation. Nevertheless, the developer of the program will generally have a copyright on the program (even if it is not registered with the Copyright Office) and this may afford some limited protection in itself. Moreover, a court may find an implied agreement not to disclose the program to unauthorized parties from the very manner in which the program is licensed. If it were meant to be public property, then why is it licensed for pay? It is, nevertheless, a sound

Duty of employees to keep secrets

Duty of licensees

110 LAW AND THE COMPUTER

idea for any software developer to include a strong nondisclosure provision in any sale or lease of one of his programs.

Problems with employee contracts

Employee contracts do present some problems though. What of the program the employee develops on company time, but which is not related to the work he or she was hired to do? How much is an employee free to bring in his or her head to use in the service of a new employer? Can a nondisclosure clause be so restrictive that it will seriously interfere with the employee's ever working for any other software developer? We consider these questions below.

Development on company time

If an employee develops a product on the employer's time, even if it is not directly related to his or her actual job, the employer has at least a right to a nonexclusive license to that product. This means that the employer can freely use the product without express authorization from the employee who developed it, but that the employee may be free to license the use of the product to others. This is the general rule in the absence of contractual provisions to the contrary. In some instances, a contract of employment specifies that the employer has an exclusive right to all new products, including software, that the employee creates on company time. Conversely, an employee may get permission from the employer to spend a certain amount of time each week "frying his own fish." In any event, the employee still must avoid injuring the employer's interest; for example, even the employee who was allowed a certain amount of time to use as he or she pleases would not be free to write programs for the employer's competitors. Needless to say, there has been considerable litigation in this area of employer-employee relations. The employee who develops a valuable product will insist that he or she did it all on weekends in his or her garage, while the employer will loudly argue that the employee did nothing at his or her desk except work on the product. Or the employer could also argue that the product in question was, indeed, what the employee was hired to develop, and so the whole thing belongs to the employer. As a practical matter, there is probably some truth on both sides. If the employee is so clever as to develop a particularly important idea, it is in the employer's interest to arrive at some accommodation that will keep the employee happy and productive. From the employee's point of view, a continuing relationship with an employer who can furnish the capital resources and support services that he or she cannot personally afford is also beneficial. Compromise is often the best policy in this situation, as it is so often in matters of potential litigation.

Switching employers

The question of what an employee is free to bring from one employer to another is a troublesome one and not always easily resolved. Obviously, an employer is not free to prevent an employee from exercising a general skill, such as coding in FORTRAN, for a later employer. Another way of saying this is that an employer cannot appropriate for him- or herself alone what, in fact, is already in common usage throughout an industry. Merely calling information a trade secret does not, as we shall see later, make it a trade secret. Likewise, the employee is not free to disclose to another employer that which truly is some unique property of a former employer. If the program or technique in question is not really "common knowledge" in the trade, then the programmer may be compelled to avoid disclosure. The problem, of course, from the employee's point of view, is that he or she cannot forget all he or she has learned. The employee may not have a copy of the "secret" program, but he or she is surely familiar with most of its techniques, and will want to feel free to use these in solving problems for later employers. Indeed, later employers may hire that person particularly for the skills they believe he or she has acquired in those prior positions. From the prior employer's point of view, it is difficult, if not impossible, to prove that a former employee has disclosed a trade secret to a competitor, especially since trade secrets may be freely used by others who find them independently for themselves. Any subsequent employer, however, who improperly causes an employee to disclose a trade secret of a former employer may share liability with that employee.

Employers must be careful not to write nondisclosure clauses in employment contracts that are too restrictive because a court is likely to throw out the entire clause. For example, the following clause would be held unenforceable by virtually every court in the United States:

Too restrictive clause may be void

> Programmer-employee hereby agrees as part of the conditions of employment that he will not program for any subsequent employer at any time, anywhere in the United States or Canada, using any language, including FORTRAN and COBOL, used in this firm during the employee's period of employment.

Such a clause as that above is literally unconscionable because it is so broad as to deprive a programmer of any subsequent possibility of working as a programmer for another employer. On the other hand, if a service bureau is the principal source of bookkeeping and inventory computer services in a limited geographic area, its employment contract might contain a clause restricting its employees from writing programs likely to compete with its own in that same geographic area at least for a limited time after they leave employment with the service.

If you have the uneasy feeling that there may be few clear-cut answers to questions in this area, then you have accurately read what this writer is saying. And just as there are often no clean answers in

Trade secrecy

contract protection of software, so too there are similar difficulties in the area of trade secrecy. Trade secrecy law also varies widely from state to state, and there is currently no federal trade secrecy legislation whatsoever, even though many have advocated that Congress should pass such legislation so that the law in this important area would be uniform throughout the United States. If you have a trade secrecy problem, consult your local lawyer. Still, there are some general guidelines that are valid almost everywhere.

It does not overtax the reason to conclude that if a program is to be a trade secret, it must be a secret. What then is a secret? More than one company can know a secret without losing the property of secrecy. Secrecy is maintained as long as those to whom the secret is revealed are bound not to reveal the secret to others. Even if a competitor develops the same program, the secrecy is preserved as long as it remains a secret with the competitor as well. If, however, the secret should come into the possession of one who is not obligated to maintain the secrecy, the secrecy can be lost forever. Secrecy once lost is all but impossible to regain.

The mere fact that a company claims some program, or any information, is a secret, or confidential, does not make it so. If the information is standard knowledge within the trade, or the program in question is in common use in many locations, it is likely public knowledge and not secret. A software developer then must take great pains to insure that any product he or she wishes to protect retains its secret character, assuming at the outset that it is indeed known only to those in his or her organization, or elsewhere, who are bound by a duty not to reveal it. Each copy of the program should be labeled *Secret, Not to Be Disclosed Without Written Authorization of this Company*, or words of similar effect. Pains must be taken to keep unauthorized copies of the program from "leaking." The developer who is found to be negligent in the manner in which the secrecy of the program is protected, may lose whatever protection trade secrecy may offer. To be taken as a secret by a court, the program must be treated as a secret by its owner. The owner must be able to prove that every reasonable care was taken to prevent unauthorized persons from coming into possession of a copy of the program.

However, the mere fact that a program is secret does not make it a trade secret. For example, an in-house program to keep track of bets on the office football pool may be secret, but is not a trade secret for several good reasons. David Bender, in a comprehensive review of trade secrecy that he wrote in 1970, points out that a program must be in "continuous use in the operation of a business" before most jurisdictions will accord it trade secrecy protection.

If a trade secret does not have some novel aspect, it is unlikely that it will give its possessor a valuable competitive edge. Most courts, therefore, require some degree of novelty before they will find a true trade secret or award damages if the item is misappropriated. The purported trade secret is usually required to represent a real economic interest and investment on the part of its owner, or the effort of its development must be more than trivial. If a program is provably commercially valuable, as by showing what clients are willing to pay for a license, and if it represents a considerable investment of time and resources by the owner in its development (or purchase from another), then a court is likely to find a protectable interest as a trade secret, provided, of course, that the all-important secrecy aspect is present.

There are several problems with trade secrecy protection from the software developer's point of view. First, the law is not uniform throughout the United States; this is a distinct disadvantage to any company that does business in many states. Second, the law has never fully addressed the novel questions raised by computer technology, and therefore has uncertainties similar to those encountered with patents and copyrights. Third, the developer must adequately protect the secrecy of the product, even if it is for his or her use alone. Failure properly to protect a trade secret is fatal in a suit for damages. Fourth, once secrecy is lost, there is no protection for the program. Even the limited protection that might be afforded by copyright is no longer available. Furthermore, because programmers are so mobile and the developer cannot prevent former employees from using their general skill, experience and memory in the service of others, secrecy may effectively be lost as soon as the first employee who helped write the secret program moves on to another job. Finally, as was the case with patent and copyright, the plaintiff has the difficult job of determining whether the program was misappropriated and then proving that misappropriation to the satisfaction of a judge or jury. Because the developer has none of the presumptions of copyright registration or letters patent, his or her burden is especially heavy. The developer would fail even after proving that the defendant actually copied the program verbatim, if the defendant convinced the court that the plaintiff did not take adequate measures to guard the program's secrecy. Yet, despite its drawbacks, trade secrecy is the most prevalent form of protection relied upon by the software industry, particularly if one considers that nondisclosure clauses in licensing contracts are as much devices to preserve the secrecy aspect of a trade secret as they are agreements which, if broken, can give rise to suits for breach of contract.

Trade secrecy problems

POSSIBILITIES FOR THE FUTURE

CONTU and possible legislation

Effect of 1976 copyright law

When Congress drafted and passed the new copyright law, it recognized that there were major problems that the legislation did not resolve, computer program protection being one of the foremost of these. The Copyright Act of 1976 therefore, was written to "freeze" program copyrightability basically at what it was (whatever it was!) prior to the passage of the new law. At the same time, Congress mandated the establishment of the National Commission on New Technological Uses of Copyrighted Works, commonly known as CONTU, to study some of the major problems modern technology had created in the area of copyright law and to recommend solutions. In 1978, the fourteen-member Commission released its Final Report. The recommendations pertinent to computer programs are as follows:

CONTU recommendations

1. That section of the copyright law that freezes the law concerning program copyrights should be repealed; that is, the freeze should be lifted.
2. For copyright purposes a program should be defined as "a set of statements or instructions to be used directly or indirectly in a computer in order to bring about a certain result."
3. A new section should be added to the copyright law, the new section to read:

   §117: *Limitations on exclusive rights: computer programs* Notwithstanding the provisions of § 106 [that section which defines what constitutes an infringement of a copyright], it is not an infringement for the rightful possessor of a copy of a computer program to make or authorize the making of another copy or adaptation of that computer program *provided:*
   1. that such a new copy or adaptation is created as an essential step in the utilization of the computer program in conjunction with a machine and that it is used in no other manner, or
   2. that such new copy or adaptation is for archival purposes only and that all archival copies are destroyed in the event that continued possession of the program should cease to be rightful.

      Any exact copies prepared in accordance with the provisions of this section may be leased, sold, or otherwise transferred, along with the copies from which such copies were prepared, only as part of the lease, sale, or other transfer of all rights in the program. Adaptations so prepared may be transferred only with the authorization of the copyright owner.

Reasons for proposed changes

The reason the proposed changes are necessary is that merely loading a copyrighted program into a computer may, without the changes, be an unlawful infringement, since it involves making a copy of the program, even if the user is in rightful possession of the program.

Moreover, the user might wish to modify the program to make it more suited to his or her own purposes, and such modification and use of the modified program might also be found to be an infringement. Obviously too, a user would want to keep back-up copies of the program, or copies of the program in different media, and this would also run the risk of infringing as the law currently stands. As of this writing, the CONTU recommendations have been embodied in legislation, the Computer Software Copyright Act of 1980, which is being considered by the House of Representatives' Judiciary Subcommittee on Courts, Civil Liberties, and the Administration of Justice. Data bases are also copyrightable under the proposed legislation, but these have never presented the same severe difficulties that applications program copyrights have.

Even if the law is passed, it does not change the fact that copyright remains inherently unsuitable as a means of protecting programs. There is little indication that software developers will greet the new law with anything more than a yawn and continue on with business as usual, relying almost exclusively on contract and trade secrecy for protection. There is, however, some small danger that Congress may pre-empt other forms of protection and make copyright the exclusive form of protection available for programs. Congress could do this, and the courts also have the authority to interpret what Congress does as having this effect even if Congress does not specifically address the federal pre-emption issue in the legislation. But it must also be pointed out that the CONTU Report, on which the proposed Software Copyright Act is based, explicitly recommends that copyright *not* be the sole means of protecting software. One can only hope that Congress and the courts will follow CONTU's suggestion in this regard.

Copyright still unsuitable

This does point up the fact that the law concerning software protection is very much in a state of flux at this time, as is most computer law. With new legislation in the mill, and two critically important cases before the United States Supreme Court, what is written here may become largely obsolete, or at least of purely historical interest, in the near future.

Some further reflections

The question of legal protection for software is inherently extraordinarily complicated. To gain a balanced view, one must, among other things, take into account the purposes of legally conferred protection for any creative work. The Constitution's mandate to "promote the progress of science and useful arts" does little to clarify the matter. It is equally simplistic to say that the Constitution demands that patent and copyright look first to the public interest, for that interest is often

Software protection issues complex

difficult to identify and is also closely related to the welfare of industry. If no significant financial rewards follow from creation of new ideas and inventions, then technology will stagnate, and the public will necessarily be the poorer.

Moreover, one cannot merely consider only the public interest versus the interest of the computer industry. The interests of the hardware manufacturers compete with those of the software developer. The clients of the computer industry have their own needs. The impact that any form of protection may have on the courts and the administrative agencies such as the Patent Office must also be taken into account.

Other recommendations

The CONTU Report recommends that copyright protection be extended to programs in a special, strong form under the Copyright Act of 1976, and the hardware producers, anxious to avoid any form of protection that might hinder the sale of their machines, agree. Others propose that patent protection be available for programs, and the software houses, anxious to gain monopolies for their own programs, concur. Others conclude that trade secrecy is the best. Some suggest federal trade secrecy is desirable. Yet others propose a system of compulsory licensing—that is, anyone could use any copyrighted program, but would have to pay a pre-set fee for that use, such as that adopted under the Copyright Law for phonograph records. Who is right? Is new legislation in this area really needed? The question must be answered by considering the arguments of those proposing and opposing such legislation.

Software houses argue that patent protection should be available for software because such protection has long been available for hardware, and hardware and software are easily interchangable. Such an argument, however, is easily answered. An invention is not patentable until it is presented in patentable form. Until then, the courts may consider it to be too abstract, too close to being a mere idea. An analogous situation exists in copyright law: a work is not entitled to copyright until it is fixed in a tangible medium of expression, even though it may be fully developed in the mind of its author.

Arguments against secrecy

Many argue that protection other than secrecy is needed to encourage an open transfer of information and to enable the technology to develop more efficiently. Given the unprecedented rapidity with which the computer industry has grown, it is difficult to believe that secrecy has really restrained that growth. Nevertheless, trade secrecy does discourage a free interchange of ideas in the private sector. There is, however, an interchange of ideas through academic research, publications in journals, presentations at meetings, and the movement of computer personnel from one employer to another. From the evidence presented to CONTU, the availability of copyright still would not change the emphasis on secrecy where it currently exists. Patents require open publication. It is questionable whether program developers would seek them because of the ease with which patented programs could be obtained by potential infringers, the difficulty of detecting and proving infringements, the high risk associated with patent litigation, and the length of time and the expense normally associated with obtaining a patent in the first place. To add insult to injury, the Patent Office might well require full documentation for any program on which a patent is granted, and this documentation would also be public even though withholding documentation is one of the standard procedures that software developers use to maintain control over leased programs. Paradoxically, the availability of patent or copyright protection might have the effect of intensifying secrecy by those who wish to avoid potential suits for infringement, particularly if the availability of a patent or copyright were held to be the sole form of legal protection available to the developer.

Patent or copyright protection for programs might mean lower costs to the consumer. Trade secrecy incurs costs by making manufacture of software less efficient. Because of secrecy, many programmers must spend time repeating work others have done. However, aside from the fact that the availability of copyrights and patents might increase secrecy and add to whatever costs secrecy might actually entail, such availability must also escalate the legal costs of the software industry. Moreover, fees for use of a copyrighted or patented program might be higher than if the program were merely under a contract that prohibited disclosure. A program protected by secrecy becomes available to the general public once the secrecy is lost, but fees for programs protected by copyright or patent could continue until the copyright or patent expires; it is doubtful that any program could remain secret that long.

Lower costs questionable

Some argue that copyright or patent protection is necessary for the growth of the software industry. But this industry is growing by leaps and bounds without it. It is doubtful that the industry could absorb much more work now because of the shortage of trained personnel.

Most software development is custom-tailored to particular users. Even software packages are often modified to include features needed by an individual client, or to run on a different machine. Clients are often willing to pay licensing fees, not because a licensor has a stranglehold on the program, but because it makes sense economically. Many small firms do not have the expertise to write their own software, or even to run someone else's without outside help. The software house not only provides a program at a price much lower than what it would cost the client to write it, but it also installs the program in the client's computer, and maintains, updates, and per-

Most software custom designed

haps even warrants the program as well. The client is buying expertise and service as much as a particular piece of software. The practice of marketing hardware without a discrete charge for the included software is no longer prevalent. Software houses can compete with hardware manufacturers for the software market.

<small>Administrative problems</small>

If copyright protection were available for programs, there would probably be few additional problems for either the courts or the Copyright Office. This, of course, stems from the fact that the software industry has shown almost complete indifference toward copyrights. The administrative problems associated with patents for software, however, was one of the principal reasons that led the President's Commission on the Patent System to recommend against them:

> The Patent Office now cannot examine applications for programs because of a lack of a classification technique and the requisite search files. Even if these were available, reliable searches would not be feasible or economic because of the tremendous volume of prior art being generated. Without this search, the patenting of programs would be tantamount to mere registration and the presumption of validity would be all but nonexistent.

Should software patents be allowed, then, the courts' current problems with the exotic technology and novel questions raised by computer-related suits would be intensified beyond toleration by the proliferation of infringement suits.

<small>Much already protectible</small>

Much of value to the computer industry can already be protected by patent or copyright. Hardware has been patented. Data compilations and directories, instruction manuals, program documentation, warranties, and other important documents all may clearly be copyrighted under the new law. Because most complex programs have significantly less value without supporting documentation and such documentation can be copyrighted, copyright protection can now be obtained indirectly even if the copyrightability of the program itself is open to question.

But is is not enough to look at both the past and the present. What legislation is called for is in part determined by what the future holds for the computer industry. What are the directions in computing?

First, the use of computers will continue to expand and touch virtually every segment of society. This increased computer usage will create a demand for more software that software houses are likely to satisfy in large part, particularly for the smaller computer users who cannot afford to hire their own computer staffs. The market for software packages for home use may grow substantially in the next few years, especially when the home television set doubles as a CRT and the phone line is the link to time-sharing computing. These trends are likely to stimulate a healthy competition among software developers. Patent protection would stifle that competition whereas continuation of the *status quo* would encourage software developers constantly to improve their products.

Second, more programs are likely to be converted to hardware and stored as a part of the computer itself. Such program modules should not be patentable if the underlying program is not, although the Supreme Court may soon decide the question. A lack of patent protection will encourage competition and drive the price for such program modules down.

Third, the increasing power of the machines, the more sophisticated hardware and increased size of the memory, will enable computers to handle programming languages that resemble ordinary speech. The more a program approximates ordinary speech, the harder it will be for a court to analyze the nature of the program. Computers themselves will be able to write complex programs and design improvements to their operating systems. This development would raise profound philosophical questions and further confound the courts.

Despite the CONTU recommendations and the often bewildering variety of schemes thus far proposed for software protection, contract and trade secrecy seem to have the most advantages for the industry and the public as well as the fewest problems in their administration. They are, moreover, the means of protection which the software industry has itself chosen and used thus far with great success.

RECOMMENDED READINGS ON LEGAL PROTECTION OF SOFTWARE

Some additional readings on copyright include: Final Report, National Commission on New Technological Uses of Copyrighted Works (CONTU Report), published by the Copyright Office, Washington, D.C. (1978); and Note, "Copyright Protection for Computer Programs," *Columbia Law Review*, Vol 64(1964), pp. 1274-1300. This paper by John Banzhaff is an early, trail-breaking work on this subject. Most of it is still relevant today.

For more material on patent protection, see H. Davis, "Computer Programs and Subject Matter Patentability," *Rutgers Journal of Computers and the Law*, Vol. 6(1977), pp. 1-25.

On the subject of trade secrecy, see D. Bender, "Trade Secret Protection of Software," *George Washington Law Review*, Vol. 38(1970), pp. 909-55, updated as "Trade Secret Software Protection," *Computer Law Service*, Section 4-4, Article 2 (1977).

The following are instructive cases on various aspects of legal protection of software: *Synercom Technology, Inc. v. University Computing Co.*, 462 F.Supp. 1003 (N.D. Tex. 1978) (the only reported case to date involving copyrightability of programs), *Gottschalk v. Benson*, 409 U.S. 63 (1972) (the Supreme Court's first opinion dealing with program patents); and *Lundy Electronics & Systems, Inc. v. Optical Recognition Systems, Inc.*, 362 F.Supp. 230 (E.D.Va. 1973) (a comprehensive review of patent law is included in this opinion.

CRIME

THE NATURE OF CRIME

Crimes in general

A tort is a form of wrongful act that results in injury to someone other than the wrongdoer. If some act is simply a tort, the government, state or federal, will not get involved in the dispute between the parties except to the extent that such disputes may be ultimately settled in its courts. A crime, however, is an act that the government considers injurious to society as a whole, a wrong against itself. Therefore the government will attempt to prevent such acts, not by assessing liability for damages if the act is committed, but by prescribing punishments to be incurred by anyone who behaves in the forbidden manner.

In order for an act to be criminal, the government must explicitly forbid that act by means of a valid statute and attach some penalty for the commission of the act. The government may make the omission of some act criminal, of course, by legislatively ordering all persons to do that act and prescribing the penalties a person must suffer for failing to do the required act. In either case, whether the government commands certain behavior, or forbids it, that command must generally be set out in a statute, and there must be sanctions for failing to obey the statute. Valid statute required

At one time in history, there used to be so-called "common law" crimes, and in some states some such crimes still exist. Common law crimes are acts that the state considers offensive and that subject the person responsible to punishment, but whose criminal nature is determined by the opinion of courts and a general sense of public morality "Common law" crime than an act of the legislation. "Corrupting public morals" might be such a vague common law crime. Fortunately, such crimes are recognized ever more rarely. It is part of our constitutionally guaranteed right to due process of law that we be given fair notice of what precise acts are forbidden or commanded by the state. Statutes, therefore, that purport to describe criminal activity, but that are so indefinite that a person of ordinary intelligence could not read them and decide what he or she could or could not do, are generally struck down by courts as violative of due process. Likewise, a statute that interferes with some right that is guaranteed by a higher law, such as the Constitution, will also be declared void and of no effect. Congress could not pass a law that made it a crime to publish a daily newspaper.

Fair notice needed

Crimes are divided into misdemeanors and felonies. A felony is a serious crime punishable by death or a sentence of a year or longer. Minor offenses against public order such as parking violations or lesser traffic infractions are usually not classified as crimes at all and we will not classify them as such here.

Misdemeanors and felonies

What does it take to commit a crime? First, there must an act. One cannot commit a crime by merely thinking about committing a crime, or wishing to commit a crime. Even discussing the possibility of committing a crime with a potential accomplice does not necessarily constitute a crime. An act that is not a crime does not become criminal simply because the actor has a plan to commit an unlawful act later on.

Act required

In addition to some act, there must generally also be a "guilty intention." The law wishes to punish wrongdoers, and someone who is unaware he or she is doing something wrong either ought not to be punished, or be punished less severely, than someone who commits a forbidden act with full knowledge that the act is wrong. Someone who acts maliciously is more guilty in the eyes of the law than someone who unintentionally engages in criminal conduct.

Guilty intention

Nevertheless, this requirement of a "guilty mind" for commission of a crime is not quite as straightforward as it first sounds. The state of mind at issue is that at the time the act associated with the crime was carried out. If Bertha declares on Monday that she intends to kill Charlie next Tuesday, then there is probably no crime if all Bertha does on Monday is declare her intention. If she *accidentally* hits Charlie with her car on Tuesday, killing him, then her guilty intention and the act that kills Charlie do not coalesce. The killing of Charlie was, by assumption, an accident. While it may be a tort, it is not a crime, although it may be for other reasons than Bertha's desire to see Charlie dead.

Act and intent simultaneous

Also, a person is assumed to intend the natural consequences of his or her acts. If Bertha fires a gun at Charlie, she cannot act surprised if Charlie is killed. In a trial, the burden would be on the accused to prove that he or she did not intend the criminal result of the act. For example, Bertha might attempt to prove that Charlie told her that the

Assumed to intend natural consequences

gun was unloaded, or that a bee stung her arm and she pulled the trigger accidentally. If no criminal intent is present, then there may be civil liability—that is, there may be a tort—but there is no crime.

But what determines what state of mind or intent must be present for any given crime? The statute that defines the crime generally also declares the state of mind a person must have to be found guilty of the crime. There are three general classifications of crimes depending on the intent required to commit them: specific intent, general intent, and strict liability.

Specific intent implies the highest degree of blameworthiness for an action: "You really meant to do it!" Specific intent, therefore, requires the actor to actually will the act with the conscious object of causing any harm that results from the act, or at least to act knowing that the act is virtually certain to cause the harm that results. Generally, specific intent is present if an act is done knowingly or purposely. By its very nature, any specific intent crime requires that the one who commits the criminal act be fully aware of what he or she is doing. Therefore someone who is drunk, or ignorant of the law, or so emotionally agitated that he or she cannot think straight is unlikely to be able to commit such a crime. Generally, specific intent crimes are the more serious crimes carrying the most severe penalties. If a statute includes the words "willfully," "deliberately," "with intent to," or words or phrases of similar import, then the crime described in almost certain to be a specific intent crime. Suppose the statute reads, "Whoever shall enter the dwelling place of another for the purpose of committing a felony shall be guilty of burglary." Sam enters Gloria's house with no intention of committing any crime whatsoever. However, once inside Gloria's house, he sees an expensive diamond ring and steals it. Sam may have committed a felony by stealing the ring, but he did not commit burglary because he did not have the specific intent necessary for burglary when he entered the house in the first place. If he had entered the house with the express purpose of stealing the ring, he would also have been guilty of burglary as the statute defines it.

Specific intent

General intent crimes require a somewhat less blameworthy state of mind, although someone who acts with specific intent acts with general intent as well. The requirement for general intent is satisfied if the actor proceeds in the face of a known, substantial, and unjustifiable risk that the harm envisioned by the statute will occur, or if the actor is criminally negligent. Criminal negligence, as opposed to simple negligence, occurs when the actor's conduct varies so much from what a reasonable person would do under the same circumstances that it demonstrates a disregard or lack of concern for the consequences of the act. A high degree of "recklessness" of some sort then characterizes general intent. If Sam fires a bullet through Carla's window, believing that Carla is not at home and with the intent of merely scaring her into

General intent

moving to another neighborhood, but the bullet does hit Carla and kills her, then a court might well find that Sam fired the shot knowing that there was a substantial risk that someone would be hurt, and that the motive for the shooting certainly did not justify it; hence it could find that Sam had a general intent to kill Carla. Similarly, if Shirley drives at 80 miles per hour in the wrong direction on a one way street, a court could find that the conduct was so grossly negligent that Shirley has the general intent of hurting or killing anyone she runs into. If no specific intent is set forth in a criminal statute, then general intent may be presumed.

Strict liability
There are a very few crimes for which the actor will be strictly liable. The owner of a tavern may be strictly liable if anyone under 21 is served intoxicating beverages even if the owner was unaware the minor was being served, or even if he or she was not present at the time. Similarly, a meat packer may be held strictly liable for shipping adulterated meat, even though the packer exercised proper caution in handling the product. Normally, there is only a fine as a penalty for a strict liability crime, and it may be unconstitutional to impose a jail sentence in such a case. Statutes imposing strict liability are usually related to the welfare of the general public and often concern acts where criminal intent would be all but impossible to prove. The strict liability is intended to cause certain types of businesspeople to use greater care in their work and to help protect the public thereby.

Transferred intent
If someone has the intent to commit a crime, that intent can be transferred to make up the intent necessary for the commission of another crime other than the one the actor initially set out to commit. For example, if Edna intends to kill Al, but kills Bill instead, mistaking him for Al, then the fact that Edna has killed the wrong person does not make the murder any less a crime of specific intent.

Defenses related to intent

Invalid statute
Someone accused of a crime may defend him- or herself in several ways. He or she may argue that the statute that defines the crime is too vague, and is therefore void, or that the statute was not validly passed, or that there is no crime such as that with which he or she is charged. If there is a valid statute that applies to the case, then he or she may argue that the act required for the crime was not performed, or that he or she did perform the act, but did not have the intent that the crime requires. It is this latter defense we will examine more closely now.

Lack of act or intent

Incapacity
The accused may argue that he or she was unable to form the intent required, or was otherwise relieved of responsibility for the action,

due to some incapacity of mind such as insanity, deficient intelligence, or illness. Lack of mental capacity is not likely to figure prominently in defenses of computer professionals, so we will not dwell much on this. Needless to say, if someone is, for any reason, mentally incompetent to form the requisite intention for a crime, then a conviction cannot be obtained, although it is quite likely, under such a condition, that the accused would be committed to custodial care of some sort.

What of the accused who claims either that he or she made a mistake concerning some fact—for example, thinking incorrectly that the man killed was attacking the accused with a knife—or that he or she made a mistake as to the law—for example, not knowing that it was against the law to carry marijuana. Any mistake of fact, no matter how bizarre, is sufficient to negate specific intent, provided the mistake pertains to an "element" of the crime. An element of a crime is a condition or fact that must be present for that crime to occur. Theft, for example, involves taking the property of another. That the property taken belongs to someone other than the one who takes it is an element of theft. If Sam takes a car that actually belongs to Alice, but Sam mistakenly believes that it really belongs to him, then Sam has not formed the specific intent necessary for theft. He does not knowingly believe he is taking the property of another. This is true even if Sam's belief that the car is his is wholly unfounded. If Sam's mistake is reckless, then he may be guilty of a general intent crime—criminal conversion, for example—but he will not be guilty of theft. Mistake of fact

If the mistake is a reasonable mistake of fact, then it is even possible that there is no general intent, because general intent requires recklessness or gross and criminal negligence, which are basically unreasonable. For example, if Alice's car looks exactly like Sam's and is parked in the same lot, and if, by coincidence, Sam's key fits both cars, then Sam can use his reasonable mistake as a defense if he accidentally takes Alice's car. His reasonable mistake would negate general intent. For strict liability crimes, any mistake, no matter how reasonable, is not a defense. The fact that the meat packer had good cause to believe the product was not adulterated is not a defense if it turns out that it was, in reality, adulterated.

Everyone is assumed to know the law (but then why have lawyers?); therefore, ignorance of, or a mistake in the law is usually not a defense to a violation of a law of which the accused was truly ignorant. This may seem like an unfair rule, and, in some cases, it is. There are, therefore, certain exceptions to it that take care of some of the more troublesome cases. Mistake of law

1. There is a defense based on a mistake as to what the law is if the accused relied upon some court order, court opinion, official interpretation of an administrative order, or statute, even if the Reliance on authorities

statute was no longer in effect, or the court order was reversed, or the court opinion was overruled, provided that such reliance was reasonable in the first place. Be warned that mere advice of counsel may not be enough. The attorney who gave the wrong advice may be guilty of malpractice, but the client may still be guilty of a crime.

<small>Ignorance of administrative order</small>

2. Orders of administrative agencies, such as the Internal Revenue Service or Federal Trade Commission, may have the force of law, and even carry criminal penalties. The accused who has violated just an administrative order of which he or she was unaware, rather than a validly enacted statute, may use ignorance of the order as a defense, unless he or she was somehow at fault in his or her ignorance, for example, his or her business required staying current on orders of the administrative agency involved.

<small>Mistake as to legal status</small>

3. A good faith belief that one has the legal status to carry out a certain act may, at least in some instances, be a defense even if that belief is wrong. For example, a citizen may believe he or she has the right to go into another's home to search for property he or she believes is stolen, even though such is not the law. Such a person, arrested for breaking and entering, might plead that defense. He or she may, or may not, be successful. Such right of search is usually reserved for police authorities armed with a search warrant.

<small>Ignorance of required act</small>

4. Ignorance is a defense in the event the statute violated requires some positive act, rather than merely refraining from certain conduct. If a statute orders that a tax be paid on every privately owned pistol, and someone is arrested for not paying the tax, then ignorance of that law would be a defense. The person arrested would still be liable for the tax plus any civil penalties for late payment, but there would be no crime because the person was unaware of the positive duty to pay the tax.

Inchoate crimes

<small>Solicitation</small>

We will study certain particular crimes later in this chapter. Related to many crimes, there are other crimes, however, that may be committed preparatory to the crime, even if the first crime never even takes place. One such crime prior to another crime is solicitation. Solicitation, as its name implies, occurs when a person encourages another person to engage in criminal activity. Solicitation is a specific intent crime and is complete even if the person solicited will have nothing to do with the crime which he or she is being urged to commit.

<small>Conspiracy</small>

Conspiracy is another crime of which one hears much in the newspapers, but which is rather hard to define. Conspiracy requires a group of persons who must agree among themselves to commit a crime or unlawful act and to help one another further the unlawful enterprise. Conspiracy is a specific intent crime and is often punished more severely than the crime the conspirators are planning to commit under the theory that those who are willing to plot criminal activity together pose a special danger to society. However, in order to have a conspiracy, it takes more conspirators than are required to commit the crime being planned. Two men cannot conspire to commit sodomy with one another because it would be impossible for less than the two of them to commit the crime itself.

Finally, the attempt to commit a crime is itself a crime, even if the attempt fails. Attempt is an act that is less than that act needed for the commission of a crime, but done with the specific intent to commit the crime, going beyond mere preparation. Shirley calls up Joe and says, "Let's rob the First National Bank on Sunday." Shirley is guilty of solicitation to rob a bank. Joe says, "OK," and the two plan the job together. Shirley and Joe are guilty of conspiracy. They buy the guns needed for the job. They have not gone beyond mere preparation so they are still not guilty of an attempt. They jump in the car and drive to the bank, fully intent on carrying out the robbery. When they arrive, they notice the bank is closed because it is a Sunday. Shirley and Joe are now also guilty of an attempt to rob the bank because they have now gone beyond mere preparation. Their mistake of fact, which prevented them from robbing the bank, is not a defense. If, after arriving at the bank, Shirley and Joe are converted to the paths of righteousness and resolve not to rob the bank because it is the wrong thing to do, and they voluntarily abandon their plan to rob that bank and any other bank, they have the defense of abandonment. If they rob the bank, the attempt is "merged" into the completed robbery, and they cannot be charged with both attempted robbery and the robbery itself. Shirley can still be charged with the separate crime of solicitation, and both can be charged with conspiring to rob the bank.

Attempt

Defense of abandonment

Having taken a quick look at some general ideas associated with criminal law, we pass on to a discussion of specific forms of crime.

THEFT

Because a crime is almost invariably only a creature of a particular statute, and statutes, in turn, are creatures of the legislative body of each state and of Congress, the criminal law will vary from state to state, and federal crimes may differ from crimes of any particular state. If you suspect that some particular act is criminal, you need to check the laws of the state where the act is committed, as well as the

Criminal code varies

federal criminal code if that might apply, to find out if it is. In some states too, you must be aware that there are still common law crimes that are defined in court opinions and not in legislation. An act which is legal in Indiana does not become a crime because it is illegal in Ohio. If the act is legal where it is done, the person responsible usually cannot be prosecuted for that act elsewhere.

Because the criminal law is a local matter, you must obtain local expertise in dealing with it. Because an act is legal or illegal in one location does not mean it has the same character in another. Gambling is legal in Nevada, illegal in Utah, and partly legalized in New York, and the definition of what constitutes gambling may be markedly different in all three states.

The warning given above carries special weight when speaking of computer crime. Some computer crimes are straightforward and present few problems anywhere. The law in any state has little trouble coping with someone who shoots a programmer, or torches a computer center. But some types of criminal activity associated with computing have presented law enforcement officials, courts, and lawmakers with novel questions that traditional laws and legal concepts could not answer. We will see some of these questions in this chapter.

New forms of old crimes

Moreover, the forms in which some traditional crimes occur are unique to computing. One form of theft by computer is known as the "salami technique." This involves taking a small amount, like thin slices of a salami, from a large number of sources. The computer of a large bank may handle hundreds of thousands of accounts. The perpetrator of a theft employing the salami technique would arrange for the computer to transfer very small amounts of money from randomly selected accounts into an account that he or she controls. Only $.10 might be transferred in a given month from any one account, and the number of accounts affected at any one time would be but a fraction of the total accounts the bank services, but the overall amount of money siphoned off would be sizeable.

Banks usually find it more convenient simply to credit an account alleged to be short $.10 if a customer complains; and, of course, most customers will simply assume that they themselves made an error and never notify the bank at all. The small patch of program that effects the transfers will probably be skillfully concealed in an enormously large and complex program or made a part of the operating system of the computer, thus defying easy detection, assuming that someone is really interested in finding it.

Because the perpetrator of the swindle in this case would presumably have access to, and intimate knowledge of, the bank's computer system, he or she could destroy or modify the program as necessary if he or she found that a detailed audit was about to take place. In actual fact, the bank would almost certainly find it cheaper to just pay the small sums and not even conduct the time-consuming and expensive investigation needed to confirm that a theft was taking place.

The blunt fact is that few prosecutions ever result from computer crime. Even the scope of the problem is not entirely clear. Donn Parker, in his exhaustive study of computer abuses, found only several hundred cases, and not all of those could be confirmed. Nevertheless, the average loss per instance of computer abuse, not counting the massive Equity Funding caper where the "take" was well above $1 billion, is $450,000, more than four times the average loss sustained in 1971 from more traditional embezzlement schemes.

Few prosecutions

Why, with computers so prevalent and the opportunities for gain so apparent, are there not more reported cases of computer crime? It may be that computer specialists are more honest than average. Then too, many computer systems do have significant security mechanisms that serve to deter abuse. But even in many instances where a thief has been caught red-handed, employers have often been unwilling to prosecute. Why?

Why few reported computer crimes

First, there is the embarrassment that an employer would suffer from publicly acknowledging that he or she and the customers have been cheated, using the employer's own, supposedly reliable, computer. Second, many prosecutors and judges do not like to handle cases involving computers for the same reason that many students avoid mathematics courses: they simply do not understand them. The evidence in computer cases is difficult to gather and harder to understand and explain to a judge or jury in a comprehensible way. Furthermore, the clever programmer who is nickle-and-diming his or her way to a fortune seems far less a danger to society than gun-toting Bonnies and Clydes. In some instances, computer criminals fired for dishonesty from one job go right into another position of even greater trust and responsibility. Third, it is just a plain fact that the law has not yet caught up with computer technology. Concepts that served the courts well in the nineteenth century have been outstripped by the rapid change in the twentieth. But some states have begun to address this issue with special computer crime legislation and such legislation is currently before Congress at the federal level. As the courts and lawmakers deal more and more with the novel questions presented by computer crime, prosecution may become routine in the future.

Statutes related to perhaps the most common of all crimes, theft, differ substantially from state to state. There are, moreover, fine distinctions in many states regarding various ways in which property can be illicitly taken, while in other states crimes against property have been merged into just a few well-written statutes. Common law theft, or larceny, is the "felonious taking and carrying away of personal

Theft

property of another with intent to deprive the owner of his property permanently." The term "felonious" in this definition may be interpreted as "without the valid consent of the owner." Many states, perhaps the majority, still adhere to this common law definition, or its equivalent. Theft is a specific intent crime in all states.

Theft and computing

Nonetheless, it is clear, even from a first reading, that this common law definition poses special problems for the computer industry. If one causes an electrical signal to be sent from one place to another, does this really amount to a taking and carrying away of personal property? But that is really all one does when copying a competitor's files without permission, using the computer to do the "dirty work." Likewise, when files are copied, the owner does not generally lose the files. Sometimes he or she may actually be using them at the very instant that the illicit copies are being made. If a car or piece of jewelry is stolen, the rightful owner can no longer drive the car, or wear the jewelry. But taking computer time, or file space, or files that belong to another person, may give the appearance of not depriving that person of anything at all.

Larceny charge may fail

Susan Nycum believes that there are but two instances in which theft of a program may not be prosecutable as larceny. The first occurs when the thief copies the program onto his or her own materials, but does not carry off the original. In this instance, the original program is never brought under the direct or indirect control of the thief, and may not even be touched. An indictment for larceny may also fail if the only thing taken is something as intangible as electrical impulses. Some states have demanded that an object must have tangible form in order to be the subject of larceny. Remember that it is statutes that determine what theft is, or is not, and someone cannot be prosecuted for a crime that is not set forth explicitly in a valid law. Thus, if the statute that defines theft of a motor vehicle, for example, declares that the subject matter of the crime is vehicles powered by gasoline, then someone who steals an electrically powered car cannot be prosecuted under the statute. It is also courts that interpret the meaning of the statute whenever there is a dispute. The legislature may wish to include electrical signals under the heading of property subject to theft, but if the theft statute does not make that intent clear, a court that relies on old common law notions may acquit an accused of larceny if he or she took only electrical signals.

Subject matter of larceny

David Bender, in an article published in 1970 and updated in 1977, divides the fifty states and the District of Columbia into four groups according to the kind of property that can be the *res*, that is, the object, of larceny. Mr. Bender's classification is now outdated in many instances—the law is changing constantly—and there are states that actually fit equally well into two or more categories. Nevertheless, the classification scheme is useful for an analysis of the various kinds of larceny statutes. The first group of states are those that retain the common law definition, restricting the subject matter of theft to property. It is in such states that computer criminals might have maximum opportunity to use archaic law to their own advantage.

Other states, those making up the second group, modify or extend the notion of property by providing lists that indicate what is to be considered property for purposes of defining theft. Because laws dealing with criminal acts are to be interpreted strictly, the usual reading of these statutes would indicate that if a certain object could not be placed among the listed items, then that object could not be the subject matter of theft.

The third group of jurisdiction is composed of those which hold that the subject matter of larceny is a "thing of value." Computer programs obviously fit rather well under this heading.

David Bender notes two problems that must be addressed not only in "thing of value" jurisdictions, but in those in the first two groups as well. The first problem arises when something is taken without an intent of permanently depriving its owner of possession, that is, when it is taken with the idea of replacing it after a copy of it has been made. The intent to return, or the actual return of the object taken, may in some jurisdictions preclude a charge of larceny, or require that some lesser charge be filed. Because theft is a specific intent crime, the intent spelled out in the statute must be present when the wrongful act is committed, or theft is not present (even though a lesser crime may have been committed). No permanent deprivation

A second problem is establishing the value of the item taken. In the case of *Hancock* v. *Texas*, the value assigned to a set of misappropriated copies of programs was their commercial value as evidenced by expert testimony. In "thing of value" states, all that needs to be proved is that whatever was taken has some value, but there does not necessarily have to be a proof of some hard and fast worth. In at least one instance a defendant was convicted of stealing computer time, even though no explicit value was able to be assigned for what was taken. Value of thing taken

In addition to the two problems cited above, there is also the problem of the manner of theft. The thief who fails to make off with the program, or even move it, has not deprived the owner of any possession, even for a brief moment. The thief who relies only on electronic signals may not have even made a tangible copy of the program. Of course, someone who misappropriates a copy of a program has by his or her action deprived the owner of something, specifically, the secre- No carrying off cy attached to the program as well as the commercial gain that might have been had by selling the program to the thief. But not all courts would be willing to recognize secrecy or potential gain as property capable of theft, although interference with these rights may well form the basis for an action in tort.

The case of *Lund* v. *Commonwealth of Virginia* furnishes a helpful example. Charles Lund, a Ph.D. student at Virginia Polytechnic Institute and State University (VPI), was convicted of grand larceny for use of VPI's computer without proper authorization. Lund's thesis research required the use of the computer, but, through an oversight, his advisor failed to provide an account for him. Lund began using accounts assigned to other persons and departments without their permission. The director of VPI's computer center estimated that by the time Lund was caught, he may have used more than $26,000 in unauthorized computer time. The director also admitted that the value of the cards and paper obtained from Lund was worth "whatever scrap was worth."

Lund admitted that he used the computer without proper authority, but he and four faculty members, including his department chairman and faculty advisor, testified that the work done was for his thesis and that he would have been given authorization had he asked for it. Lund appealed his conviction on the grounds that there was no evidence that the articles in question were stolen, or that they had a value of $100 or more, and he further argued that, in any event, computer time and services were not the subject matter of larceny.

The Virginia statute at issue states:

> Any person who: (1) Commits larceny from the person of another of money or other thing of value of five dollars or more, or (2) Commits simple larceny not from the person of another of goods and chattels of the value of one hundred dollars or more, shall be deemed guilty of grand larceny. . . .

and

> If any person obtain, by any false pretense or token, from any person, with intent to defraud, money or other property which may be the subject of larceny, he shall be deemd guilty of larceny thereof. . . .

The Supreme Court of Virginia found that labor or services could not be the subject of larceny "because neither time nor services can be taken and carried away." Even though some states had amended their criminal codes to make taking services by false pretenses a crime, Virginia had not done so. Also, the unauthorized use of a computer was found not to be the subject of larceny because it did not involve the "taking and carrying away of a certain concrete article of personal property." The court also would not accept the prosecution's argument that the value of the print-outs should be measured by the cost of production. The court concluded that where there is no market value for an article that has been stolen, the prosecution is obligated to prove its value. The print-outs had no ascertainable value to VPI or to the computer center. Lund's conviction was therefore overturned and the indictment against him was dismissed.

There is little doubt that the result in the Lund case was fair and that the prosecution may have acted somewhat overzealously in going after him in the first place. Yet, if there is to be consistency in the interpretation of the law, the same result should have been reached even if Lund had been using the state's computer to sell homework assignments to computer science students, or to print Snoopy calendars to sell in the dormitories. If Lund, however, had been engaged in activity for personal profit, the court might then have used that profit as a measure of the value of the time and services that he took.

A fourth group of states consists of those states that have legislation dealing specifically with trade secrets. The fact that a state has a statute that makes a misappropriation of a trade secret criminal, does not foreclose prosecution under other statutes, such as the theft statute, for the same offense.

Theft of trade secrets

As one might expect, California and New York, because of their size and the complexity of their technology and industry, have trade secret statutes. California, in fact, has one of the most detailed such statutes in the nation. This statute reads in part:

California statute

> (b) Every person is guilty of theft who, with intent to deprive or withhold from the owner thereof the control of a trade secret, or with the intent to appropriate a trade secret to his own use or to the use of another, does any of the following:
> 1. Steals, takes, or carries away any article representing a trade secret.
> 2. Fraudulently appropriates any article representing a trade secret entrusted to him.
> 3. Having unlawfully obtained access to the article, without authority makes or causes to be made a copy of any article representing a trade secret.
> 4. Having obtained access to the article through a relationship of trust and confidence, without authority and in breach of the obligations created by such relationship makes or causes to be made, directly from and in the presence of the article, a copy of any article representing a trade secret.

The statute further proscribes conspiracy to obtain a trade secret, and explicitly declares that the return or intent to return the article representing the trade secret is not a defense.

Loopholes

Despite its precision and seeming comprehensiveness, the California statute still leaves possible loopholes for the computer thief, because both "article" and "copy" as defined elsewhere in the statute seem to refer only to tangible objects. If this is true, then transferring a trade secret from one memory file to another would not be copying. The theft law does not seem to forbid the employee from using a program memorized for his or her own personal benefit, although conspiracy may be involved in a sale to third parties.

How have the California courts interpreted this statute? In *Ward* v. *Superior Court of the State of California*, the accused Ward, an employee of a computer service bureau, used a telephone to transfer a secret program from a competitor's computer to that of his employer. He then caused his employer's computer to print a copy of the stolen program and carried the copy to his office. He was charged under both the trade secret and grand theft statutes of California. The court found that the "article" taken must be tangible, "even though the trade secret which the article represents may itself be intangible." The electronic impulses representing the stolen program were not sufficiently tangible to constitute an article of theft. But Ward had gone beyond merely transferring electronic signals from one computer to another. His act of making a tangible copy of the program and then carrying the copy even the short distance to his office sufficed to establish the necessary elements for prosecution for theft of a trade secret; furthermore, making the copy was in itself sufficient as a violation. The court also concluded that the enactment of the trade secret statute made a trade secret property that was subject to theft, and, therefore, a misappropriation of any trade secret, or article representing a trade secret, can also be charged as a theft under the larceny statute. The lesson for would-be thieves, at least in California, is that they should not make tangible copies of the programs they steal. If Ward had merely transferred the competitor's program to his computer and used it, possibly to his great profit, without bothering to print it, he might have gotten away free, although there might have been a tort, breach of contract, or a copyright infringement.

New York statute

The New York larceny statute includes trade secrets and secret scientific materials as articles of theft. Copying is itself an offense prosecutable apart from, or in addition to, stealing. New York also seems to have a very broad notion of property that may be subject to theft. New York also seems to follow the same valuation rule as California and Texas, that is, the commercial value of the object governs. All this points up the key fact that criminal law may vary markedly from state to state and there are few generalizations that will be valid across the nation.

In addition to the state criminal codes, there is Title 18 of the United States Code, which is the federal criminal code. The principal federal statute which deals with theft is Section 641 of Title 18:

Federal criminal code

> Whoever embezzles, steals, purloins, or knowingly converts to his use or the use of another, or without authority, sells, conveys or disposes of . . . anything of value of the United States or any department or agency thereof, or any property made or being made under contract for the United States or any department thereof, or whoever receives, conceals, or retains the same with intent to convert it to his use or gain knowing it to have been embezzled, stolen, . . .

is subject to certain criminal penalties.

The statute is clearly very comprehensive in both the kind of activity it forbids and in the kind of property subject to theft. Forbidden activity includes embezzling, which is the fraudulent or unauthorized conversion or appropriation of property that has rightfully or lawfully come into the converter's possession, as opposed to stealing, in which the property comes into the converter's possession in a wrongful manner. The statute also forbids stealing, knowingly converting to the use of the actor or a third party, as well as selling, disposing of, or conveying without authority "anything of value" that belongs to the United States or any of its departments or agencies, or even any property that has been made or is being made under contract for the United States or any of its departments. The statute also proscribes receiving and hiding stolen property if it is known to have been stolen.

Conversion was a notion encountered and defined in the chapter on torts. Stealing is a narrower notion than conversion. The United States Supreme Court has said, "To steal means to take away from one in lawful possession without right with the intention to keep wrongfully."

Stealing v. conversion

> Conversion, however, may be consummated without any intent to keep and without any wrongful taking, where the initial possession by the converter was entirely lawful. Conversion may include misuse or abuse of property.

Certain phrases in Section 641 are "jurisdictional," that is, they provide the grounds on which the federal government can enter a particular case. Merely because some crime has been committed does not mean that it is a federal crime. In actual fact, most crimes are only violations of state law and the accused in such a situation cannot be brought to trial in federal court. For a crime to be a federal offense, the crime must somehow affect the United States, and not just some particular state. Remember that a crime is a wrong against the public; if

Federal jurisdiction

the public is to be interpreted as all of the citizens of the United States, then there must be some reason for that interpretation. The jurisdictional phrase in Section 641 is "of the United States or any department or agency thereof, or any property made or being made under contract for the United States or any department thereof." This basis for federal jurisdiction can be quite broad. For example, if the government has a license for the use of certain programs and the programs are stolen from their developer (and not necessarily directly from the government itself), then that would suffice to bring in federal jurisdiction. Section 641 also states that the measure of value of any item misappropriated is the "face, par, or market value, or cost price, either wholesale or retail, whichever is greater." This implies that the commercial value of a stolen program would be accepted by a court as a measure of its worth; or, if the program were completely lost to its owner, the cost of rewriting it might be used.

<small>Other federal statutes</small>

Other federal statutes apply to theft-related offenses in addition to Section 641. Section 659 of Title 18, for example, deals with theft from an interstate common carrier, and applies regardless of who owns the goods stolen. The goods become "interstate," and hence subject to federal jurisdiction, when the goods are segregated for interstate commerce and are turned over to those who will be transporting them; such interstate character continues until the goods arrive at their destination and are delivered by being unloaded or being placed to be unloaded. The act in question under Section 659 must be either stealing or embezzling them. This section does not seem to include unauthorized copying.

<small>Transportation of stolen property</small>

Section 2314 of Title 18 forbids interstate transportation of stolen property. The stolen article must actually cross state lines to trigger federal jurisdiction. In *United States* v. *Lester*, a conviction was upheld even though the defendant had merely transported misappropriated copies of commercially valuable geological survey maps across state lines. This implies that the statute could be invoked if someone carried an unauthorized copy of a computer program as well. There are also additional federal laws, such as that which covers conversion by a government employee of property entrusted to his or her care, that may be helpful to curb computer crime in carefully defined situations.

OTHER STATE AND FEDERAL STATUTES

<small>Misappropriation</small>

Although theft of software constitutes one of the largest potential sources of loss due to computer crime, there are other ways to lose than theft and other ways to misappropriate things than simply carting them off. A common problem, for example, at university computing facilities is unauthorized use of the machine, which may be characterized as misappropriation of computer time. Because computer time is a "thing of value," it is likely that, even in this case, many state larceny statutes might be applicable. There are, however, usually other state statutes as well that could be used to handle this situation, at least if a court could be convinced to interpret such statutes in a reasonable, though possibly broad, manner. For example, even an unauthorized user must usually provide an account number to which the use of computer resources will be charged. Furnishing this information is, in effect, fraudulently tendering a credit card because, presumably, the account the unauthorized person is using is not his or her own. This, in turn, could lead to prosecution under a credit care fraud statute. If a false name or identification is used, then forgery might also be involved. Forgery, generally, is the fraudulent making or altering of a writing for a fraudulent or deceitful purpose. The mere making of the fraudulent writing is sufficient to complete the crime. If the writer then proceeds to use the writing to defraud someone—such as cashing a forged check—then a second crime is involved that is known as uttering a forged instrument. This raises the question of what constitutes a writing in dealing with a computer. Of great legal significance too, along these same lines, is what constitutes a signature, a matter of critical importance with the advent of electronic funds transfer systems.

Credit card fraud

Forgery

Damaging information stored on a magnetic tape, such as by garbling that information by passing it through a strong magnetic field, is also most certainly prosecutable under a malicious mischief statute, provided that the court can accurately be made aware of the precise nature of the damage done. Anyone who breaks and enters a computer facility with the express purpose of doing substantial damage, or committing some other felony, is subject to prosecution for burglary. "Breaking and entering," under most modern statutes, is to be interpreted very broadly, so that breaking might even occur in opening an unlocked door. Virtually any unauthorized entry of a building for the purpose of committing a serious crime therein would involve burglary, even if the crime originally contemplated never comes to pass. Most people associate burglary with theft, but this is incorrect. The crime the burglar may intend can be any felony; moreover, the burglar may be found innocent of the intended crime, but be found guilty of burglary as a separate crime in itself.

Malicious mischief

Burglary

Some states have "telephone abuse" statutes that might be used to prosecute someone who attacks a computer or its contents from a remote site via a telephone line. Although the laws of each state are different, there is no state which does not have a substantial arsenal of statutes which can be used against the computer criminal. Some of

Telephone abuse

these laws are fairly obvious: statutes dealing with larceny, fraud, invasion of privacy, etc. Other statutes are less obvious, but might still prove to be valuable weapons. Among these would be statutes dealing with credit card fraud, fraudulent destruction of recordable instruments, or tampering with records.

Other federal laws besides those related directly to larceny can also be employed against computer crime. Some of the more important such statutes are discussed briefly below.

Mail and wire fraud

The two principal statutes that deal with abuse of federal channels of communication are Sections 1341 (mail fraud) and 1343 (wire fraud) of Title 18 of the United States Code. Both statutes have two essential elements: 1) the actor must use the mail (wire) for the purpose of executing, or attempting to execute, 2) a fraud or scheme to obtain money under false pretenses. Fraud has been liberally interpreted by the federal courts, and it is likely that they would find fraud in a scheme to obtain an unauthorized copy of a program. All cases tried to date under the wire fraud statute have involved calls which have crossed state lines.

One such wire fraud case was *United States* v. *Seidlitz*. Seidlitz, who operated his own computer business in Virginia, had obtained access codes to the computer of his former employer, Optimum Services, Inc. (OSI), located in Rockville, Maryland. OSI had developed a sophisticated program that Seidlitz misappropriated for his own personal gain. He obtained the electronic signals that represented the program through interstate telephone lines. Once the transmission had been made, he could, of course, print copies from the stored information. Seidlitz also had a computer terminal in his home in Maryland. As events turned out, he would have been better off had he stolen the program using that terminal. Seidlitz's theft was discovered, as are most computer crimes, purely by accident.

Jarvis Finney, the federal prosecutor for the district in which the crime was committed, pointed out some of the serious problems associated with trying to win a conviction in this kind of case under existing state and federal law. He made these observations in a report to a Senate committee that was considering possible new legislation to deal with computer crime. First, there is the problem of proving that Seidlitz actually called the computer from which he was stealing programs. Even once this is established, "it is also incumbent to establish, with precision, what material is being retrieved from the computer. Unless the victim company has certain specialized equipment available, this may pose an extreme burden which can seriously hamper any attempt to obtain a search warrant."

Suppose it had even been determined that Seidlitz had indeed phoned OSI's computer and that OSI knew precisely what information had been transmitted to Seidlitz's phone. Although Seidlitz was actually found with copies of the stolen programs in his possession, we will suppose too that a search of his premises had not revealed any identifiable copies. The incriminating evidence could have been entirely concealed on magnetic tapes or in invisible memory in the depths of the computer. The program might have been scrambled in such a way that only Seidlitz could decode it by means of another secret program; hence an exhaustive search of his home and business might have revealed no clear evidence of any crime, this even if the entire contents of his computer's memory had been "dumped" and given to a computer specialist to read. But such a blanket seizure and examination of all of Seidlitz's records and of all of the information stored in his computer might have run afoul of the Fourth Amendment, a consideration we will discuss in the next chapter.

If Seidlitz had not transmitted the programs to Virginia, then the wire fraud statute would have been useless because there would not have been a crossing of state lines. Moreover, a charge of interstate transportation of stolen property was dismissed by a judge because the judge held that there was nothing carried off in the sense needed for an act of stealing. The programs that Seidlitz misappropriated were not really "carried off" at all; they still resided snugly inside OSI's computer. Seidlitz had merely reproduced them by means of an electronic signal over the phone. The case was thus distinguished from those in which a copy had first been made and then transported interstate.

_{Need state lines crossed}

A conviction for what must appear to most sensible people to be a crime was nearly avoided because what was stolen was not carried off; in technical language, the "asportation" required for theft was not present. Would the court have found the necessary asportation if Seidlitz had erased the program in OSI's computer at the same time that he copied it into his own? It would certainly seem that the gratuitous destruction of OSI's files should not be required to classify the act as a theft. The courts would do well to reexamine the concept of asportation in a case such as this, but it does highlight the problems in applying antiquated notions to modern technology.

Federal statutes concerning trespass and burglary refer to specialized situations, e.g., banks and post offices, but not to the more general notion of "federal enclave." A federal enclave is property specially defined in the criminal code, Section 7, to fall under the jurisdiction of the federal government, at least for purposes of law enforcement. Probably the most important form of federal enclave is land obtained with the permission of a state legislature for the express purpose of some important federal project, such as construction of a fort or military installation. It also seems that the language of Section 2113(a), which deals with burglary of a bank, refers only to common law theft and not to the more extensive notion of theft that might en-

Federal enclaves

able a court to find say misappropriation of a trade secret. The Supreme Court, moreover, has held that federal criminal law in this respect is not to be interpreted in the light of what the state law is at the location of the crime. For these reasons, the federal statutes dealing with burglary and trespass are not as helpful as one might think in coping with computer crime. There is, however, the Assimilative Crimes Act, which adopts state criminal law to fill in the gaps in federal criminal law for each federal enclave in the state. Thus, even though the federal law may be deficient considered in isolation, state law may remedy that deficiency at least for federal enclaves.

Assimilative Crimes Act

Several federal statutes relate to deceptive practices, but by far the most comprehensive of these is Section 1001 of Title 18, which reads in part:

Deceptive practices

> Whoever, in any matter within the jurisdiction of any department or agency of the United States, knowingly and willfully falsifies, conceals or covers up by any trick, scheme or device a material fact, or makes any false, fictitious, or fraudulent statements or representations or makes or uses any false writing or document knowing the same to contain any false, fictitious or fraudulent statement or entry,

shall be subject to certain criminal penalties. All that Section 1001 requires is some "false, fictitious, or fraudulent statement, knowingly and willfully made." Note this is a specific intent crime. The statute embraces both oral and written representations. Because an entry of a password or authorization code into a computer is very much a statement that the one who enters it is entitled to what that person orders the computer to give him or her, this statute would seem to be a likely weapon with regard to misappropriation of computer services or information in any case in which the user misrepresents his or her identity or status.

An instructive case relating to computer abuse by fraud is *United States* v. *Jones.* Through a sophisticated scheme, again discovered solely by chance, the defendant's brother had a computer generate checks payable to the defendant that should have been payable to the defendant's employer. Because the payor of these checks was Canadian, the defendant was charged with transporting in foreign commerce checks valued at more than $5000, knowing the same to have been taken by fraud (Section 2314), and of unlawfully converting these checks knowing them to be fraudulent (Section 2315). Note how specific criminal statutes can get. Mrs. Jones moved that the charges be dismissed on the grounds that the checks in question were actually forgeries and, therefore, did not fall under the provisions of the statutes under which she had been indicted, because these statutes expressly did not apply to any "falsely made, forged, altered, counterfeited or spurious representation of . . . an obligation . . . or promise to pay . . . by a bank or corporation of any foreign country." Note how technical the criminal law can be. Note too that if Mrs. Jones' act did not precisely fit the act described in the statute as necessary for the crime, then she could not be charged under that statute (even though she might well be chargeable under some other statute). Recall that a forgery is essentially a fraudulent writing made with intent to defraud. The district court held that the checks were indeed forgeries and dismissed the charges; the government appealed.

The legal issue was whether "the alteration of accounts payable documents fed into a computer which resulted in the issuance of checks to an improper payee constituted 'falsely made, forged, altered, counterfeited or spurious' security." The Court of Appeals reversed the district court, holding that the act which caused the computer to print the fraudulent checks did not constitute the making of a false writing, "but rather amounted to the creation of a writing which was genuine in execution but false as to the statements contained in such writing." In other words, this was a situation where the alteration of invoices, which led, in turn, to a computer issuing checks to an improper party, was fraud rather than forgery, even though the perpetrator of the theft was, in some sense, merely using the computer as a pen to issue checks to which she had no right.

Fine distinction drawn

Jones was prosecuted in Maryland, the district of U.S. Attorney Jarvis Finney, mentioned above in connection with the *Seidlitz* case. Mr. Finney thus has the distinction of being a federal prosecutor associated with two major computer crime cases, although some prosecutors have not been involved with any at all. Mr. Finney pointed out to a Senate committee that if the checks had been found to be forgeries, and the indictments against Mrs. Jones had been dismissed, then there probably would not have been any federal statutes under which she could have been charged. The mail fraud statute might have been another possibility, but this would have required some proof that checks were placed in the mail in a scheme to defraud, whereas no checks at all might have been sent through the mails, only invoices. "Thus," said Mr. Finney, "there may be instances where computer-related criminal activity has no criminal sanction."

Federal statutes which deal with the destruction of property seem well-styled to handle a broad spectrum of possible offenses; Section 1361 of Title 18, which deals with the malicious destruction of government property, is the widest in its scope. It was used in the trial of the Catonsville Nine, who poured blood on selective service records during the Viet Nam War. In that particular case, the value of the property injured was taken to be the cost of restoring the damaged records.

Destruction of property

Despite the seeming availability of statutory protection, prosecution of computer "criminals" is often difficult. Susan Nycum also gave testimony before a Senate committee exploring possible computer-related legislation. She recounted a personal experience concerning computer abuse that might not have been prosecutable. While Mrs. Nycum was in charge of a computer center, one of her staff detected a user attempting to erase the volume table of contents for the system. The destruction of this master file would, of course, have created havoc in the computer operation, and, according to Mrs. Nycum's estimate, would have cost $50,000 to recreate. The attempt at destruction was made from a terminal outside the computer center itself using intrastate telephone lines and was frustrated only because of prompt action taken to disconnect the caller. Despite the large amount of damage and inconvenience that would have resulted had the attempt succeeded, local law enforcement agencies were not sure that there was any law under which they could prosecute. The best they could do was a suggestion that the person be charged with making an obscene phone call. No charges were filed. Though state authorities were involved in the incident cited, it is not clear that under the circumstances federal authorities would have even had the option of prosecuting for an obscene phone call.

Aiding and abetting

A person who encourages or aids another in the commission of an indictable offense may also be indicted as an aider and abettor, or if that person assists the actor after the commission of the crime, he or she may risk prosecution as an accessory after the fact. There are also the crimes of attempt to commit a felony, or conspiracy, mentioned in the first section of this chapter. Section 371 of the United State Criminal Code makes it a crime for two or more persons to conspire together to commit a crime to defraud the federal government. The notion of fraud upon the government is very broad and does not imply any monetary loss to the government. Yet, as we have seen, with all the vast statutory arsenal already in existence, more legislation, drafted especially to meet the challenge of computer crime, may be needed. We discuss some existing new legislation as well as some proposed new legislation of this sort in the next section.

Conspiracy to defraud

NEW LEGISLATION

Law changing rapidly

Several states have already passed statutes specifically directed against computer crime and other states are considering such a move. The situation concerning new legislation is changing so rapidly that the best that can be done at this point is to survey some representative laws, not necessarily good laws, to see what might be done in this area. Computer professionals should be aware if new legislation that might affect their industry is being considered in their state, and they should not be afraid to make their voices heard for or against such legislation since they are probably those most qualified to discuss its potential impact and the technical problems it will cause. While most lawmakers might argue that most professionals in the computer field are ignorant of the law, most legislators are even more ignorant of computer technology, and even some of the "modern" statutes drafted to try to meet the complexities of computer crime suffer from defects that are obvious to anyone having even a passing acquaintance with computing. We consider first an important bill that is being considered as of this writing by a committee of the Senate.

S.240

S.240, otherwise known as the "Federal Computer Systems Protection Act of 1979," was first introduced in a slightly different form in 1977 by Senator Abraham Ribicoff. As of this writing, S.240 has been transmitted by the Senate Criminal Justice Subcommittee to the full Senate Committee on the Judiciary for further consideration. It remains the subject of a running debate in such professional publications as *Computerworld*; first, as to whether any new law is needed at all; and, if one is needed, whether this bill will do the job properly.

S.240 states as follows the acts it wishes to curb:

(a) Who knowingly and willfully, directly or indirectly accesses, causes to be accessed or attempts to access any computer, computer system, computer network, or any part thereof which, in whole or in part, operates in interstate commerce or is owned by, under contract to, or in conjunction with, any financial institution, the United States Government or any branch, department or agency thereof, any entity operating in or affecting interstate commerce, for the purpose of:
1. devising or executing any scheme or artifice to defraud, or
2. obtaining money property, or service, for themselves or another, by means of false or fraudulent pretenses, representations or promises, shall be fined a sum of not more than two and one-half times the amount of the fraud or theft and imprisoned not more than 15 years or both.

(b) Whoever intentionally and without authorization, directly or indirectly accesses, alters, damages, destroys, or attempts to damage or destroy any computer, computer system, or computer network described in subsection (a), or any computer software, program or data contained in such computer, computer system or computer network, shall be fined not more than $50,000 or imprisoned not more than 15 years or both.

The bill continues with an extensive and fairly broad list of definitions. "Access" is defined so broadly that it could include any use of almost anything having something to do with a computer:

> "Access" means to approach, instruct, communicate with, store data in, retrieve data from, or otherwise make use of any resources of, a computer, computer system, or computer network.

On the other hand, "computer" is given a rather restrictive interpretation in that it is limited to electronic devices that manipulate data via electronic or magnetic impulses, thus excluding some of the major new forms of computers, such as those that employ fluidics. But the definition is also too broad in that it does not restrict its scope to general purpose machines, thus opening the way for rulings that electronic watches and automated traffic signals are covered by the bill. However, in the version voted out of the Senate Criminal Justice Subcommittee in late 1979, automated typewriters, home computers, and hand-held calculators were exempted from coverage by the bill. In place of the many paragraphs of definitions in the original draft of S.240 dealing with computers, computer systems, computer networks, and the like, the subcommittee defined a computer to be "a device that performs logical, arithmetic and storage functions by electronic manipulation and includes any property and communication facility directly related to or operating in conjunction with such a device." But because reference is still made to "any property or communication facility directly related to or operating in conjunction with such a device," it appears that software and even telephones are to be treated as part of the computer itself. Yet despite this seeming breadth, it is not obvious that the most serious potential source of loss, illicit copying of a printed program, is even covered at all.

S.240 duplicative and overboard

Two conclusions are evident. First, the proposed legislation duplicates much existing legislation. Second, and almost antithetical to the first conclusion, this bill ranges so broadly and is written so unclearly that it is hard to say with any degree of certainty exactly what the bill would make a crime. Because anyone considering a particular act must be fairly clearly advised by the law whether the proposed act subjects him or her to possible criminal liability, S.240 may be struck down as unconstitutionally vague. The extremely harsh penalties of the original draft—up to a $50,000 fine and 15 years in prison for perhaps stealing but $.25 worth of computer time—have been redrawn by the Senate subcommittee to bring them into line with penalties applicable to mail and wire fraud. Yet even these penalties can be severe for acts that might be common practice within the computer industry, such as printing a Snoopy calendar on company time.

There seems to be little disagreement among experts, both in computing and law enforcement, that existing legislation is indeed inadequate. But, although most of the witnesses at the hearings on S.1766, the predecessor of S.240, felt that some legislation was needed, almost no one was satisfied with S.1766 itself. Senator Ribicoff redrafted S.1766, incorporating suggestions made by then Assistant Attorney General Benjamin Civiletti, and reintroduced the modified bill as S.240 in 1979.

<small>Existing laws inadequate</small>

The scope of federal jurisdiction is one of the most striking features of S.240. It seems even broader than that of Section 641 of Title 18, discussed earlier in this chapter, which is quite broad indeed. If jurisdiction is a problem in the application of existing federal criminal law to computer abuses, the problem should be virtually nonexistent with regard to S.240. Note that the grounds for jurisdiction include:

<small>Scope of federal jurisdiction</small>

1. the computer (which, according to the bill, includes anything having something to do with the computer as defined in more traditional terms) operates in interstate commerce;
2. the computer is owned by, under contract to, or in conjunction with
   a) any financial institution,
   b) the United State government or any branch, department, or agency thereof, or
   c) any entity operating in or affecting interstate commerce.

Because hot dog stands operating in the middle of nowhere using locally produced products can be considered to operate in and affect interstate commerce, there is virtually nothing that could have anything, however remote, to do with computers and not fall under the scope of this bill. Thus, someone causing a computer to print some obscene comment on a terminal being used by a friend might be subject to federal prosecution. Carried to its extreme, this bill would cover the theft of a digital wristwatch, and might even cover running an automated red traffic light. The subcommittee tried to pare down the jurisdiction somewhat by extending coverage to all computers used by the federal government, by financial institutions or in interstate commerce. But a moment's reflection upon the scope given "interstate commerce" by the courts would warn that this may not be much of a limitation after all.

The vast scope of the federal jurisdiction and the breadth of the definitions (while, at the same time, seeming to ignore items and acts that truly belong under the coverage of the law), as well as the ambiguity of what is forbidden conduct, are all significant problems with this bill. As a further example, the bill appears to make it a crime if one merely devises a scheme to defraud, even if the schemer makes no attempt to carry out the plan and no conspiracy is involved. It is common practice within computer operations, of course, for "systems jocks" to attempt to devise ways to beat the system, cause it to crash, or obtain data to which they are not entitled. Some computer operations tolerate such antics, even though the consequences can be annoying, because they help locate and correct security flaws. It is virtually standard practice as well, particularly with university systems, for students to play unauthorized games such as "Star Trek," print calendars of various sorts, compile statistics for bowling leagues, or do other jobs that the rules of the system, and possibly laws of the state, definitely forbid. These rules, however, are virtually unenforceable, and abuses are sometimes winked at to encourage students to gain greater experience in the use of the computer. To make such pranks crimes seems a bit excessive. It is well to say that the law would never move against such petty offenses, but it would not be wise to put temptation in the hands of those seeking some means of bringing "campus radicals" to their knees.

We now turn our attention to two representative pieces of state computer crime legislaion.

Arizona

The definition of the relevant computer-related terminology in the Arizona statute, *Arizona Revised Statutes* Section 2301(E), is quite similar to that of S.240 in its original form, and thus suffers from the same defects. The main body of the legislation creates a new crime, computer fraud. The statute bears a striking resemblance to S.240, but is not quite as sweeping in its scope. Section 13-2316 of the Arizona Criminal Code reads in part:

> A. A person commits computer fraud . . . by accessing, altering, damaging or destroying without authorization any computer, computer systems, computer network, or any part . . . with the intent to devise or execute any scheme or artifice to defraud or deceive, or control property or services by means of false or fraudulent pretenses, representations or promises.

> B. A person commits computer fraud . . . by intentionally and without authorization accessing, altering, damaging or destroying any computer, computer system or computer network or any computer software, program or data contained in such computer, computer system or computer network.

Although this statute is not quite as broad as S.240, it suffers from many of the same ailments. It is not clear what specific acts are forbidden; and it is admitted by the Arizona Attorney General that student use of computer time without authorization would be a violation. The Attorney General would rely upon prosecutorial discretion to avoid abuse of the law, a risky business at best. Likewise, just as was the case with S.240, the law does not seem to make unauthorized copying of a program a crime under many common circumstances.

But the law suffers from yet another defect. Some of the terms in this new law are defined in pre-existing statutes. The computer fraud statute speaks of the "intent to . . . control property." In Section 13-1801 of the Arizona Statutes, "control" is defined to be an action which excludes others from using their own property except on the defendant's own terms. In stealing a copy of a program for personal use, an actor would not control the program in this sense. No doubt Arizona courts will have to determine whether the new law has actually extended the notion of control.

Depends on prior statutes

Florida

Florida, on the other hand, instead of using the S.240 definitions, has chosen to use definitions similar to those proposed by the Association for Computing Machinery. "Computer" is taken to be an internally-programmed, automatic device that performs data processing. Although similar to the ACM definition, it is, unfortunately, not the same. It obviates the "electronic" limitation of S.240, but it lacks the important provision of "general purpose." Thus, it would appear that Florida too could find computer crime in unlikely places such as wristwatches. The Florida law defines three categories of offenses: offenses against intellectual property, offenses against computer equipment and supplies, and offenses against computer users.

Definitions

Offenses against intellectual property include knowing and unauthorized modification, alteration, or destruction of programs, data or supporting documentation, as well as the taking of computer-related documents that are trade secrets (generally, see *Florida Statutes* Section 815.03 to Section 815.06). Presumably this latter category would include making off with an unauthorized copy of a secret program. Offenses against computer equipment include taking, injuring, or damaging the tangible objects associated with a computer system. The heart of the section which deals with offenses against computer users is the following paragraph:

Offenses against intellectual property

> Whoever willfully, knowingly and without authorization accesses or causes to be accessed any computer, computer system, or computer network; or whoever willfully, knowingly and without authorization denies or causes the denial of computer services which, in whole or in part, is owned by, under contract to, or operated for, on behalf of, or in conjunction with, another commits an offense against computer users.

148   LAW AND THE COMPUTER

Tries to avoid duplication

The Florida statute is unquestionably the best of the three laws considered in its ability to define and address computer abuse. Also, the Florida legislation attempts to address special computer-related questions that are not likely to be answered by other existing law. In other words, the Florida law has tried to avoid duplication in forbidding acts already well covered by prior legislation. If someone alters a program so that it will not run, it is a crime under Florida law if the act is done knowingly and willfully and the program is that of another. One need not argue the value of the damage done, the cost of correcting the damage, or whether the owner was deprived of control. The altering is prosecutable as an offense against intellectual property.

Ideal bill

What would an ideal computer abuse bill be like? First, it ought to be general and flexible enough to lend itself to the rapidly exploding computer technology and new uses to which computers might be put. Yet the law ought to be narrow enough to exclude watches, traffic signals, and pocket calculators. Second, it should address those special questions that computers raise without unnecessarily infringing on areas well-covered by existing law. Third, it ought to specify in a form that can be understood by computer users and the judicial system alike what acts constitute crimes under the law and which do not.

Two approaches

At least two approaches are possible. The first is to draft statutes which expand upon the common law notions of property, asportation, and the like, at least in the case of computer-related items, to enable acts of computer abuse to be treated under existing penal codes. The second alternative is to draft laws specifically creating new offenses related to computer abuse. The advantage of the first approach, of course, is that it takes advantage of existing law, law with which the courts and attorneys have already had experience. An example of a statute of this type would be the following:

> For purposes of application of any statute in which the taking of, or damage to, property is an essential element, property shall include computer programs, whether internal or external to, a computer. A computer program will have been asported or taken if an unauthorized copy is made, it being sufficient that the copy, if not reduced to tangible form, is embodied internal to a computer system, even though the owner of the program thus copied remains in possession and control of his original. If the value of such program asported is to be established, it shall be the commercial value of the program as established by expert witnesses.

As an example of model legislation embodying the second approach, the author offers the following Model Computer Crime Bill which is based heavily on the Florida law and ACM definitions.

Model computer crime bill

As used in this chapter, unless the context clearly indicates otherwise:

"Intellectual property" means data including programs.

"Computer program" means an ordered set of data representing coded instruction or statements that, when executed by a computer, cause the computer to process data.

"Computer" means an internally programmed, general purpose, automatic device that performs data processing.

"Computer software" means a set of computer programs, procedures, and associated documentation concerned with the operation of a computer system.

"Computer system" means a set of related, connected or unconnected, computer equipment, devices, or computer software.

"Computer network" means a set of related, remotely connected devices and communications facilities including more than one computer system with capability to transmit data among them through communications channels.

"Computer system services" means providing a computer system or computer network to perform useful work.

"Property" means anything of value and includes, but is not limited to, financial instruments, information, including electronically reproduced data and computer software and programs in either machine or human readable form, or any other tangible or intangible item of value.

"Financial instrument" means any check, draft, money order, certificate of deposit, letter of credit, bill of exchange, credit card, or marketable security.

"Access" means to approach, instruct, communicate with, store data in, retrieve data from, or otherwise make use of any resource of a computer, computer system, or computer network.

The "value" of property is its commercial value, reasonable retail value, or cost of production, whichever is greatest. The assessment of "value of damage" to property is determined by the cost of restoring the property to its condition immediately prior to being damaged.

Offenses against intellectual property

1. Whoever willfully, knowingly, and without authorization modifies data, programs, or supporting documentation residing or existing internal or external to a computer, computer system, or computer network commits an offense against intellectual property.
2. Whoever willfully, knowingly, and without authorization destroys data, programs, or supporting documentation residing or existing internal or external to a computer, computer system, or computer network commits an offense against intellectual property.
3. Whoever willfully, knowingly, and without authorization discloses or takes data, programs, or supporting documentation that is a trade secret, or is confidential as provided by law, residing or existing internal or external to a computer, computer system, or computer network commits an offense against intellectual property.

4. An offense against intellectual property is a Class B misdemeanor. However, the offense is a Class A misdemeanor if the value of the property acted upon is at least two hundred fifty dollars ($250) but less than two thousand five hundred dollars ($2500), and a Class D felony if
    (i) the value of the property acted upon is at least two thousand five hundred dollars ($2500),
    (ii) the damage causes a substantial interruption or impairment of utility service rendered to the public,
    (iii) the owner of the property is a bank or financial institution, or
    (iv) the offense involves property that is confidential as a matter of law.

Offenses against computer equipment or supplies
1. Whoever willfully, knowingly, and without authorization modifies equipment or supplies used or intended to be used in a computer, computer system, or computer network commits an offense against computer equipment or supplies.
2. An offense against computer equipment or supplies is a Class B misdemeanor. However, it is a Class A misdemeanor if the cost of restoring the equipment or supplies to their condition immediately prior to modification is at least two hundred fifty dollars ($250) but less than two thousand five hundred dollars ($2500), and a Class D felony if
    (i) the cost of restoration is at least two thousand five hundred dollars ($2500),
    (ii) the modification causes a substantial interruption or impairment of utility service rendered to the public,
    (iii) the equipment or supplies belong to a financial institution, bank, or health care facility, or
    (iv) the modification poses an unreasonable danger to other property or to human life.
3. Whoever willfully, knowingly, and without authorization destroys, takes, injures, or damages equipment or supplies used or intended to be used in a computer, computer system, or computer network; or whoever willfully, knowingly, and without authorization destroys, injures, or damages any computer, computer system, or computer network commits an offense against computer equipment or supplies.
4. The penalties for the offense described in (3) shall be the same as those described in (4) of the section concerning offenses against intellectual property.

Offenses against computer users
1. Whoever willfully, knowingly, and without authorization accesses or causes to be accessed any computer, computer system, or computer network; or whoever willfully, knowingly, and without authorization denies or causes to be denied computer system services to an authorized user of such computer system services, which, in whole or part, is owned by, under contract to, or operated for, on

behalf of, or in conjunction with another commits an offense against computer users.
2. An offense against computer users is a Class B misdemeanor. However, this offense is a Class D felony if the act
    (i) causes a substantial interruption or impairment of utility service rendered to the public,
    (ii) interferes with the operation of a bank, financial institution, or health care facility, or
    (iii) involves an intent to devise or execute any scheme to obtain by fraud property the value of which exceeds one thousand dollars ($1000).

Chapter not exclusive—Nothing in this chapter shall be construed to preclude the applicability of any other provision of the criminal law of this state that presently applies or may in the future apply to any transaction that violates this chapter, unless such provision is inconsistent with the terms of this chapter.

If any provision of this act or the application thereof to any person or circumstance is held invalid, it is the legislative intent that the invalidity shall not affect other provisions or applications of the act that can be given effect without the invalid provisions or applications, and to this end the provisions of this act are declared severable.

SUGGESTED ADDITIONAL READINGS ON COMPUTER CRIME

A classic work on this subject is Donn Parker, *Crime by Computer* (New York: Scribner's, 1976).

Susan Nycum wrote two surveys, one dealing with state and the other with federal legislation, concerned with existing laws that might be used to combat computer crime. These two articles appeared in Volume 5 (1976) of the *Rutgers Journal of Computers and the Law* at pages 271 and 297.

For a congressional study dealing with computer security, see Staff Study of *Computer Security in Federal Programs*, Committee on Government Operations of the U.S. Senate, 95th Congress, 1st Session, 1977.

For a survey of methods of computer security, see R. Slivka and J. Darrow, "Methods and Problems in Computer Security," *Rutgers Journal of Computers and the Law*, Vol. 5(1976), 217-69.

For more than you really want to know about Senator Ribicoff's Computer Crime Bill, see *Federal Computer Systems Protection Act: Hearings on S.1766 Before the Subcommittee on Criminal Laws and Procedures of the Senate Committee on the Judiciary*, 95th Congress, 2d Session (1978).

Two reported cases dealing with computer crime are *Hancock v. State*, 402 S.W.2d 906 (Ct. Crim. App. Tex. 1966), affirmed in *Hancock v. Decker*, 379 F.2d 552 (5th Cir. 1967); *U.S. v. Jones*, 553 F.2d 351 (4th Cir. 1977). *U.S. v. Seidlitz*, 589 F.2nd 152 (4th Cir. 1978).

EVIDENCE

DISCOVERY

The United States has an adversary system of justice. Each party to any dispute that comes before a court will set forth its evidence to support its particular position. If the issue is solely one of law, the parties will present arguments on behalf of their positions, citing as many and as weighty authorities as they can. If the issue is one of fact, they will attempt to convince judge or jury, whoever is "trying" the fact, by arguments and evidence that things happened as each party claims it did. This is not necessarily the best system of justice. Perhaps it would be better if attorneys for each side worked impartially with the court to try as best they could to determine the "truth" of the matter in controversy. But that is not what we have, and not what parties to lawsuits in this country face.

In order to have evidence to present in support of his or her position, the party must gather that evidence. In order to have that evidence weighed in any verdict, a party must be able to present that evidence in court, preferably in a convincing and comprehensible manner. There are thus two distinct phases in the evidentiary process. The first is the evidence-gathering phase, which is generally termed "discovery"; the second is the evidence-presenting phase that occurs when the party states his or her case in court. The two are quite different not only in style and nature, but in the legal rules which govern them. Moreover, the rules that govern criminal cases are quite different from those that govern civil cases. This section will discuss discovery, first in a criminal proceeding, and then in a civil proceeding.

Gathering evidence in a criminal proceeding

Fourth Amendment safeguards

Most Americans are aware that a police officer cannot simply walk up to anyone at all and arrest that person, charge him or her with a crime and put that person in jail. Likewise, law enforcement officials are not free to select a house at random, break into it, and begin searching for evidence of criminal activity. One of the most important safeguards we have against a "police state" is the Fourth Amendment to the United States Constitution, which reads:

> The right of the people to be secure in their persons, houses, papers, and effects, against unreasonable searches and seizures shall not be violated, and no warrants shall issue, but upon probable cause, supported by oath or affirmation, and particularly describing the place to be searched, and the persons or things to be seized.

Although the first eight amendments to the Constitution were originally held to limit only the powers of the federal government, leaving state governments free to ignore the protections the Bill of Rights granted their citizens against the federal government, the Supreme Court has held that most of these same protections have been extended against the states as well by the Fourteenth Amendment.

Vast treatises have been written on the Fourth Amendment alone. Other significant rights are granted in the Fifth, Sixth, Seventh, and Eight Amendments as well, these amendments together with the Fourth forming the foundation on which this nation's entire system of criminal justice administration is built. Obviously, this book cannot even begin to cover this enormous area. We must focus instead on some of the central themes that might be of interest to the computing industry.

Reasonable expectation of privacy

In order to gather evidence of criminal behavior, police may wish to conduct a search. The Supreme Court has stated that the Fourth Amendment protects people, not places. If a person is in a place where he or she has a reasonable expectation of privacy, then any attempt to violate that privacy to gather information is a search. It was even held that eavesdropping on a caller in a public phone booth is a search, although visual observation of the fact that the caller was in the phone booth was not a search, since that act did not carry the expectation of privacy.

Search warrants

If the police wish to conduct a search, they must generally obtain a warrant (more about this in a moment). Under certain conditions warrantless searches are permitted, and evidence may be seized without a warrant. If a police officer has a right to be where he or she is, and notices evidence of a crime, the officer may seize it if the evidence is in plain view. Many a computer criminal has been caught because he or she carelessly left printed records that signaled the illicit activity in places where the criminal had no right to expect privacy. Certain industries subject to heavy federal regulation may have their premises and records inspected without a warrant under the theory that engaging in that business is an implicit waiver of privacy. It is not clear what the limits of this doctrine are. It has been made clear by the Supreme Court, however, that even routine administrative searches, that is, searches by administrative agencies such as OSHA, which are conducted for the purpose of checking compliance with regulations rather than apprehending criminals, still require a warrant, although the standards for issuing such a warrant are somewhat less rigorous than for a police search warrant. Also, the Fourth Amendment carries no protection against searches by private individuals. If someone sneaks into your house, uncovers evidence of a crime, and then takes that evidence to the police, then, unless that informant is an agent of the police, the Fourth Amendment does not forbid use of that evidence even if the entry into your house was entirely illegal.

How do police obtain a search warrant? They must go before a judge or other authorized judicial officer who is not associated with prosecuting the case in question and present a sworn affidavit in which facts within the affiant's (the one who swears to the affidavit) personal knowledge or about which he or she has trustworthy information, are set forth that would justify a person of reasonable caution to believe that the evidence in question will be found. The evidence must be described with some particularity, as must the place to be searched. The warrant must direct the police concerning what they are looking for and where to look for it. Even when they are searching the place described, they are restricted to look only in those locations in which the evidence might reasonably be found. For example, if they are looking for a stolen car, they cannot open a dresser drawer hoping to find the car inside.

Unless a computer criminal is foolish enough to leave evidence of the crime lying around in hard copy form, or in a format that the nonprofessional can understand, the search for computer evidence unquestionably creates special problems for law enforcement officials. Evidence of computer crime is most probably to be found, if at all, in the internal storage of a machine, or perhaps on disks, tapes, or cards that do not look anything at all like the traditional "smoking gun" or packet of heroin. Needless to say, any police officer who served a search warrant upon a computer operation would almost certainly have to bring along a computer expert, probably one, in fact, with expertise in the particular hardware and operating system of the ma-

Special problem of computer search

chine to be "searched." One can easily imagine too the enormous volume of material that such a search might produce. Nevertheless, there is at least one instance of a search warrant that included among the "personal property" to be sought as evidence of an alleged theft of a computer program:

1. Key punch computer cards, punched with the Information Systems Design remote plotting programs;
2. computer printout sheets with printouts of Information Systems Design remote plotting programs; and
3. Computer memory bank or other data storage devices magnetically imprinted with Information Systems Design remote, plotting computer programs

Among the items taken pursuant to the search in question were a total directory of all files; a "dump" of the description directory of the files, a number of computer tapes, and a program listing. Note that what was sought is rather specific, namely, items associated with Information Systems Design. It would have almost certainly been a violation of the Fourth Amendment to call for a general search and a taking of all materials of whatever kind stored within the defendant's computer.

Because the activity within a computer can be monitored by various forms of electronic surveillance, at least a brief mention of the law in this area is desirable. An electronic surveillance is a search and requires judicial supervision, at least in the form of a proper warrant, as is the case with any search. A conversation or transmission of data where one of the parties to the exchange of information has given permission for eavesdropping on, or recording, the exchange is not considered a search, because each party to such an exchange must assume the risk that another party will reveal the nature and substance of what is transmitted. Sections 2510 to 2520 of Title 18 of the United States Code, otherwise known as Title III of the "Omnibus Crime Control and Safe Streets Act of 1968," gives detailed rules concerning wiretaps and other forms of electronic surveillance. States are bound to standards at least as strict as those contained in these sections. In any event, such techniques may not be used as mere "fishing expeditions" to try to find evidence of some criminal activity.

Exclusionary Rule

What happens if illegally obtained evidence does come into the possession of law enforcement agencies or prosecutors? Suppose, for example, a search is conducted without a warrant, but such that the search does not fit into any of the recognized situations for which a warrant might be waived. What can be done with any evidence that such a search produces? The answer to this question is given by the

"Exclusionary Rule," a highly complex and controversial rule of law. In essence, the Exclusionary Rule states that any evidence that is obtained in violation of the Constitution may not be used against the person whose constitutional rights were violated. Not only may the evidence directly obtained from the violation not be used, but no evidence that would not have been obtained but for the violation and the evidence gained from it can be used either. Thus, if an illegal search reveals an address book, which in turn leads to a cache of stolen property, the stolen property cannot be admitted as evidence if the only reason it was found was because of the improperly obtained address book.

As is always the case with any rule of law, there are exceptions. If the evidence has also been obtained from a source that is independent of the constitutional violation, or if the evidence obtained is sufficiently far removed from the constitutional violation that a court considers the evidence to be no longer "tainted" by the violation, or where the evidence has been mistakenly used against the defendant, but a court determines that the error was "harmless," that is, the defendant could have been convicted anyway, then the Exclusionary Rule does not apply to exclude the evidence at trial or to force the government to grant the defendant a new trial in which the evidence will not be admitted. Certainly, anyone unfortunate enough to be a defendant in a criminal trial needs an attorney, and one of the first things an attorney for such a defendant must look for is whether any of the evidence obtained against the client has been obtained in a constitutionally impermissible fashion so that the attorney can move to have it excluded completely from the trial. Because the manner of "searching" a computer and the types of surveillance that might be employed to monitor computing activity have not been explored by the courts, this should be an area of special interest to the computing industry. Is it permissible, for example, even under the federal wiretap statute, to arrange to "dump" all of the activity of a given computer through some "trapdoor" or "Trojan horse" technique? If a computer operates in time-sharing and the defendant is but one of many users, what are the rights of those not under suspicion, but whose files are also invaded during a surveillance, even with a warrant?

Surveillance of computing activity

In the federal judicial system, indictments for more serious crimes must come from a grand jury. The Exclusionary Rule does not apply in grand jury proceedings and illegally seized evidence may be used in convincing a grand jury to indict, even though that same evidence cannot later be introduced at trial. Grand juries may also summon witnesses and order them to bring specific documents with them. The

Grand jury

Fifth amendment protection

Fifth Amendment protects people against having to be witnesses against themselves, that is, give personal testimony that is likely to incriminate themselves, but a grand jury or prosecutor may arrange for a witness to obtain "use immunity," which means that any testimony that the witness gives or any evidence gained directly from it cannot be used to prosecute that witness for any crime; if such immunity is granted, the witness must testify or risk jail for "contempt." Furthermore, business records that are merely in the custody of an employee of a business are not protected by the Fifth Amendment in most circumstances. For example, the treasurer of a corporation may not withhold the books of the corporation if these are properly sought by a grand jury or an investigator with a court order because they contain information that the treasurer knows will show he has been embezzling. Nor will a computer operator be able to shield illicit activity by appealing to the Fifth Amendment if ordered to produce files that will show that she has been defrauding the company she works for.

Computer investigation difficult

Nevertheless, the discovery of evidence in criminal investigations of computer crime is often extraordinarily difficult. Most successful prosecutions for computer-related crime have been successful only because of carelessness on the part of the defendant, information obtained from an informant, or brazen self-confidence and pride that led the defendant to admit openly what he or she was doing. The real limits of search and seizure relative to computer files have yet to be tested.

Civil proceedings

Pretrial discovery

We now look at the pretrial process of gathering evidence in cases that are merely civil in nature. Each state and the federal government has its "Rules of Civil Procedure" or the equivalent, which include the discovery rules applicable in that jurisdiction. The purpose of pretrial discovery is to enable the parties to a suit to gain as much of the evidence they need to properly present their respective cases, sharpen the issues for trial, and avoid "surprise" as a trial tactic. The sharpie lawyer holding several cards up his or her sleeve to drop upon an unsuspecting opponent at an opportune moment during the trial, leaving the opponent confounded and the jury dazzled, is contrary to the spirit of modern discovery, where, at least in theory, the ideal is for both sides to lay their cards face up on the table before trial so that the trial can be conducted with a minimum of surprise. In fact, the party who tries to withhold vital evidence improperly from the opposing party may find that that evidence will not be permitted at trial, or that the entire case may go against the party who will not cooperate in the discovery process.

In point of fact, discovery, in the sense of trying to ascertain the "facts" of a particular case, should begin even before suit is filed. No attorney should file suit unless and until he or she is reasonably convinced that there are adequate grounds for the suit. This involves more than simply listening to a client; it involves fact-finding to see if the client's complaint is well-founded in fact and law, whether the law recognizes a cause of action that will address the client's grievance, and whether there is at least a genuine dispute as to what the facts of the dispute really are. This may involve contacting the potential defendant informally to determine the other side of the story, or other witnesses to gain other views as to the facts. It may involve consulting an outside expert to determine how strong a case can be made for the client from a technical point of view. Most potential litigation does not reach the courtroom. The client may be advised that he or she simply does not have a case, or a recognized cause of action, or the matter may be resolved informally outside the courtroom.

Need proper grounds for suit

Be fully aware, however, that the process of discovery, even before the institution of a suit, can be fairly expensive, although its cost does not generally begin to compare with the cost of discovery after suit is filed. Even if an attorney agrees to accept a case on a contingency fee basis—that is, the attorney will receive a certain percentage of any recovery, and nothing at all if no recovery is made—out-of-pocket expenses such as filing fees and costs for a private investigator must be reimbursed by the client. The cost of a deposition alone, particular the fees of a court stenographer for recording the session and making a transcription, can run into the hundreds of dollars; this is a cost the client must bear even if he or she fails to recover a dime.

Cost of discovery

Before suit is formally brought by the filing of a complaint in an appropriate court, a party has little rights in the way of discovery; the client must primarily depend on the potential defendant's goodwill and desire to avoid litigation. Once a complaint is filed and the defendant answers by denying those assertions by the plaintiff with which he or she disagrees or about which he or she has insufficient knowledge and by raising various defenses, discovery begins. The general scope of discovery is described as follows in the federal Rules of Civil Procedure:

> Parties may obtain discovery regarding any matter, not privileged, which is relevant to the subject matter involved in the pending action, whether it relates to the claim or defense of the party seeking discovery or to the claim or defense of any other party, including the existence, description, nature, custody, condition and location of any books, documents, or other tangible things and the identity and location of persons having knowledge of any discoverable matter. It is not ground for objection that

the information sought will be inadmissible at the trial if the information sought appears reasonably calculated to lead to the discovery of admissible evidence.

Note that the material that can be sought in discovery is extremely broad; basically, it is virtually anything at all that relates to the claim or defense of either party in such a way that it might reasonably be expected to lead either directly or indirectly, to evidence that is admissible at trial. The question of what material is privileged—that is, what information is sheltered from legally compelled disclosure—is a rather technical one, and is determined by state law, both in state and in federal cases. As an example of a privilege applicable universally, communications between an attorney and his or her client concerning the litigation are privileged and may not be discovered by the opposing party. If one party feels that the other party is attempting to discover information to which it has no right, that party may apply to the court for a protective order that bars the party seeking that information from obtaining it. If the court should declare that the information is properly discoverable, then the party must produce it or risk sanctions up to and including losing the lawsuit.

Privileged material

Could a party institute an improper lawsuit merely for the purpose of gaining information about the other party through discovery? Perhaps, but if the lawsuit were truly improper, both the plaintiff and his attorney would incur potential liability. The case might well be thrown out of court and the defendant could counterclaim for damages as well as seek appropriate protective orders from the court. Moreover, the defendant could "retaliate" by using the discovery process to find out information damaging to the plaintiff. Judges are also empowered to protect trade secrets.

Improper lawsuits

The basic forms of discovery are depositions, both written and oral; written interrogatories; production of documents or things; permission to enter upon land or other property, for inspection or other purposes; physical and mental examinations; and requests for admissions.

Forms of discovery

Oral depositions may be conducted at the request of either party to a suit. The person "deposed" can be either a party to the suit or just someone who may have useful information, probably someone a party intends to call as a witness at trial, or whose testimony a party would like to have for the record in case that person is not available at time of trial. Persons may be subpoenaed to appear for a deposition and even ordered to bring specified documents with them. A subpoena is an order to appear for some specific purpose under penalty of being held in contempt of court for failure to appear. In actual practice, attorneys try to cooperate to arrange for necessary depositions at mutually convenient times. Depositions involve direct and cross-examination by both parties, much as at an actual trial, with a court stenographer present to record what is said. Deposing a witness is a rather formal and fairly expensive method of trying to obtain information needed for trial. The deposition thus obtained, that is, the written transcript of the various questions and answers, is not intended to be used as a substitute for an in-person appearance by a witness at trial. It may be used in place of personal at-trial testimony by the witness only in case the witness becomes unavailable, or in very limited instances if the witness does testify at the trial; for example, it may be used to attack a witness' credibility if the witness says one thing at trial and said something else at the deposition.

If an oral deposition is not practical, then the Rules of Civil Procedure allow for deposing a witness using written questions. This is usually less satisfactory than an oral deposition in several respects. First, the questions are determined in advance so that there is little chance for follow-up should any one question reveal information that should be pursued at once. In an oral deposition, an attorney can pursue any lines of questioning that are suggested by answers to previous questions. Second, any element of spontaneity and surprise is lost. If the written questions are directed at a party to the suit, the answers will almost certainly be checked and perhaps even written by his or her attorney. This may be true as well for witnesses who are not parties. Answers that are thoughtfully prepared are likely to be more bland and contain less startling information than answers that must be provided on the spur of the moment. In both oral and written depositions, there are opportunities for attorneys to object to questions proposed by the other side, and, if necessary, to seek the guidance of the court as to whether a given question should be answered.

Written depositions

One of the most important of all discovery devices are written interrogatories. Only parties can serve interrogatories upon one another. A set of interrogatories cannot be served upon a witness who is not a party to the suit. Interrogatories are simply sets of questions that one party wants the other to answer. Drafting interrogatories can be an art form in itself, and lengthy sets of interrogatories can be time-consuming and expensive to answer. Generally, of course, the attorney for a party helps prepare the answers. Because interrogatories can be used effectively to harrass another party and to go on fishing expeditions, many courts have rules which limit the use of interrogatories, for example, by specifying that no more than thirty questions, including subparts, may be submitted by any party. A party who feels that interrogatories are being used to harrass, or that any question is improper, may seek the protection of the court.

Interrogatories

Recovery of expenses

A party is obligated to answer interrogatories that may lead to admissible evidence, and may not simply declare that the answer is too difficult or expensive to obtain. Nevertheless, it is not the purpose of discovery to place the burden of preparing the opponent's case on the other party. In certain instances, the court may make the party seeking discovery bear the inconvenience and cost of gleaning the information it seeks. For example, the federal rules provide:

> Where the answer to an interrogatory may be derived or ascertained from the business records of the party upon whom the interrogatory has been served or from an examination, audit or inspection of such business records, or from a compilation abstract or summary based thereon, and the burden of deriving or ascertaining the answer is substantially the same for the party serving the interrogatory as for the party served, it is a sufficient answer to such interrogatory to specify the records from which the answer may be derived or ascertained and to afford to the party serving the interrogatory reasonable opportunity to examine, audit or inspect such records and to make copies, compilations, abstracts or summaries.

A party served with a particularly burdensome interrogatory may, therefore, in certain circumstances, be justified in simply carting a moving van full of computer print-outs over to the other party, unloading them, and stating, "Here, the answer to your question is contained somewhere in all this material. It is as easy for you to find as for us. Good luck!" It must also be noted that the Fifth Amendment protections do not apply to civil suits. A party cannot refuse to provide information or answer questions merely because it may subject him or her to civil liability. If there is the possibility of criminal prosecution based on the answers that may be given, the guidance of and some suitable protection from the court may be sought.

Requests for documents

One party may seek from another party permission to

> inspect and copy, any designated documents (including writings, drawings, graphs, . . . and other data compilations from which information can be obtained, translated, if necessary, by the respondent through detection devices into reasonably usable form), or to inspect and copy, test, or sample any tangible things

that are discoverable and in the possession of the other party. It is evident that this may be a powerful means of discovery in computer-related suits since the respondent (party to whom the request is directed) may be required not merely to provide material in the form in which he or she has it (which may be encoded or in some format comprehensible only to him- or herself), but must provide the material in "reasonably usable" form; thus, a party could require that encoded material be decoded, or that a key to understanding a nonstandard format be provided along with the print-outs. A party would not be able to avoid discovery by providing a machine language dump of a complex data file in response to a request for meaningful documents.

One means of discovery intended to cut down on costs and inconvenience in gathering evidence is request for admissions. One party may ask the other party to admit a particular fact so that it will not have to be proved. Not every fact important to a case is a matter of dispute between the parties, and the admission of certain specific facts will often accelerate both the trial and the entire discovery procedure. Both parties, for example, may agree that an accident occurred at Fifth and Main at approximately 4 P.M. on September 24. Admissions to this effect will obviate having to establish these facts at trial. Admissions that pertain to a specific suit are valid only to that specific suit and may not be used as evidence in other law suits. This is to encourage the parties to agree on as much as possible so that the matters of real dispute and critical importance can be reached expeditiously at trial. One party may not really believe a certain fact is as the opposition presents it, but will admit to it anyway to save time if he or she does not believe it is important to his or her case. If a party is unreasonable about admitting something that ought to be admitted, something that is clear and obvious, then that party may be assessed the cost of proving that fact later at trial.

<small>Request for admission</small>

Some courts require a pretrial conference between the opposing attorneys with the judge to help sharpen the issues for trial, agree on admissibility or inadmissibility of certain evidence, and prepare any orders concerning how the trial is to be conducted. By the time of trial, a good attorney should be well aware of what the opposing counsel intends to present and the strengths of weaknesses of his or her own, as well as the opposing party's, case. At the pretrial conference, the judge may encourage the attorneys to settle the case before trial. Trials are expensive for both the parties and the government. But if the matter goes to trial, each party will have evidence to present gathered during the discovery process. We next look at evidence at trial, particularly as it relates to computer-related matters.

<small>Pretrial conference</small>

EVIDENCE AT TRIAL

It is basic common sense, as well as sound law, that an attorney cannot ask a witness any question whatsoever, or introduce into evidence anything that strikes the attorney's fancy. Evidence that may be introduced at trial is said to be admissible; evidence that must be excluded is said to be inadmissible. In order to be admissible, evidence must first and foremost be relevant. It must relate to one or more of

<small>Admissibility</small>

the issues in dispute and tend to lend credibility to one side or the other. Even relevant evidence can be excluded on various grounds. For example, it may be redundant; the fact that it is intended to prove may be important, but it may have already been admitted, or established by better evidence. Or the evidence may be relevant but much too prejudicial to one side for reasons having nothing to do with the dispute at hand. For example, a criminal defendant may have a record a mile long of bank robbery convictions, and this may have some bearing on whether that defendant is a solid citizen worthy of trust and confidence, but it cannot be introduced by the prosecution as part of its case against the defendant unless the defense first provides some opportunity for its admissibility, for example, by introducing evidence of its own about what an honest person the defendant is. The reason for exclusion of the previous convictions is that a jury may assume that if a defendant had committed previous crimes for which he or she was convicted, that defendant surely must be guilty of the one with which he or she is charged now, and they will prejudge the matter without listening to the rest of the evidence, which may show that this time the defendant was really a hundred miles from the bank when it was robbed.

Reliability

Furthermore, if evidence is to be introduced, there must be some basis for believing that the evidence may be reliable. A more technical way of saying this is that a foundation must be layed for evidence if a court is to find it admissible. At this time, however, it must be noted that a great deal of technically inadmissible evidence is presented at trials. The mere fact that evidence *can* be excluded does not automatically mean that it *will* be excluded. If one party attempts to introduce inadmissible evidence, the other party must object and must state the specific grounds why it believes that evidence should not be admitted. If the party fails to object, it is deemed to have waived its right to exclude that evidence, and the possibly inadmissible evidence then becomes admissible. If the judge mistakenly admits inadmissible evidence, but the grounds stated in the objection for excluding the evidence are inadequate—that is, there are grounds for excluding the evidence, but they are not those stated in the objection—then the evidence will stand. There is also the situation where inadmissible evidence is introduced before the opposing party has a chance to object, for example, when a witness blurts out some inadmissible fact or opinion. If that evidence is objected to as soon as possible and the judge sustains the objection, he or she will also ask the jury, if there is one, to disregard that information. Unfortunately, of course, it is all but impossible for the jury to disregard what they have heard, particularly if it is especially shocking, despite what the judge tells them.

Objection necessary

In any event, laying the foundation for evidence is critically important. In order to introduce eyewitness testimony about an accident, the party seeking to have that testimony admitted will generally first have to establish, at least by suitable questions to the witness, that the witness did, in fact, personally see the accident in question. In order to introduce a photo of a wrecked automobile, it will have to be established, among other things, that the automobile pictured is actually that involved in the accident being litigated. A proper foundation is essential for computer-generated evidence. The means of laying that foundation will differ with the nature of the case and of the evidence, but certain general principles can be established. Before considering these principles and in order to understand them better, we first consider some important rules of evidence.

Laying a foundation

The Hearsay Rule is the bane of judges, attorneys, and law students, and is considered by many legal scholars to have outlived whatever usefulness it may have originally had. It is a rule, moreover, now so riddled with exceptions that its applicability has been sharply limited. The statement and application of the Hearsay Rule varies from state to state, but, in a general way, it may be stated as follows:

Hearsay rule

> Hearsay, which is defined as a statement made out of court offered to prove the truth of what the statement asserts, is not admissible.

Suppose Sam hears Shirley say, "Carl robbed the First National Bank." Sam is then called as a witness in Carl's trial for the robbery of the First National Bank. Can Sam testify to what he heard Shirley say? The answer is no. The reason is that the statement, "Carl robbed the First National Bank," was made out of court and could not be offered to prove the truth of what it asserts, namely, that Carl robbed the bank. It is hearsay and inadmissible. Suppose now that Shirley is on trial for defaming Carl by calling him a bank robber. Can Sam now testify at the trial that he heard Shirley make the statement? Yes, because now the testimony would not be offered to prove that Carl is a bank robber, but rather to show that Shirley published (spoke) the slanderous statement. The statement then is not introduced to prove what it asserts, but is offered to prove that a slander actually took place.

What has the Hearsay Rule to do with computers? What happens when computer print-outs are introduced as possible evidence at a trial? The print-outs represent out-of-court statements. The computer itself cannot testify as a witness at trial, and the "statements" are not those of a machine because they ultimately depend on statements made by human beings who programmed the computer and supplied the data from which the statements were produced. If the statements, the print-outs, are offered to prove the truth of the information they contain, then they are hearsay, and will be inadmissible unless they fit under some one of the many exceptions to the Hearsay Rule.

Such print-outs almost invariably do fall under one or more exceptions to the Hearsay Rule, however, and may, therefore, be admitted into evidence. If the print-outs were prepared by a party opponent, then they are admissible under the federal Rules of Evidence and in most states. An admission of a party opponent, such as documents supplied by that party, are not hearsay at all under the federal rules. They would fit under exceptions to the Hearsay Rule in most states that would consider them hearsay. Note that in order to fall outside the Hearsay Rule, or to fit under an exception to it, such documents must be prepared by the opposing party. You, as one party to a suit, cannot simply prepare such documents, declare them to be admissions, and introduce them into evidence. If such were the case, any party could prepare self-serving evidence and use it at will. But if the opposing party has generated the print-outs, you are free to use them against that party, if you wish. One moral here is beware of creating print-outs that might come back to haunt you.

Perhaps the most important exception to the Hearsay Rule as far as the admissibility of computer-generated evidence is concerned is the so-called Business Records Exception. Exceptions to the Hearsay Rule have come about when there is reason to believe that the evidence, although hearsay, is still reliable. Businesses normally keep reliable records if such records are made in the regular course of doing business. Federal Rule of Evidence 803(6) describes the types of records which fall under this exception:

> A memorandum, report, record, or data compilation, in any form, of acts, events, conditions, opinions, or diagnoses, made at or near the time by, or from information transmitted by, a person with knowledge, if kept in the course of a regularly conducted business activity, and if it was the regular practice of that business activity to make the memorandum, report, record, or data compilation, all as shown by the testimony of the custodian or other qualified witness, unless the course of information or the method or circumstances of preparation indicate lack of trustworthiness. The term "business" as used in this paragraph includes business, institution, association, profession, occupation, and calling of every kind, whether or not conducted for profit.

The Business Record Exception is phrased and treated somewhat differently in different jurisdictions, but the federal rule gives the flavor. Essentially, what this exception demands is that someone who has actual knowledge of the information in question has entered it into the regularly kept records of the business close to the time at which the information was obtained, and that someone, not necessarily the person who entered the data in the records in the first place, testify to the method and reliability of such record-keeping, or that there be other evidence attesting to this reliability. One important fact should be particularly noted: Data generated specifically in preparation for litigation is not produced in the ordinary course of business, and is, in any case, sufficiently self-serving that it is highly unlikely that any court would permit it to be introduced by the party that prepared it, at least under the Business Records Exception to the Hearsay Rule. Another important note: The print-out itself, which sets forth the business records, does not need to be prepared close to the time that the data is entered. It is understood by courts that data may be stored for a long time before use. What is important is that the data be fresh when it is entered in the official records so that its reliability upon entry is less subject to question.

Another rule of evidence not related to hearsay as such, but of importance to computer-generated evidence is the Best Evidence Rule. One way of stating this rule is:

Best Evidence Rule

> If the content of some writing is to be proved, then evidence to this end other than the original writing itself can be introduced if and only if the original writing itself is shown to be unavailable.

A key question involved with the Best Evidence Rule is "What is an original writing?" "Writing" is to be taken very broadly; the term includes writings in the ordinary sense as well as photographs, tape recordings, phonograph records, and almost certainly such items as computer tapes, discs, and card decks. An "original" is the writing itself, or any counterpart executed at the same time and intended to have the same effect as the original. If two parties to a contract exchange two copies of the contract at the time it is executed, each to have the same legal effect, each contract will be considered an original, even if one happens to be a photocopy of the other. Two prints from the same photographic negative are each originals. The federal Rules of Evidence (Rule 1001(3)) explicitly state that, "If data are stored in a computer or similar device, any print-out or other output readable by sight, shown to reflect the data accurately, is an 'original.'"

Consider the following example in which both the Hearsay and Best Evidence Rules come into play. ABC Company sues XYZ Corporation claiming that XYZ failed to pay $15,000 due ABC on March 11. ABC offers into evidence the fact that it keeps regular records of payments received from all sources. As each payment is received in the Treasurer's Office, the Treasurer forwards a slip giving relevant details of the payment to data processing, which enters the information in the "payments received" file of the ABC computer. ABC produces a print-out showing that in the month of March no payment was received from XYZ. XYZ produces its computerized "accounts paid" file print-out as well as a photocopy of its cancelled check for $15,000 made out to ABC and dated March 11. The photocopy was obtained from XYZ's bank, because XYZ claims that the check itself was destroyed in an office fire. What, if any, of this evidence is admissible?

The absence of an entry in the regular business records of ABC does not fit under the Business Records Exception to the Hearsay Rule because that exception refers to actual entries. However, there is another exception to the Hearsay Rule which allows such absences into evidence to show that something did not happen (under the theory that if it did happen, it would surely have been recorded). XYZ's print-out with the payment shown can be admitted under the Business Records Exception. The bank's photocopy of the cancelled check can be admitted for several reasons. First, it is part of the regular business records of the bank. Second, the original writing is not available, so that, in this case, the "best evidence" of the content of the check (the payee and the amount) is the photocopy. Also, the photocopy of the check itself can be offered as evidence that payment was made by XYZ to ABC in March, and, therefore, ABC's records are in error. This use of the photocopy would not involve using the photocopy to prove the contents of the check, but to reduce the credibility of ABC's evidence.

Foundation for computer-generated evidence

We return now to the problem of laying the foundation for the admission of computer-generated evidence. Inasmuch as such evidence will be hearsay, the foundation must be directed not only at showing that the evidence is reliable, but that it fits under an exception to the Hearsay Rule as well. To show reliability, it must be shown that from entry to retrieval, there was sufficiently little chance of error or tampering that the evidence should at least be presented to the trier of fact, be it judge or jury, who can then give it what weight and credibility they deem fitting.

Areas of foundation testimony

William Fenwick and Gordon Davidson, in an excellent analysis of the use of computerized business records as evidence, list nine areas in which foundation testimony will have to be given. This testimony will have to come from someone who is familiar with the way the records were originally made, how they were stored, and how they were retrieved for use in hard copy form. The nine areas include:

1. reliability of the computing equipment itself;
2. the manner in which the data in question was entered into the computer system;
3. that the data in question was entered in this manner in the regular course of business;

4. and that the entry occurred "within a reasonable time after the events recorded by persons having a personal knowledge of the events";
5. methods by which the business checks its data for accuracy upon entry into the system;
6. the method of storing the data within the system and any precations taken to insure that the data is not lost or its accuracy compromised while it is in storage;
7. the reliability of the programs or other methods used to process the data;
8. the measures taken to verify that the programs or other methods are correct and are operating properly when in use;
9. the time and method of preparing the print-outs.

Similar lists of foundational evidence are given in various court opinions. If the evidence generated by computer is admitted, but a court of appeals rules that a proper foundation was not laid, then the case may be sent back to the trial court for a new trial. In one New Jersey case, the trial was reopened for presentation of additional evidence because the plaintiff's witness concerning the computer-generated evidence

> did not provide information on the type of computer used and its acceptance in the field as standard, efficient and accurate equipment. This witness did not testify as to the competency of those who program the computer and process the daily output, nor did he fully explain the input controls or the mechanics of the machines.

In addition, the witness was not familiar with the procedure for handling the entry of the data that was part of the matter in dispute.

A central theme of this section is that computer print-outs, however impressive they may appear to the nonprofessional, will not even get into court unless someone can convince the court they are reliable, and that they fit under some exception to the Hearsay Rule. As can be seen from the number and complexity of the areas that must be touched upon to lay the foundation for the introduction of such evidence, convincing the court of the reliability is not a trivial task. It is, therefore, very important that a business that keeps records by means of a computer thoroughly document and test its procedures so that if these records ever do need to be entered into evidence at a trial, the court can be given enough information to be satisfied that they are admissible. It may even be beneficial to have an attorney assist in setting up the computerized record keeping system so that any weak spots in the admissibility of records produced by the system can be identified and corrected before the business finds that a court will not accept its records as reliable. As a further precaution, a fall-back system might be available, using original documents, in the event the computerized system does not pass evidentiary muster.

TRIAL AND AFTER

Because the reader may someday be involved in a trial either as a party or as a witness, or perhaps as a juror, it seems reasonable to include a few words about the basic structure of a trial, a few thoughts about the examination of witnesses, and what can happen after a trial is over when one of the parties is not satisfied with the outcome.

The structure of a trial

We have already considered a pretrial process. If the parties cannot settle their dispute during that time, the matter comes to trial. We will assume it is a trial before a jury. In basic outline, here is what will take place.

Jury selection

1. Citizens who are to form the "panel" from which the jury will be selected are given notice by the clerk of the court to appear at a specified date and time. The lawyers for both sides examine prospective jurors in a process called "voir dire." In some courts, particularly the federal courts, the judge may do most of the examination. Each party may request some prospective juror be struck "for cause," that is, because the prospective juror has some real or potential bias that makes him or her unlikely to be impartial; for example, he is the brother of the defendant. The judge rules whether the cause given is sufficient to excuse the juror. Each side has a certain number of jurors it can excuse for no reason whatsoever; these are called peremptory challenges.

Preliminary instructions, opening statements

2. Once the jury is chosen and sworn in, the judge may give the jurors preliminary instructions to give them some idea of the law of the case and how to behave as jurors. Each party may also make an opening statement, usually for the purpose of acquainting the jury with its theory of the case and outlining how it will proceed to substantiate that theory.

Cases-in-chief

3. The plaintiff (or the prosecution, in a criminal trial) then presents its case-in-chief. This involves calling its witnesses and setting forth any exhibits it wishes the jury to consider. At the close of

the plaintiff's (state's) case-in-chief, the defendant may ask the court to grant a directed verdict (acquittal), on the grounds that the plaintiff has failed, as a matter of law, to establish a sufficient case. If the motion is denied, the defendant then presents his or her case-in-chief. At the end of the defendant's case-in-chief in a civil case, both sides may ask the court for a directed verdict in their favor. In a criminal trial, the defendant may ask for a directed verdict of acquittal, but the state may not ask for a directed conviction. Only the jury can find a criminal defendant guilty.

4. If no motion for a directed verdict is granted, each side may have a limited opportunity to present rebuttal evidence. The parties then make closing statements to the jury intended to sum up their respective theories of the case and remind the jury of what they have shown at trial as well as the weakness of the opponent's evidence. Rebuttal

5. Before or after the closing arguments, the judge instructs the jury concerning the law of the case. In some instances, a judge is permitted to make comments concerning the evidence. Instructions are, in some sense, one of the weakest links in the jury system since they are often so complex and so legalistic in their wording that virtually no jurors can really understand them. The judge may spend an hour or more delivering a mini-course in law to jurors who barely understand a word said. Final instructions

6. The jury then retires to deliberate and, hopefully, to render a fair and just verdict. Verdict

There is no question in this writer's mind that virtually all jurors are exceptionally conscientious about their task and are as anxious to see justice done as any attorney or judge could wish. The strength of the jury system and its greatest fault as well is that the jurors are laypeople without any expertise in the complexities of the case being tried, from either a technical or legal point of view. If judges and attorneys have trouble coping with computer-related issues and evidence, one can only surmise what the jurors do with it. Yet jury trials are guaranteed as a matter of right in certain kinds of cases, and there is little likelihood that this will change in the foreseeable future. Attorneys must gear their presentations to this well-intentioned, but untrained, group of people to whom the law has given the power to decide facts that trouble even the greatest experts in the field. The problem of highly technical cases being tried by inexpert judges and juries has led to proposals for a special "science court" for such cases, but attempting to abolish the right to a jury may well lead to constitutional difficulties.

Direct and cross-examination of witnesses

Direct examination

The party who calls a witness has the right to examine that witness first. This is the direct examination of the witness. Generally, such an examination begins by asking the witness several easy questions, such as his or her name, occupation, and address, to try to put the witness at ease. Most witnesses are at least nervous on the stand, and some are just plain terrified. The party calling the witness tries to elicit from its witness the information the witness has that is important to its case. Generally, a foundation must be laid that establishes the witness as a reliable source of that information. If the witness is a so-called "expert witness," an authority, say, in computing, and the parties have not yet stipulated that the witness is indeed an expert in the area in which he or she is to testify, then the examination will have to begin by laying the foundation for asking the judge to recognize the witness as an expert. Usually this is done by questioning the witness about his or her academic background, experience, publications, and recognition by professional organizations. Even if the witness is not an expert witness, but merely someone who is alleged to have special information that is relevant to the case, it must be established on direct examination that the witness does have first-hand knowledge of the information about which he or she is to testify.

Expert witness

Cross-examination

Once the direct examination is finished, the opposing party is entitled to cross-examine. Cross-examination cannot range over any material whatsoever relevant to the case, but rather its scope is usually determined by what was covered on direct examination. Cross-examination is an art in itself. The cross-examiner does not wish to have the witness repeat the evidence favorable to the other party because the more times they jury hears it, the more likely they are to believe it. So the cross-examiner's primary goal is to discredit the witness, if possible, or bring out other information that is damaging to the other side. If he or she feels that no damaging information can be brought out, particularly if the witness has done little to further the opponent's case, the attorney may simply choose not to cross-examine at all.

Because of the extensive discovery procedures available to both sides, an attorney should know the answer to virtually every question he or she asks any witness, either on direct or cross-examination. There may be some surprises, but if there are too many, it is probably because the attorney did not prepare properly for the trial. An attorney who does not know what a witness for his or her side is going to say may well be guilty of malpractice if he or she calls that witness. Nor is it unethical for an attorney to review with the witnesses what their testimony will be on the stand, so long as he or she does not attempt to get them to lie or present testimony the attorney and the witnesses know to be false.

Following cross-examination, there may be redirect examination on matters raised on cross-examination, followed by re-cross-examination, and so on.

Some general rules for witnesses:

Rules for witnesses

1. Be honest.
2. Do not volunteer information. Answer the questions which are asked of you and no more.
3. Be natural, but recognize too that if you are talking to a jury, they need to understand what you are saying if it is to have effect. Try to phrase things so that the jury will understand you.
4. Remember that if inadmissible evidence is to be excluded, it must be objected to. If the opposing counsel is examining you, it might be well to wait a second or two before responding to a question to permit the counsel for your side to object if he or she thinks the question is improper. An answer once given is hard to withdraw from the minds of the jury, even if the judge instructs them to disregard it.

Appeals

If a party is dissatisfied with the outcome of a trial, then it may try to appeal the decision. Appellate courts do not sit as triers of fact, but, instead, decide matters of law. In some sense, appellate courts make law by interpreting what the law really is.

In order to carry on an appeal, the appellant (party seeking the appeal) must formulate the grounds for the appeal. These must be in terms of some mistake or error of law that the trial court made during the time it had control of the case. The alleged errors that the appellant wants considered must be specifically set forth, because a court of appeals will only very rarely consider any error other than one raised by the appellant.

Grounds for appeal

The appellant must support allegations of error with relevant portions of the trial transcript and a legal brief that contains the arguments which favor his or her position together with citations to appropriate authorities such as other opinions of the appellate court. The appellee (party against whom the appeal is directed) will usually also write a brief in defense of his or her contention that the appellant's allegations of error are wrong.

Prior objection needed

An appellant is almost always precluded from raising any error to which he or she did not object earlier as well as from introducing new evidence that the trial court did not have an opportunity to consider. If new evidence is found after trial that might have substantially affected the outcome of the trial, the trial court must be given an opportunity to consider it through a motion for a new trial. The denial of the motion for a new trial can then be appealed. The appeals court does not conduct a trial; it hears argument concerning questions of law. Was evidence which the judge admitted really inadmissible? Was the party unfairly prevented from introducing evidence critical to its case? Did the judge make improperly prejudicial remarks in front of the jury? How is a particular statute to be interpreted in the light of the facts established at trial, that is, did the trial judge properly instruct the jury as to the law?

An appeals court then decides the appeal and usually supports its decision with a written opinion that sets forth the reasons why it ruled as it did. Such opinions can then be used as the basis for study by lawyers and law students who wish to learn the thinking of the appeals court on the issued raised.

Further appeal

If the appeals court rules against the appellant and there is a higher appeals court yet, the disappointed appellant can seek review by that court. Usually, however, such review is discretionary and the higher appeals court can choose to refuse review, if it wishes.

If a court of appeals finds error, it may hold that the error was "harmless," that is, it did not substantially affect the outcome of the trial. Or it may hold that the error was "reversible error," that is, it is so serious that corrective action of some sort must be taken, which, very often, turns out to be the granting of a new trial. If a new trial is granted, it is just as if the old trial did not take place. The judge in the new trial will, presumably, have the guidance of the appellate court's opinion so as not to make the same mistake that led to the granting of the new trial. The judge may still make other mistakes, however, and the case may be appealed yet again with perhaps yet another trial granted.

Appellants usually lose

In actual practice, the majority of appellants lose their appeals. An appeals court will give the trial court the benefit of the doubt. If there is a correct reason for a trial judge to act as he or she did, even though the reason the judge gave for his or her action was incorrect, that judge will not be reversed. For example, if a judge admits certain evidence under one exception to the Hearsay Rule that is not really applicable, but the evidence could have been legitimately admitted under another exception, the evidence will be held admissible even though the trial judge was technically wrong. Furthermore, unless a finding of fact could not possibly have been made from the evidence presented, a court of appeals will accept as given all findings of fact made at the trial.

Obviously, trials and appeals are terribly expensive and time-consuming processes. It is much better to avoid litigation, if at all possible. By knowing something of the law, and having a good attorney to assist you, litigation can often be avoided. That is a point that began this book, and that is the note on which we end.

SUGGESTED ADDITIONAL READINGS ON EVIDENCE

A sample examination of an expert witness at trial is presented by R. Freed, in *Computers and Law* (privately published; see recommended readings for Chapter II), pp. 61–82.

Volume 52, Number 3, of the *Chicago-Kent Law Review* (1976) contains several papers under the heading "Law and Technology Symposium: Coping with Computer Generated Evidence in Litigation." Paper titles are "Evaluating the Credibility of Computer-Generated Evidence," "Data Processing Evidence: Is It Different?" "Computer Generated Evidence Specially Prepared for Use at Trial," and "The Use of Models in Litigation: Concise or Contrived?"

For other valuable discussions of computer-related evidentiary law, see W. Fenwick and G. Davidson, "Use of Computerized Business Records as Evidence," *Jurimetrics Journal*, Vol. 19, No. 1(Fall 1978), pp. 9–27, adapted from an article published in Volume 14 of *American Jurisprudence Proof of Facts* 2d.; and P. Abelle, "Evidentiary Problems Relevant to Checks and Computers," *Rutgers Journal of Computers and the Law*, Vol. 5(1976), pp. 323–87.

Two opinions containing discussions of the foundation required for computer-generated evidence at trial are found in the appendices. Two additional such cases are *Transport Indemnity Co. v. Seib*, 132 N.W.2d 871 (Neb. 1965)(one of the very first cases addressing this issue); and *King ex rel. Murdock Acceptance Corp.*, 222 So.2d 393 (Miss. 1969).

APPENDIX 1

A BRIEF GUIDE TO LEGAL REFERENCES AND CITATIONS

One of the most important tools of the attorney's trade is a law library. Three years of law school is barely enough to teach a lawyer-in-training some basic principles of law, how to analyze a fact situation to pinpoint the central legal issues and questions it raises, and where to look to find the answers. This appendix is intended to help you understand the peculiar means of citing sources you will encounter in legal works, give a quick introduction to a few of the more important sources, and provide some clues where you yourself might start to look if you want to research a problem in a law library.

Court cases

When a judge or group of judges reaches a decision about a case before them, they will often write an "opinion." The opinion contains the facts of the case, the issues in dispute, how the court decides on each of these issues and the reasons for the court deciding as it does. The most important opinions are usually those which are written by the appellate courts since these are the courts that guide the lower (trial) courts in their interpretations of the law. If an appellate court is the highest court in its jurisdiction, as the Supreme Court of the United States is the highest court of appeals in the federal judicial system, then its interpretation of the law is definitive, at least in its own jurisdiction, until it should change its mind, or the legislative body that writes the statutory law changes the law.

Because court opinions are so important as a source of the law, the opinions of most appellate courts and even of some trial courts are published in court "reporters."

The principal reporter series for the federal system today is the *United States Reports*, which is the official reporter for opinions of the Supreme Court of the United States; the *Federal Reporter*, now in its "second series," which publishes opinions of the various United States Courts of Appeals and of several other federal courts, including the Court of Customs and Patent Appeals; and the *Federal Supplement*, which publishes selected opinions of the federal district courts. Supreme Court opinions are available in other sources as well, including the Supreme Court Reporter and the United States Supreme Court Reports (Lawyer's Edition), now in its second series, which are put out by competing publishers, and which often are available more quickly than the official reporter series. *U.S. Law Week*, a weekly summary of new law and opinions, supplies the text of more important Supreme Court opinions very shortly after they are released.

As regards opinions of state appellate courts, there is a "National Reporter System," established by the West Publishing Company, which divides the nation up into seven regions: Atlantic, Pacific, Northeastern, Southeastern, Northwestern, Southwestern and Southern. One should not take these geographic denominations too seriously since some states are found in surprising series. Some states use these reporters as their official reporters for appellate decisions; other states will publish only their more important appellate opinions. Many states have their own reporter series, sometimes one series for each appellate level. For example, Indiana has the *Indiana Appellate Court Reports* for the Indiana Court of Appeals as well as the *Indiana Reports* for the opinions of the Supreme Court of Indiana. The two most populous states have special West reporters, the *California Reporter* and the *New York Supplement.* California and New York each have a variety of state reporters.

In addition to the more general reporter series, there are specialized reporters as well such as the *Tax Court of the United States Reports,* but this brief overview cannot begin to list every conceivable source of court opinions.

Naturally, no lawyer wants to write *United States Supreme Court Reports* every time he or she wants to refer to an opinion contained therein. A special form of legal citations has been developed which, once understood, is not difficult to follow, and which also saves much time and space in referencing sources.

First of all, each reporter series has a specific abbreviation. A complete citation to an opinion in a court reporter has the following format:

Volume #   Reporter (abbreviated)   page
(Court, if not clear; year given)

Thus, 345 U.S. 65 (1965) would refer to whatever opinion begins on page 65 of Volume 345 of the *United States Reports,* that opinion being issued in 1965. The court rendering the opinion is clear in this instance. On the other hand, 68 N.E.2d 357 (Ind. App. 1935) would lead you to the *Northeast Reporter,* Second Series, Volume 68, page 357, and an opinion of the Indiana Court of Appeals issued in 1935. Generally too, the reference to the reporter citation is preceded by the name of the case with which the opinion was concerned, as in *Albertson v. Qumquat Piano Co.*

A second series for a reporter is started if the volume numbers in the first series have become so large that the publisher simply wants to start at Volume 1 all over again. Court opinions are being issued all the time, so eventually it will be necessary to have a third series, fourth series, and so on. Some reporters are already in their third series. You must be careful to distinguish which series you are looking for; for example, 3 N.E. 45 and 3 N.E.2d 45 look very similar, but they represent opinions years apart in time and shelves apart in the library.

The abbreviations for the national reporters are fairly straightforward; for instance, S.W. stands for Southwest. *Federal Supplement* is abbreviated by F.Supp, and the *Federal Reporter* by "F.," or "F.2d" for the second series. If you cannot figure out what a particular abbreviation stands for, just ask the librarian.

Statutes

There are several sources of federal statutory law, that is, laws passed by Congress. A statute when first passed is available in "slip law" form, that is, as a separate "handout." At the end of each Congressional session, the various slip laws are bound chronologically in the *Statutes at Large*. Most statutes also find a place in the *United States Code*, a compilation of federal statutes divided into various "Titles." Each Title deals with some general area of the law; for example, Title 18 is the federal Criminal Code.

The official version of the *U.S. Code* just sets forth the text of the statutes without comment. There are versions of the *Code* marketed by private publishers, namely, the *United States Code Annotated* and the *United States Code Service*, which give not only the text of the statutes, but references to various court opinions that have settled various questions on each section. Because the courts keep rendering opinions and Congress keeps passing new legislation, these Code services update their texts on a regular basis by issuing "pocket parts," supplements that fit into the back of the hard-bound volumes, or even independently bound supplementary volumes. Every so often, a completely new set of materials is issued.

State statutes may be found in various forms. Most, if not all, states have "session laws," which are the state versions of the *Statutes at Large*. All states have an official version of their *Codes*, and most have an annotated version as well, which may or may not be the official version. As is the case with the federal annotated code versions, state annotated sets give references to court opinions for that state that help explain and clarify the meaning of each section of the Code as the courts have read it. Both official and annotated versions have indices that help direct the reader to those statutes that deal with any subject in which he or she might be interested. Once again, there are supplements. Someone using any version of the Codes, federal or state, must be certain to check the supplement as well as the main text in order to make certain that the information is as current as possible.

The format for citing federal statutes is

                  Title #   Source abbreviation   Section

For example, 18 U.S.C.A. § 2345 refers to Section 2345 of Title 18 found in the *United States Code Annotated*. It should also be noted that the *Internal Revenue Code* (I.R.C.) is Title 26 of the *U.S. Code* but is almost always referred to as the I.R.C.; thus, I.R.C. § 1021 is Section 1021 of the *Internal Revenue Code*. Each state has its particular format for citing references to its particular statutes, but it should not be too hard to pick up the reference system that your state uses.

Administrative regulations

Rules and regulations issued by administrative agencies often have the force of law and are of great importance, in any event, because they indicate how the governmental agency that issued them feels on a particular matter under its jurisdiction. The legislation passed by Congress granting some agency authority over some area and outlining the policies that should guide it may be a matter of paragraphs. The regulations issued by that agency may run into volumes. The Internal Revenue Act takes up one fairly thick volume, but the regulations run on three times as long.

While they are under consideration for adoption, and right after they are, in fact, adopted, proposed and new regulations will be published in the *Federal Register* (Fed. Reg.), an almost daily publication available from the Government Printing Office (but not for free). Regulations in force are published in the *Code of Federal Regulations* (C.F.R.), also published by the Government. The C.F.R. is published annually and is arranged by "Titles" similar to those used in the *U.S. Code*. As an example of a citation to the C.F.R., 42 C.F.R. § 2401.5 (1978) refers to Section 2401.5 of Title 42 of the 1978 edition of the *Code of Federal Regulations*.

Law reviews

Most law schools, and some other institutions or associations, publish journals containing articles and other pieces of a scholarly nature pertaining to various areas of the law. Two such reviews of special potential interest to computer users are the *Rutgers Journal of Computers, Technology & The Law* and *Jurimetrics*, the journal of the Section of Science and Technology of the American Bar Association. Citations to law review articles are given in the following format:

> Volume #   Name of review(abbrev.)   Page   (Year)

Preceding the above, the last name of the author is given, followed by the name of the article being cited. For example, Sprowl, *Evaluating the Credibility of Computer-Generated Evidence*, 52 CHI.-KENT L. REV. 547 (1976) refers to an article by Sprowl with the title given, which appeared in 1976 in Volume 52 of the *Chicago-Kent Law Review* beginning on page 547. There are a number of variations on this theme, but you should have no trouble deciphering citations with a little practice. For example, Note, *Computers and New Legislation*, 1976 HAMBONE L. REV. 1, a mythical publication, refers to a "Note," a work by a law student (students rarely get their names attached to what they publish in law reviews) in the 1976 issue of *Hambone Law Review*. When no volume number is available, the year of the issue is used as a substitute.

This peculiar form of citing works from periodicals is used for journals and magazines other than law reviews as well. It is not clear why those who dreamed up this format chose to leave off the first name of the author, or to include the month of publication. This is not a reasoned presentation, just a brief summary of how lawyers do these things.

Digests, encyclopedias, and dictionaries

The West Publishing Company markets "The American Digest System," as well as several special digests. The digests are meant to complement the reporter series that West also publishes. West has given a large number of legal topics "key numbers." The key numbers go with the "headnotes" to court opinions in the reporters to indicate what area of the law the headnote deals with. A headnote is a brief statement supplied by West, which is not part of the actual opinion, but which is intended to summarize some special point of law contained in the opinion. A complex opinion may have scores of headnotes with many different key numbers. The digests are arranged by topics and key numbers so that reporters and digests can be coordinated. A digest is essentially a compilation of headnotes by key number for a specific time period, or perhaps a specific court, or perhaps a specific geographic area. Of special interest are the "Words and Phrases" volumes of the digests, which help locate materials related to given terminology, and the volumes that list cases alphabetically by plaintiff and by defendant.

Law encyclopedias are what their name implies, encyclopedic works that cover various legal topics. They are essentially compilations of treatises and research papers. There are two major law encyclopedias, *American Jurisprudence* and *Corpus Juris Secundum*. Each of these encyclopedias have new volumes added periodically, and much of their older material becomes obsolete. There are, as one might suspect, tricks to getting the maximum benefit from these encyclopedias. Unless you know exactly where you should look, as when you have a specific article you want to look at, or you have a very patient librarian who is willing to help you, you may not find these compendia all that helpful. Even then, they are such general surveys and go out of date so quickly that they are not always a good source anyway. They are ordinarily used by attorneys who need a fast start on where to look elsewhere for opinions that deal with some questions they are researching. West has also published encyclopedias and digests for many states, as well as the *Federal Practice Digest*.

Legal dictionaries are, of course, dictionaries of legal terms. These often give a citation to a case which supports the definition given by the dictionary. The two best-known dictionaries are Black's and Ballentine's.

Looseleaf services

There are many special services available intended to update those subscribing to them in specialized areas of the law. Since most of these services supply their product in looseleaf form on a periodic basis, to be entered into a ring binder, they are known as "looseleaf services." One of these is the *Computer Law Service*, edited by Robert Bigelow. Bigelow also edits the *Computer Law Service Reporter*, which specializes in cases dealing with some aspect of computer law. There are three major publishers of looseleaf services: Prentice-Hall (P-H), Commerce Clearing House (CCH), and Bureau of National Affairs (BNA). There are so many looseleaf services that a listing would be impractical, and, in any event, most libraries will carry only a fraction of what is available. If you want to know what is carried by your local law library that might be of interest to you, a trip there should tell you. Each looseleaf service has its own method of indexing and of finding pertinent material. You should learn this for any service you expect to use on a regular basis.

Most looseleaf services have a special form of citation and of pagination; for example, paragraph or section numbers are often used instead of or in addition to page numbers. Again, my advice is to decide what looseleaf services, if any, you are really interested in and then learn the system for that service.

APPENDIX 2

IBM v. CATAMORE ENTERPRISES

The opinion presented in edited form here illustrates the harm that faulty computer services can bring upon a business as well as the pitfalls and problems in trying to establish liability for that harm. IBM relies upon the various protective devices it built into its contract, while Catamore tries to circumvent these devices through a variety of the means discussed in Chapter 2.

Note that this is an opinion of a Court of Appeals. Catamore had won a huge verdict (more than $11 million) at the trial of this case. The appellate court overturns that verdict and sends the case back for another trial. The opinion is an excellent review of many of the concepts introduced in Chapter 2.

IBM v. CATAMORE ENTERPRISES,
548 F.2d 1065 (1st Cir. 1976).

The events at issue here spanned the years between 1967 and 1971 and concern the efforts of Catamore to computerize, and thus expand, its operations with leased IBM equipment and the assistance of IBM services—the scope and quality of which are the heart of this suit.

Suit began in October, 1972, with the filing of a simple complaint by IBM in which it sought to collect $68,453.23 from Catamore for rental of equipment and payment for services. Catamore filed an answer containing a simple denial of the facts that would give rise to liability and a counterclaim asserting that IBM had breached numerous express and implied warranties of performance and claiming damages of $250,000. A year and a half later, Catamore filed eight additional counterclaims, principally identifying different elements of alleged damage but adding specific allegations of breach of contract and false representations and claiming damages of $15,554,210. Trial began on March 10, 1975. On or about May 16, 1975, Catamore again amended its counterclaims in various particulars, adding a ninth counterclaim charging IBM with wanton, reckless, and negligent conduct and claiming $18,887,800 in actual damages and $7,293,234 in punitive damages. After fifty-six days of trial and nine days of deliberation, the jury returned a verdict for IBM on its claim against Catamore in the amount of $68,453.23 and a verdict for Catamore on its counterclaims in the amount of $11,400,000. IBM now appeals from the $11,400,000 judgment entered against it.

IBM argues on appeal that, as a matter of law, there is no basis for liability for breach of contract or for negligence. In addition, it challenges the evidence and instructions as to damages and maintains that a number of rulings at trial and the allowance of excessive latitude to Catamore's counsel contributed to confusion and error.

[Despite the fact that all did their best to be fair at the trial, we must overturn the judgment and remand to the trial court for a new trial.] For reasons that are stated below, we deal only with questions of contract liability.

What we might term the contract history of this case is the following. In the mid-1960s Catamore was a thirty-year-old family company, which had specialized in selling religious jewelry to wholesalers and was in the process of expanding and diversifying its business. It was not only selling a general line of jewelry but, by 1965, was experimenting with a new sales method, "program selling," in which wholesalers were bypassed and, after market tests were run, prepackaged units of jewelry items were placed directly in retail stores of some of the large chains. Reordering would take place several times a year.

Catamore's tests led to increasing sales and expectations and the recognition that for it to develop capacity to process dramatically increased quantities of retail orders, and to coordinate production with demand, it would require a system of production control using electronic data processing equipment. Conversations between Catamore's President, Robert Catanzaro, and an IBM salesman, Davitt, led to a study of Catamore's needs by an IBM systems engineer. Thereafter, IBM's representative staged a presentation for Catamore, in which he explained—through the use of schematic charts—the different steps necessary to computerize Catamore's production control system. At this point, in September, 1968, Catamore decided to adopt such a system. It proceeded to sign a Machine Service Agreement, providing for the lease of a computer. Both parties understood that it was to be installed in December of 1969, after the necessary preparatory work had been done.

The core of this dispute is the opposite understandings of the parties as to who had the responsibility for doing this preparatory work, which consisted of general systems design (as to the overall flow of the system), a more refined detail systems design, and programming.

It is Catamore's contention that IBM orally agreed to furnish, along with the computer, a completely computerized production control system on a "turnkey" basis, so that Catamore personnel (who would have had training in operating the system) could take over all operations. Even the ordinarily time-consuming task of programming was allegedly assumed by IBM since it would use and merely modify preexisting programs already in its library of programs. Catamore had only the obligations of hiring a programmer/maintenance man to run and keep updated the system after installation and of converting basic data used in its manual system so that the data could be used by the computer.

It is IBM's view that, on ordering the computer equipment, Catamore would have available to it, at no extra cost, both the education of Catamore's employees in data processing and assistance in systems engineering design. The latter, according to one IBM witness, Davitt, meant that, to take one of the four operations of production control, the order entry system [the other three operations were invoicing (what had been shipped); inventory control (what was on hand); and a bill of materials system (what components are required to fill incoming orders)], IBM, working with Catamore, would develop a "systems design flow chart of entry order," i.e., more detailed design of this function, on the basis of which a programmer could begin to work. The programmer then would write even more explicit instructions and then translate those into a coding language understood by the computer. Catamore would be allowed to use IBM facilities for testing. But all programming would be Catamore's responsibility, IBM not at that time performing this service for customers. IBM did, however, offer Catamore any of the package programs in its library that might be useful.

These contrasting views as to who was to do what are the seeds of what followed. While a chart of the steps to be taken, and times within which they should be taken, to prepare for the December 1969 installation of the computer and start-up of the new system had been part of IBM's sales presentation, little seemed to be happening by way of joint consultation or implementation by either party during the next nine months. Some work on the systems design was done by IBM; in April of 1969 Catamore had hired a controller, Correra, to supervise its data processing project; a start had been made on converting the items of Catamore's inventory to computer-compatible numbers; and a larger computer had been placed on order. But no Catamore employee had obtained any data processing education. In the meantime, Catamore had pushed ahead with its new sales approach, bringing back a significantly increased number of orders as the result of testing its product lines and packages in many retail outlets. It also prepared for expansion by making arrangements for additional facilities, financing, and new products.

In June 1969 IBM announced a new policy to all its customers, stating that systems engineering services would be supplied on a charge basis, except that assistance which had earlier been mutually planned would be continued to be supplied without charge until January 1, 1970. In addition, rental charges would be reduced 3 percent. This came to be called "unbundling." Catanzaro testified that he was assured by IBM's Davitt that unbundling would not affect Catamore since IBM's commitments would be fulfilled before January 1, 1970. When a new IBM marketing representative, O'Reilly, took over the Catamore account in September, 1969, from Davitt, he saw that the time remaining until December was inadequate to perform all the tasks necessary to launch the new system, and recommended to Catamore that delivery of the equipment be deferred to March or April of 1970. This was agreeable to Catamore, which was seeking a new building and which would not face another business season until the fall of 1970. It set an outside installation date of September 1970.

In November of 1969 IBM wrote Catamore, referring to the provision in the unbundling announcement that services earlier "mutually planned" would be continued without charge until January 1, 1970. It listed the areas so agreed upon as: "Production Control, Inventory, Order Entry, Invoicing, Accounts Receivable, and Accounts Payable." It then noted that "the system design for production control has been 90 percent completed with the remaining accounting application systems [presumably Accounts Receivable and Accounts Payable] to be designed." It concluded by stating that after January 1, 1970, services in the noted areas would be on a charge basis "as stated in our Agreement for IBM Systems Engineering Services." The parties disagree as to the message conveyed by this letter, Catanzaro testifying that he had been told by IBM personnel that the 90 percent included programming, IBM witnesses insisting that this referred only to systems design.

Shortly thereafter, on December 9, 1969, Catamore signed IBM's form "Agreement for IBM Systems Engineering Services"(SES). This agreement stated that it was to govern all assistance in the installation and use of data processing products; that it was "the complete and exclusive statement of the agreement between the parties, which supersedes all proposals oral or written and all other communications between the parties"; that the customer's exclusive remedy should be limited in nature and amount to the amount paid for services under the applicable Service Estimate, that IBM would not be liable for lost profits or other claims, or for consequential damages; and that no action "arising out of the services under this Agreement may be brought by either party more than one year after the cause of action has accrued."

On the same date Catamore signed a Service Estimate, or authorization, in the amount of $4,884 for work to be done by October 31, 1970—in contrast to the September, 1970, date which was orally agreed upon—on the production control system and other items. The forms stated that authorization was given "under the terms of the captioned Agreement for IBM Systems Engineering Services." Catanzaro testified that in authorizing his subordinate to sign this agreement, he did so because "we had commited our company to a course of action that was irrevocable" and, having been told that the remaining 10 percent of work to be done would cost about $5,000, felt that all he would be giving up was the difference between this added obligation and the 3 percent reduction in rental Catamore would receive.

On January 29, 1970, Catamore executed a second authorization in the amount of $2,508 for work to be done by March 30, 1970, in performing "the detail design and definition of the order entry/Inventory Control System previously developed. . . . Included in this estimate are: 1. Program Descriptions. 2. Transaction Analysis. 3. Major Report Layouts. 4. Record and File Specifications[.] At the termination of this scope of effort, an estimate will be submitted covering programming implementation and documentation of the systems." This authorization contained the same explicit reference to the SES as did the previous authorization.

At this point the focus shifts. In early 1970 Catamore not only had seen its program selling continue to expand but seized an opportunity to enter the costume jewelry field. When one of its customers (a costume jewelry firm that had bought fine jewelry from Catamore to supplement its line) ceased to do business with it, Catamore hired the customer's experienced sales force and Catanzaro brought about the creation of two new corporations, M. V. Creations, Inc., which was to purchase costume jewelry, and Vicario, Inc., which was to be a selling company (hereinafter referred to as MV/Vicario). A new and urgent need for a data processing merchandise control system arose. According to Catamore an oral agreement was reached in mid-March 1970 for the creation of a merchandise control system to be completed in eight weeks. A larger computer was ordered and beginning on March 30, 1970, a series of SES Estimates was entered into by MV/Vicario. All of these contained the above mentioned reference that "authorization for the above work is given under the terms of the captioned Agreement for IBM Systems Engineering Services."

The subsequent unfolding of events may be even more telescoped, since they are not germane to the issues we deem presently controlling. The system supplied to MV/Vicario, according to Catamore witnesses, failed to reflect inventory accurately, with the result that it ended 1970 with a badly overinventoried position. When September 1970 arrived, Catamore was still without a production control system and, faced with a deluge of orders, resorted to extreme efforts to cope with a crisis but was unable to process many orders. "Locked" into IBM equipment and system, Catamore, according to Catanzaro, was forced to wait for a 1971 delivery. The MV/Vicario sales representatives, faced with reduced advance "draws" against commissions, left. Catamore again faced the busy fall season of 1971, unable to cope with orders and losing customers. An IBM study of Catamore's problem, presented in December 1971, revealed, according to Catanzaro, only the problems he knew existed three years earlier. Various threats, cancellations, restrictions, promises, demands, and negotiations occupied the latter part of 1971 and much of 1972.

While this narrative is extensive, we have omitted reference to voluminous testimony bearing on acts IBM may or may not have done which would be relevant to Catamore's allegations of fraud, misrepresentation, or negligence. In so compressing our presentation of the facts, we have not captured the full flavor of Catamore's case, in its assertions and evidence as to negligence,[1] fraud and misrepresentation,[2] or damages.

At this point we summarize in more detail both the theories of liability that were submitted to the jury and the parties' present positions with respect to them. Catamore's contract claims arise from its allegation that it and IBM entered into two separate oral contracts, each of which could be enforced consistent with the Statute of Frauds; the 1968 oral agreement for a production control system and the 1970 agreement for a data processing merchandise control system for MV/Vicario. A pivotal issue, of course, is the applicability of SES agreement's limitations of liability clauses to these causes of action. The district court refused to rule that these contract claims were subject to the limitation of liability clauses in the SES agreement as a matter of law. It thought there was sufficient evidence of misrepresentation for a jury to find that Catamore had been induced to enter the SES agreement by fraud, rendering the

---

1. Catamore relies on such items as the assignment by IBM of a mere trainee to design Catamore's system, the choice of a particular computer before the general design had been finished, the incompatibility of the computer with the type of disk storage drive chosen, . . . , IBM's advice that Catamore not have outside consultants, [failure to provide proper backups], a failure by IBM to warn adequately of the latent dangers of adopting a system based on electronic data processing.

2. Catamore's catalogue of alleged frauds includes a "bait and switch" allegation (in that IBM, without Catamore's knowledge, cancelled the original computer order and substituted an order for a larger machine); IBM advice to change the inventory numbering system to an 8-digit system and thereby lock Catamore into computerization; the alleged misrepresentation . . . that IBM's work . . . was 90 percent complete; IBM's representation that the remaining 10 percent of the system would be completed for no more than $5,000. . . .

agreement itself voidable, and that there were no other impediments to its rescission. Whether or not the SES agreement was valid, the district court also believed there were bases for regarding the two oral agreements as wholly independent of the SES agreement and not subject to its limitations. It therefore also permitted the jury to find both that the SES agreement was in effect and that both breaches of contract claims were meritorious. Catamore, in addition, now maintains that, whether or not the SES agreement is voidable, the limitations of liability clauses in it are themselves void and may not bar its contract claims.

IBM, not surprisingly, insists that the jury should not have been permitted to consider the contract theories of recovery. In its view, neither oral contract was enforceable: the 1968 agreement was within the Statute of Frauds and the 1970 agreement was not a contract since the parties intended that it would be reduced to writing before it would become binding. In any event, IBM insists that, as a matter of law, both contract claims were subject to the SES agreement—which it maintains was valid in all respects—and were barred by it.

Catamore's negligence claim is that IBM, in its dealings with Catamore, commited numerous unreasonable acts of misfeasance, all of which were independently actionable in negligence regardless of their relation to the contract claims. Even if the SES agreement barred the contract claims, Catamore maintains that the limitations of that written agreement should not be construed to apply to its negligence count. IBM, on the other hand, contends that the negligence claim should never have gone to the jury. Its view is

1. that the district court abused its discretion in permitting the addition of a negligence counterclaim on the twenty-ninth day of trial;
2. that, under the facts of this case, Catamore's sole remedy was in contract; and
3. that even if a negligence action was maintainable, this action too was subject to the limitation of liability clauses in the SES agreement. . . .

For the present, . . . we focus in particular upon the issue whether, under New York law, the SES agreement, the voidable character of which we leave to the second trial, barred the counterclaims for the breach of the two oral contracts. We do so because these contract issues predominated at the first trial and probably were conceived by the jury as central to the resolution of this dispute. Moreover, unlike many of the other claims where we cannot now say with any certainty that egregious errors were committed, we think that—notwithstanding the care taken at trial and indeed perhaps because of the spirited, relentless thrust and parry of this extended trial— the significance to be accorded facially comprehensive written agreements between sophisticated corporate entities was undervalued.

The morass of business between two companies described on this record, their promises oral and written, the disparity of their understandings, the frustration of expectations, the inevitable recriminations and conflicting memories—all this is not unique, new, or infrequently encountered. The law in its effort to facilitate just resolutions of such controversies has, over the centuries, developed certain aids or guides to decision. Two of these are involved in the critical contracts questions at issue here. The first is the substantive principle that when, in the course of business transaction between people or corporations, free and uncoerced understandings purporting to be comprehensive are solemnized by documents that both parties sign and concede to be their agreement, such documents are not easily bypassed or given restrictive interpretations. The second is the functional principle that in our system of resolving disputes, the judge and the jury share in the decision process. In such a case as this the judge must first assess the evidence in order to decide whether, under the substantive principle as illuminated by precedents, the jury should do the weighing.

Here, we think the judge improperly permitted the jury to conclude that the SES agreement, if not voided by fraud, had no effect on Catamore's claims of breach of the 1968 and 1970 contracts. The SES agreement contained a clause providing that an action for breach of contract could not be brought more than one year after the cause of action arose. Neither of Catamore's breach of contract counterclaims were made within one year after the respective causes of action accrued. These actions were therefore time barred if the SES agreement applies to actions brought under the two oral agreements and if the limitation clause is valid. We are persuaded that the clause applies and is valid.

As to the 1968 oral agreement, the jury found in September 1968 that IBM did in fact orally undertake to deliver a completely designed and programmed, turnkey production control system. Given this finding, this contract concededly had complete vitality until December 9, 1969, when the SES agreement was signed. If all that had occurred on December 9 was the execution of the SES agreement, it may well have been open to the jury to decide that it had no effect on the September 1968 oral agreement. By its terms, SES purported to supersede "all proposals oral and written and all other communications between the parties relating to the subject matter of this Agreement." Since an executed contract, oral or written, is not a proposal, and of higher dignity than a "communication," SES would seem not necessarily to apply. At the very least there would seem to be enough facial ambiguity to justify accepting other evidence of the parties' intent.

But the execution of the SES was accompanied simultaneously by Catamore's execution of its first Service Estimate. The Estimate was, according to Catamore, for the remaining 10 percent of the work to be done. And as we have noted, the Estimate form contained the statement, immediately above the space for a customer's signature, that "Authorization for the above work is given under the terms of the captioned agreement for IBM Systems Engineering Services." Catamore's president, as we have also noted, testified that what he thought to be the remaining 10 percent of the work on the production control system was to be performed under the SES agreement. Because Catamore's claim for damages for breach of contract arises from IBM's failure to *complete* and *deliver* the production control system, and since Catamore appears clearly to have entered into an arrangement whereby the last 10 percent of the work on this system was to be performed subject to the SES agreement, its claim for breach of this promise is necessarily governed by the one-year limitation period contained therein.

Because the parties have cast this issue in such different terms, we emphasize what we have not decided. We are not deciding that the SES agreement replaced or superceded the 1968 oral agreement in its entirety. Nor have we been required to determine which of two inconsistent provisions—one in the oral contract and one in the written contract—apply. The SES provisions are new clauses, not inconsistent with any earlier ones. Catamore's argument that the SES agreement did not replace the *entire* earlier agreement misses the point. We accept the proposition that "parol evidence, which does not vary or contradict the writing, is admissible to complete the understanding of the parties." Here, however, we are concerned with the reverse situation: a writing that does not vary or contradict the evidence of the terms of the parol agreement.

Catamore objects to the application of the SES agreement to the 1968 contract on the grounds that when it entered the SES agreement it was ignorant of wrongs IBM had already committed in performing the 1968 contract. It insists that it cannot be held to have waived any rights under a contract when ignorant of wrongs already committed. This argument misses the mark. Although the evidence of wrongs IBM had already committed may well be relevant as to whether the SES agreement was fraudulently induced—at least insofar as it applied to causes of action arising under the 1968 oral contract—and this evidence may also be supportive of other theories of recovery, it is irrelevant to the question of the effect of the SES agreement, if valid, on the contract arising from IBM's failure to deliver the turnkey production control system by September 1970. In December 1969 Catamore agreed that any such action must be instituted within a year after its accrual. The present action not having been so instituted, it is barred by the SES agreement.

The applicability of the SES agreement to the performance of the 1970 oral agreement involving IBM and MV/Vicario is even more clear. Here again, the jury appears to have found that the discussions in the spring of 1970 culminated in a mid-March oral agreement providing that IBM would deliver a merchandise control system to MV/Vicario. Each such authorization contained the same notation that the authorization "is given under the terms of the . . . [SES]." Catanzaro had testified that IBM's work for MV/Vicario was on the basis of the SES agreement. . . .

Catamore argues that MV/Vicario is a separate corporation and, since it was not a party to the SES agreement, the references to SES in the Service Estimates were not sufficient to require a conclusion that the SES limitation of liability clause applied to MV/Vicario. But the entire record in this case demonstrates the intimate relationship between Catamore and MV/Vicario as interrelated parts of a common enterprise in which Catanzaro was the dominant leader. Catamore suggests that if the SES has any application to the MV/Vicario Estimates at all, it is limited to "the purpose of authorizing work to be performed." Catamore argues that this must be strictly construed against IBM and be read to refer only to a clause that states that estimates may be agreed to in writing, are not guaranteed, and do not constitute a fixed price contract. But all of this information is set forth in the Service Estimate itself; absolutely no justification exists for construing this incorporation by reference so narrowly. The SES is a two-page document containing ten provisions under ten captions. We see no ambiguity in the words "Authorization for the above work is given under the terms of [SES]" as would justify any construction that would incorporate some terms and exclude others.

Since we find the limitations in the SES agreement apply to both of Catamore's contract actions, we must now consider the validity of the provision limiting the period of IBM's liability to one year following the accrual of the cause of action. Catamore, not surprisingly, complains that it is unfair for IBM to attempt so to curtail its risks and liabilities. The short answer to their complaint is such clauses, providing the time limitation is reasonable, are valid under New York law. We observe that a small consumer may often be required to deal with a large supplier on the latter's terms—perhaps the forces of competition are the only check to one-sided dealings. In any case, it seems to us that when a supplier and its customer, neither of whom is helpless in the marketplace, agree on the terms limiting the period of liability for future services to one year, those terms must be respected. We, therefore, hold that the district court erred in permitting the jury to find both that the SES agreement was valid and that IBM was liable to Catamore for having breached the two oral agreements.

At the second trial, Catamore may attempt to escape the limitations in the SES agreement by establishing that it was induced to enter into it by fraud. We do not rule out the possibility that the trial court might permit a jury to find fraud in the inducement only insofar as the SES agreement affects actions to recover under the 1968 oral agreement. Catamore may also attempt to recover on a negligence theory. We reemphasize that we are expressing no opinion on the merits of these alternative theories of recovery.

Finally, we realize that there are hotly contested issues concerning damages—such as the sufficiency of the basis for projecting lost profits, proximate cause, duplication and confusion, and adequacy of instructions. Without scrutinizing these in detail, we limit ourselves to suggesting that in any future retrial, exhibits such as charts be prepared so as to minimize, if not avoid entirely, speculation that any elements of damage have been double counted. A jury is, in a case like this, given quite enough of a task without being unnecessarily confused.

APPENDIX 3

SELECTED SECTIONS OF THE COPYRIGHT LAW OF 1976

Some important definitions from Section 101:

A "compilation" is a work formed by the collection and assembling of preexisting materials or of data that are selected, coordinated, or arranged in such a way that the resulting work as a whole constitutes an original work of authorship. The term "compilation" includes collective works.

"Copies" are material objects, other than phonorecords, in which a work is fixed by any method now known or later developed, and from which the work can be perceived, reproduced, or otherwise communicated, either directly or with the aid of a machine or device. The term "copies" includes the material object, other than a phonorecord, in which the work is first fixed.

A work is "created" when it is fixed in a copy or phonorecord for the first time; where a work is prepared over a period of time, the portion of it that has been fixed at a particular time constitutes the work as of that time, and where a work has been prepared in different versions, each version constitutes a separate work.

A "derivative work" is a work based upon one or more preexisting works, such as a translation, musical arrangement, . . . , abridgment, condensation, or any other form in which a work may be recast, transformed, or adapted. A work consisting of editorial revisions, annotations, elaborations, or other modifications which, as a whole, represent an original work of authorship is a "derivative work."

A "device," "machine," or "process" is one now known or later developed.

To "display" a work means to show a copy of it, either directly or by means of a film, slide, television image, or any other device or process . . .

A work is "fixed" in a tangible medium of expression when its embodiment in a copy or phonorecord, by or under the authority of an author, is sufficiently permanent or stable to permit it to be perceived, reproduced, or otherwise communicated for a period of more than a transitory duration. A work consisting of sounds, images, or both, that are being transmitted, is "fixed" for purposes of this title if a fixation of the work is being made simultaneously with its transmission.

"Literary works" are works, other than audiovisual works, expressed in words, numbers, or other verbal or numerical symbols or indicia, regardless of the nature of the material objects, such as books, periodicals, manuscripts, . . . tapes, disks or cards, in which they are embodied.

APPENDIX 3   193

To "perform" a work means to recite, render, play, dance or act it, either directly or by means of any device or process or, in the case of a motion picture or other audiovisual work, to show its images in any sequence or to make the sounds accompanying it audible.

"Publication" is the distribution of copies or phonorecords of a work to the public by sale or other transfer of ownership, or by rental, lease, or lending. The offering to distribute copies . . . to a group of persons for purposes of further distribution, public performance, or public display, constitutes publication. A public performance or display of a work does not of itself constitute publication.

SECTION 102. SUBJECT MATTER OF COPYRIGHT: IN GENERAL

a. Copyright protection subsists, in accordance with this title, in original works of authorship fixed in any tangible medium of expression, now known or later developed, from which they can be perceived, reproduced, or otherwise communicated, either directly or with the aid of a machine or device. Works of authorship include the following categories:
   1. literary works . . . .
b. In no case does copyright protection for an original work of authorship extend to any idea, procedure, process, system, method of operation, concept, principle, or discovery, regardless of the form in which it is described, explained, illustrated, or embodied in such work.

SECTION 103. SUBJECT MATTER OF COPYRIGHT: COMPILATIONS AND DERIVATIVE WORKS

a. The subject matter of copyright as specified in section 102 includes compilations and derivative works, but protection for a work employing preexisting material in which copyright subsists does not extend to any part of the work in which such material has been used unlawfully.
b. The copyright in a compilation or derivative work extends only to the material contributed by the author of such work, as distinguished from the preexisting material employed in the work, and does not imply any exclusive right in the preexisting material. The copyright in such work is independent of, and does not affect or enlarge the scope, duration, ownership, or subsistence of, any copyright protection in the preexisting material.

SECTION 105. SUBJECT MATTER OF COPYRIGHT: UNITED STATES GOVERNMENT WORKS

Copyright protection under this title is not available for any work of the United States Government, but the United States Government is not precluded from receiving and holding copyrights transferred to it by assignment, bequest, or otherwise.

SECTION 106. EXCLUSIVE RIGHTS IN COPYRIGHTED WORKS

Subject to sections 107 through 118, the owner of copyright under this title has the exclusive rights to do and to authorize any of the following:

1. to reproduce the copyrighted work in copies or phonorecords;
2. to prepare derivative works based upon the copyrighted work;
3. to distribute copies or phonorecords of the copyrighted work to the public by sale or other transfer of ownership, or by rental, lease or lending . . . .

SECTION 107. LIMITATIONS ON EXCLUSIVE RIGHTS: FAIR USE

Notwithstanding the provisions of section 106, the fair use of a copyrighted work, including such use by reproduction in copies or phonorecords or by any other means specified in that section, for purposes such as criticism, comment, news reporting, teaching (including multiple copies for a classroom use), scholarship, or research, is not an infringement of copyright. In determining whether the use made of a work in any particular case is a fair use the factors to be considered shall include:

1. the purpose and character of the use, including whether such use is of a commercial nature or is for nonprofit educational purposes;
2. the nature of the copyrighted work;
3. the amount and substantiality of the portion used in relation to the copyrighted work as a whole; and
4. the effect of the use upon the potential market for or value of the copyrighted work.

APPENDIX 4

PARKER v. FLOOK

This appendix contains the text of the "slip opinion" in *Parker* v. *Flook*, which, as of this writing, represented the Supreme Court's latest word on program patents. The slip opinion is released when the Court hands down its decision. Later, the Court's opinions are compiled and published in the *United States Reports*, the official reporter of opinions of the United States Supreme Court.

Justice John Paul Stevens wrote the opinion, which a majority of justices accepted as representing the thinking of the Court on the issues raised in this case. Three of the nine justices joined in a dissenting opinion written by Justice Potter Stewart. Dissenting opinions have no legal force or effect. They sometimes represent future directions of the Court, however, should the balance of the Court change with later appointments.

This opinion also contains an example of a patent claim in an appendix.

(Slip Opinion)

> NOTE: Where it is feasible, a syllabus (headnote) will be released, as is being done in connection with this case, at the time the opinion is issued. The syllabus constitutes no part of the opinion of the Court but has been prepared by the Reporter of Decisions for the convenience of the reader. See *United States* v. *Detroit Lumber Co.*, 200 U.S. 321, 337.

SUPREME COURT OF THE UNITED STATES

Syllabus

PARKER, ACTING COMMISSIONER OF PATENTS AND TRADEMARKS v. FLOOK

CERTIORARI TO THE COURT OF CUSTOMS AND PATENT APPEALS

No. 77–642. Argued April 25, 1978—Decided June 22, 1978

Respondent's method for updating alarm limits during catalytic conversion processes, in which the only novel feature is a mathematical formula, *held* not patentable under § 101 of the Patent Act. The identification of a limited category of useful, though conventional, post-solution applications of such a formula does not make the method eligible for patent protection, since assuming the formula to be within prior art, as it must be, *O'Reilly* v. *Morse*, 15 How. 62, respondent's application contains no patentable invention. The chemical processes involved in catalytic conversion are well known, as are the monitoring of process variables, the use of alarm limits to trigger alarms, the

notion that alarm limit values must be recomputed and readjusted, and the use of computers for "automatic process monitoring." Pp. 4-12.
559 F.2d 21, reversed.

STEVENS, J., delivered the opinion of the Court, in which BRENNAN, WHITE, MARSHALL, BLACKMUN, and POWELL, JJ., joined. STEWART, J., filed a dissenting opinion, in which BURGER, C. J., and REHNQUIST, J., joined.

NOTICE: This opinion is subject to formal revision before publication in the preliminary print of the United States Reports. Readers are requested to notify the Reporter of Decisions, Supreme Court of the United States, Washington, D.C. 20543, of any typographical or other formal errors, in order that corrections may be made before the preliminary print goes to press.

SUPREME COURT OF THE UNITED STATES

No. 77-642

Lutrelle F. Parker, Acting Commissioner of Patents and Trademarks, Petitioner,
v.
Dale R. Flook.

On Writ of Certiorari to the United States Court of Customs and Patent Appeals.

[June 22, 1978]

MR. JUSTICE STEVENS delivered the opinion of the Court.

Respondent applied for a patent on a "Method For Updating Alarm Limits." The only novel feature of the method is a mathematical formula. In *Gottschalk* v. *Benson*, 409 U.S. 63, we held that the discovery of a novel and useful mathematical formula may not be patented. The question in this case is whether the identification of a limited category of useful, though conventional, post-solution applications of such a formula makes respondent's method eligible for patent protection.

I

An "alarm limit" is a number. During catalytic conversion processes, operating conditions such as temperature, pressure, and flow rates are constantly monitored. When any of these "process variables" exceeds a predetermined "alarm limit," an alarm may signal the presence of an abnormal condition indicating either inefficiency or perhaps danger. Fixed alarm limits may be appropriate for a steady operation, but during transient operating situations, such as start-up, it may be necessary to "update" the alarm limits periodically.

Respondent's patent application describes a method of updating alarm limits. In essence, the method consists of three steps: an initial step which merely measures the present value of the process variable (*e.g.*, the temperature); an intermediate step which uses an algorithm[1] to calculate an updated alarm limit value; and a final step in which the actual alarm limit is adjusted to the updated value.[2] The only difference between the conventional methods of changing alarm limits and that described in respondent's application rests in the second step—the mathematical algorithm or formula. Using the formula, an operator can calculate an updated alarm limit once he knows the original alarm base, the appropriate margin of safety, the current temperature (or other process variable), and the appropriate weighting factor to be used to average the original alarm base and the current temperature.

The patent application does not purport to explain how to select the appropriate margin of safety, the weighting factor, or any of the other variables. Nor does it purport to contain any disclosure relating to the chemical processes at work, the monitoring of process variables, or the means of setting off an alarm or adjusting an alarm system. All that it provides is a formula for computing an updated alarm limit. Although the computations can be made by pencil and paper calculations, the abstract of disclosure makes it clear that the formula is primarily useful for computerized calculations producing automatic adjustments in alarm settings.[3]

The patent claims cover any use of respondent's formula for updating the value of an alarm limit on any process variable involved in a process comprising the catalytic chemical conversion of hydrocarbons. Since there are numerous processes of that kind in the petrochemical and oil refining industries,[4] the claims cover a broad range of potential uses of the method. They do not, however, cover every conceivable application of the formula.

II

The patent examiner rejected the application. He found that the mathematical formula constituted the only difference between respondent's claims and the prior art and therefore a patent on this method "would in practical effect be a patent on the formula or mathematics itself."[5] The examiner concluded that the claims did not describe a discovery that was eligible for patent protection.

The Board of Appeals of the Patent and Trademark Office sustained the examiner's rejection. The Board also concluded that the "point of novelty in

---

1. We use the word "algorithm" in this case, as we did in *Gottschalk* v. *Benson*, 409 U.S. 63, 65, to mean "[a] procedure for solving a given type of mathematical problem...."

2. Claim 1 of the patent is set forth in the appendix to this opinion, which also contains a more complete description of these three steps.

3. App., at 13.

4. Examples mentioned in the abstract of disclosure include naphtha reforming, petroleum distillate and petroleum residuum cracking, hydro-cracking and desulfurization, aromatic hydrocarbon and paraffin isomerization and disproportionation, paraffin-olefin alkylation and the like. *Id.*, at 8.

5. *Id.*, at 47.

[respondent's] claimed method"⁶ lay in the formula or algorithm described in the claims, a subject matter that was unpatentable under *Benson, supra.*

The Court of Customs and Patent Appeals reversed. 559 F. 2d 21. It read *Benson* as applying only to claims that entirely pre-empt a mathematical formula or algorithm, and noted that respondent was only claiming on the use of his method to update alarm limits in a process comprising the catalytic chemical conversion of hydrocarbons. The court reasoned that since the mere solution of the algorithm would not constitute infringement of the claims, a patent on the method would not pre-empt the formula.

The acting Commissioner of Patents and Trademarks filed a petition for a writ of certiorari, urging that the decision of the Court of Customs and Patent Appeals will have a debilitating effect on the rapidly expanding computer "software" industry,⁷ and will require him to process thousands of additional patent applications. Because of the importance of the question, we granted certiorari,—U.S.—.

III

This case turns entirely on the proper construction of § 101 of the Patent Code, which describes the subject matter that is eligible for patent protection.⁸ It does not involve the familiar issues of novelty and obviousness that routinely arise under §§ 102 and 103 when the validity of a patent is challenged. For the purpose of our analysis, we assume that respondent's formula is novel and useful and that he discovered it. We also assume, since respondent does not challenge the examiner's finding, that the formula is the only novel feature of respondent's method. The question is whether the discovery of this feature makes an otherwise conventional method eligible for patent protection.

The plain language of § 101 does not answer the question. It is true, as respondent argues, that his method is a "process" in the ordinary sense of the word.⁹ But that was also true of the algorithm, which described a method for

---

6. *Id.*, at 60.

7. The term "software" is used in the industry to describe computer programs. The value of computer programs in use in the United States in 1976 was placed at $43.1 billion, and projected at $70.7 billion by 1980 according to one industry estimate. See Brief Amicus Curiae for the Computer and Business Equipment Manufacturers Association, at 17–18, n. 16.

8. 35 U.S.C. § 101 provides:
"Whoever invents or discovers any new and useful process, machine, manufacture, or composition of matter, or any new and useful improvement thereof may obtain a patent therefor, subject to the conditions and requirements of this title."
Section 100 (b) provides:
"The term 'process' means process, art or method, and includes a new use of a known process, machine, manufacture, composition of matter, or material."

9. The statutory definition of "process" is broad. See n. 8, *supra.* An argument can be made, however, that this Court has only recognized a process as within the statutory definition when it either was tied to a particular apparatus or operated to change materials to a "different state or thing." See *Cochrane* v. *Deener*, 94 U.S. 780, 787–788. As in *Benson*, we assume that a valid process patent may issue even if it does not meet one of these qualifications of our earlier precedents. 409 U.S., at 71.

converting binary-coded decimal numerals into pure binary numerals, that was involved in *Gottschalk* v. *Benson*. The holding that the discovery of that method could not be patented as a "process" forecloses a purely literal reading of § 101.[10] Reasoning that an algorithm, or mathematical formula, is like a law of nature, *Benson* applied the established rule that a law of nature cannot be the subject of a patent. Quoting from earlier cases, we said:

' "A principle, in the abstract, is a fundamental truth; an original cause; a motive; these cannot be patented, as no one can claim in either of them an exclusive right.' *Le Roy* v. *Tatham*, 14 How. 156, 175. Phenomena of nature, though just discovered, mental processes, and abstract intellectual concepts are not patentable, as they are the basic tools of scientific and technological work." 409 U.S., at 67.

The line between a patentable "process" and an unpatentable "principle" does not always shimmer with clarity. Both are "conception[s] of the mind, seen only by [their] effects when being executed or performed." *Tilghman* v. *Proctor*, 102 U.S. 707, 728. In *Benson* we concluded that the process application in fact sought to patent an idea, noting that:

"The mathematical formula involved here has no substantial practical application except in connection with a digital computer, which means that if the judgment below is affirmed, the patent would wholly pre-empt the mathematical formula and in practical effect would be a patent on the algorithm itself." 409 U.S., at 71-72.

Respondent correctly points out that this language does not apply to his claims. He does not seek to "wholly pre-empt the mathematical formula," since there are uses of his formula outside the petrochemical and oil refining industries that remain in the public domain. And he argues that the presence of specific "post-solution" activity—the adjustment of the alarm limit to the figure computed according to the formula—distinguishes this case from *Benson* and makes his process patentable. We cannot agree.

The notion that post-solution activity, no matter how conventional or obvious in itself, can transform an unpatentable principle into a patentable process exalts form over substance. A competent draftsman could attach some form of post-solution activity to almost any mathematical formula; the Pythagorean Theorem would not have been patentable, or partially patentable, because a patent application contained a final step indicating that the formula, when solved, could be usefully applied to existing surveying techniques.[11] The concept of patentable subject matter under § 101 is not "like a nose of wax which may be turned and twisted in any direction . . . . " *White* v. *Dunbar*, 119 U.S. 47, 51.

---

10. In *Benson* we phrased the issue in this way:
"The question is whether the method described and claimed is a 'process' within the meaning of the Patent Act." 409 U.S., at 64.

11. It should be noted that in *Benson* there was a specific end use contemplated for the algorithm—utilization of the algorithm in computer programming. See *Application of Chatfield*, 545 F. 2d 152, 161 (CCPA 1976) (Rich, J., dissenting). Of course, as the Court pointed out, the formula had no other practical application; but it is not entirely clear why a process claim is any more or less patentable because the specific end use contemplated is the only one for which the algorithm has any practical application.

Yet it is equally clear that a process is not unpatentable simply because it contains a law of nature or a mathematical algorithm. See *Eibel Process Co.* v. *Minnesota and Ontario Paper Co.*, 261 U.S. 45; *Tilghman* v. *Proctor*, 102 U.S. 707.[12] For instance, in *Mackay Radio and Telegraph Co.* v. *Radio Corporation of America*, 306 U.S. 86, the applicant sought a patent on a directional antenna system in which the wire arrangement was determined by the logical application of a mathematical formula. Putting the question of patentability to one side as a preface to his analysis of the infringement issue, Mr. Justice Stone, writing for the Court, explained:

> "While a scientific truth, or the mathematical expression of it, is not patentable invention, a novel and useful structure created with the aid of knowledge of scientific truth may be." 306 U.S., at 94

Funk Bros. Seed Co. v. *Kalo Co.*, 333 U.S. 127, 130, expresses a similar approach:

> "He who discovers a hitherto unknown phenomenon of nature has no claim to a monopoly of it which the law recognizes. If there is to be invention from such a discovery, it must come from the application of the law of nature to a new and useful end."

Mackay Radio and *Funk Bros.* point to the proper analysis for this case: The process itself, not merely the mathematical algorithm, must be new and useful. Indeed, the novelty of the mathematical algorithm is not a determining factor at all. Whether the algorithm was in fact known or unknown at the time of the claimed invention, as one of the "basic tools of scientific and technological work," see *Gottschalk* v. *Benson, supra*, 409 U.S., at 67, it is treated as though it were a familiar part of the prior art.

This is also the teaching of our landmark decision in *O'Reilly* v. *Morse*, 15 How. 62. In that case the Court rejected Samuel Morse's broad claim covering any use of electromagnetism for printing intelligible signs, characters or letters at a distance. *Id.*, at 112-121. In reviewing earlier cases applying the rule that a scientific principle cannot be patented, the Court placed particular emphasis on the English case of *Neilson et al.* v. *Harford*, Webster's Patent Cases 273 (1844), which involved the circulation of heated air in a furnace system to increase its efficiency. The English Court rejected the argument that the patent

---

12. In *Eibel Process Co.* the Court upheld a patent on an improvement on a papermaking machine that made use of the law of gravity to enhance the flow of the product. The patentee, of course, did not claim to have discovered the force of gravity, but that force was an element in his novel conception.

Tilghman v. *Proctor* involved a process claim for "the manufacturing of fat acids and glycerine from fatty bodies." The Court distinguished the process from the principle involved as follows:

"[T]he claim of the patent is not for a mere principle. The chemical principle or scientific fact upon which it is founded is, that the elements of neutral fat require to be severally united with an atomic equivalent of water in order to separate from each other and become free. This chemical fact was not discovered by Tilghman. He only claims to have invented a particular mode of bringing about the desired chemical union between the fatty elements and water." 102 U.S., at 729.

merely covered the principle that furnace temperature could be increased by injecting hot air, instead of cold into the furnace. That court's explanation of its decision was relied on by this Court in *Morse:*

> "'It is very difficult to distinguish it [the Neilson patent] from the specification of a patent for a principle, and this at first created in the minds of the court much difficulty; but after full consideration we think that the plaintiff does not merely claim a principle, but a machine, embodying a principle, and a very valuable one. *We think the case must be considered as if the principle being well known, the plaintiff had first invented a mode of applying it* . . . ." 15 How., at 115 (emphasis added).[13]

We think this case must also be considered as if the principle or mathematical formula were well known.

Respondent argues that this approach improperly imports into § 101 the considerations of "inventiveness" which are the proper concerns of §§ 102 and 103.[14] This argument is based on two fundamental misconceptions.

First, respondent incorrectly assumes that if a process application implements a principle in some specific fashion, it automatically falls within the patentable subject matter of § 101 and the substantive patentablity of the particular process can then be determined by the conditions of § 102 and § 103. This assumption is based on respondent's narrow reading of *Benson, supra*, and is as untenable in the context of § 101 as it is in the context of that case. It would make the determination of patentable subject matter depend simply on the draftsman's art and would ill serve the principles underlying the prohibition against patents for "ideas" or pheonomena of nature. The rule that the discovery of a law of nature cannot be patented rests, not on the notion that natural phenomena are not processes, but rather on the more fundamental understanding that they are not the kind of "discoveries" that the statute was enacted to protect.[15] The obligation to determine what type of discovery is sought to be patented must precede the determination of whether that discovery is, in fact, new or obvious.

13. See also *Risdon Locomotive Works* v. *Medart,* 158 U.S. 68; *Tilghman* v. *Proctor, supra.*

14. Sections 102 and 103 establish certain conditions, such as novelty and nonobviousness, to patentability.

15. The underlying notion is that a scientific principle, such as that expressed in respondent's algorithm, reveals a relationship that has always existed.

"An example of such a discovery [of a scientific principle] was Newton's formulation of the law of universal gravitation, relating the force of attraction between two bodies, F, to their masses, m and m', and the square of the distance, d, between their centers, according to the quation $F = mm'/d^2$. But this relationship always existed—even before Newton announced his celebrated law. Such 'mere' recognition of a theretofore existing phenomenon or relationship carries with it no rights to exclude others from its enjoyment. . . . Patentable subject matter must be new (novel); not merely heretofore unknown. There is a very compelling reason for this rule. The reason is founded upon the proposition that in granting patent rights, the public must not be deprived of any rights that it theretofore freely enjoyed." P. Rosenberg, Patent Law Fundamentals § 4, at 13 (1975).

Second, respondent assumes that the fatal objection to his application is the fact that one of its components—the mathematical formula—consists of unpatentable subject matter. In countering this supposed objection, respondent relies on opinions by the Court of Customs and Patent Appeals which reject the notion "that a claim may be dissected, the claim components searched in the prior art, and, if the only component found novel is outside the statutory classes of invention, the claim may be rejected under 35 U.S.C. § 101." *Application of Chatfield,* 545 F. 2d 152, 158 (CCPA 1976).[16] Our approach to respondent's application is, however, not at all inconsistent with the view that a patent claim must be considered as a whole. Respondent's process is unpatentable under § 101 not because it contains a mathematical algorithm as one component, but because once that algorithm is assumed to be within the prior art, the application, considered as a whole, contains no patentable invention. Even though a phenomenon of nature or mathematical formula may be well known, an inventive application of the principle may be patented. Conversely, the discovery of such a phenomenon cannot support a patent unless there is some other inventive concept in its application.

Here it is absolutely clear that respondent's application contains no claim of patentable invention. The chemical processes involved in catalytic conversion of hydrocarbons are well known; as are the practice of monitoring the chemical process variables, the use of alarm limits to trigger alarms, the notion that alarm limit values must be recomputed and readjusted, and the use of computers for "automatic process monitoring-alarming."[17] Respondent's application simply provides a new and presumably better method for calculating alarm limit values. If we assume that that method was also known, as we must under the reasoning in *Morse,* then respondent's claim is, in effect, comparable to a claim that the formula $2\pi r$ can be usefully applied in determining the circumference of a wheel.[18] As the Court of Customs and Patent Appeals has explained, "if a claim is directed essentially to a method of calculating, using a mathematical formula, even if the solution is for a specific

---

16. Section 103, by its own terms, requires that a determination of obviousness be made by considering "the subject matter as a whole." 35 U.S.C. § 103. Although this does not necessarily require that analysis of what is patentable *subject matter* under §101 proceed on the same basis, we agree that it should.

17. App., at 22.

18. Respondent argues that the inventiveness of his process must be determined as of "the time the invention is made" under § 103, and that, therefore, it is improper to judge the obviousness of his process by assessing the application of the formula as though the formula were part of the prior art. This argument confuses the issue of patentable subject matter under § 101 with that of obviousness under § 103. Whether or not respondent's formula can be characterized as "obvious," his process patent rests solely on the claim that his mathematical algorithm, when related to a computer program, will improve the existing process for updating alarm units. Very simply, our holding today is that a claim for an improved method of calculation, even when tied to a specific end use, is unpatentable subject matter under § 101.

purpose, the claimed method is nonstatutory." *Application of Richman*, 563 F. 2d 1026, 1030 (1977).

To a large extent our conclusion is based on reasoning derived from opinions written before the modern business of developing programs for computers was conceived. The youth of the industry may explain the complete absence of precedent supporting patentability. Neither the dearth of precedent, nor this decision, should therefore be interpreted as reflecting a judgment that patent protection of certain novel and useful computer programs will not promote the progress of science and the useful arts, or that such protection is undesirable as a matter of policy. Difficult questions of policy concerning the kinds of programs that may be appropriate for patent protection and the form and duration of such protection can be answered by Congress on the basis of current empirical data not equally available to this tribunal.[19]

It is our duty to construe the patent statutes as they now read, in light of our prior precedents, and we must proceed cautiously when we are asked to extend patent rights into areas wholly unforeseen by Congress. As MR. JUSTICE WHITE explained in writing for the Court in *Deepsouth Packing Co. v. Laitram Corp.*, 406 U.S. 518, 531:

> "[W]e should not expand patent rights by overruling or modifying our prior cases construing the patent statutes, unless the argument for expansion of privilege is based on more than mere inference from ambiguous statutory language. We would require a clear and certain signal from Congress before approving the position of a litigant who, as respondent here, argues that the beachhead of privilege is wider, and the area of public use narrower, than the courts had previously thought. No such signal legitimizes respondent's position in this litigation."

The judgment of the Court of Customs and Patent Appeals is

Reversed.

APPENDIX

Claim 1 of the patent describes the method as follows:

> "1. A method for updating the value of at least one alarm limit on at least one process variable involved in a process comprising the catalytic chemical conversion of hydrocarbons wherein said alarm limit has a current value of
>
> $$Bo + K$$

---

19. Articles assessing the merits and demerits of patent protection for computer programming are numerous. See, *e.g.*, Davis, Computer Programs and Subject Matter Patentability, 6 Rutgers Journal of Computers and the Law 1, and articles cited therein, at 2 n. 5 (1976). Even among those who favor patentability of computer programs, there is questioning of whether the 17-year protection afforded by the current Patent Act is either needed or appropriate. See *id.*, at 20 n. 133.

"wherein Bo is the current alarm base and K is a predetermined alarm offset which comprises:

"1. Determining the present value of said process variable, said present value being defined as PVL;

"2. Determining a new alarm base, $B1$, using the following equation:

$$B1 = Bo\,(1.0 - F) + PVL(F)$$

"where F is a predetermined number greater than zero and less than 1.0;

"3. Determining an updated alarm limit which is defined as $B1 + K$; and thereafter

"4. Adjusting said alarm limit to said updated alarm limit value."

App., at 63.

In order to use respondent's method for computing a new limit, the operator must make four decisions. Based on his knowledge of normal operating conditions, he first selects the original "alarm base" (Bo); if a temperature of 400 degrees is normal, that may be the alarm base. He next decides on an appropriate margin of safety, perhaps 50 degrees; that is his "alarm offset" (K). The sum of the alarm base and the alarm offset equals the alarm limit. Then he decides on the time interval that will elapse between each updating; that interval has no effect on the computation although it may, of course, be of great practical importance. Finally, he selects a weighting factor (F), which may be any number between 99% and 1%,[20] and which is used in the updating calculation.

If the operator has decided in advance to use an original alarm base (Bo) of 400 degrees, a constant alarm offset (K) of 50 degrees, and a weighting factor (F) of 80%, the only additional information he needs in order to compute an updated alarm limit (UAV), is the present value of the process variable (PVL). The computation of the updated alarm limit according to respondent's method involves these three steps:

First, at the predetermined interval, the process variable is measured; if we assume the temperature is then 425 degrees, PVL will then equal 425.

Second, the solution of respondent's novel formula will produce a new alarm base ($B1$) that will be a weighted average of the preceding alarm base (Bo) of 400 degrees and the current temperature (PVL) of 425. It will be closer to one or the other depending on the value of the weighting factor (F) selected by the operator. If F is 80 percent, that percentage of 425 (340) plus 20 percent (1 − F) of 400 (80) will produce a new alarm base of 420 degrees.

Third, the alarm offset (K) of 50 degrees is then added to the new alarm base ($B1$) of 420 to produce the updated alarm limit (UAV) of 470.

The process is repeated at the selected time intervals. In each updating computation, the most recently calculated alarm base and the current measurement of the process variable will be substituted for the corresponding numbers in the original calculation, but the alarm offset and the weighting factor will remain constant.

---

20. More precisely, it is defined as a number greater than zero, but less than 1.

SUPREME COURT OF THE UNITED STATES

No. 77-642

Lutrelle F. Parker, Acting Commissioner of Patents and Trademarks, Petitioner,
v.
Dale R. Flook.

On Writ of Certiorari to the United States Court of Customs and Patent Appeals.

[June 22, 1978]

MR. JUSTICE STEWART, with whom THE CHIEF JUSTICE and MR. JUSTICE REHNQUIST join, dissenting.

It is a commonplace that laws of nature, physical phenomena, and abstract ideas are not patentable subject matter.[1] A patent could not issue, in other words, on the law of gravity, or the multiplication tables, or the phenomena of magnetism, or the fact that water at sea level boils at 100 degrees centigrade and freezes at zero—even though newly discovered. *Le Roy* v. *Tatham*, 14 How. 156, 175; *O'Reilly* v. *Morse*, 15 How. 62, 112-121; *Rubber-Tip Pencil Co.* v. *Howard*, 20 Wall. 498, 507; *Tilghman* v. *Proctor*, 102 U.S. 707; *Mackay Co.* v. *Radio Corp.*, 306 U.S. 86, 94; *Funk Bros. Seed Co.* v. *Kalo Co.*, 333 U.S. 127, 130.

The recent case of *Gottschalk* v. *Benson*, 409 U.S. 63, stands for no more than this long-established principle, which the Court there stated in the following words:

> "Phenomena of nature, though just discovered, mental processes, and abstract intellectual concepts are not patentable, as they are the basic tools of scientific and technological work." *Id.*, at 67.

In *Benson* the Court held unpatentable claims for an algorithm that "were not limited to any particular art or technology, to any particular apparatus or machinery, or to any particular end use." *Id.*, at 64. A patent on such claims, the Court said, "would wholly pre-empt the mathematical formula and the practical effect would be a patent on the algorithm itself." *Id.*, at 72.

The present case is a far different one. The issue here is whether a claimed process[2] loses its status of subject matter patentability simply because *one step*

---

1. 35 U.S.C. § 101 provides:
"Whoever invents or discovers any new and useful process, machine, manufacture, or composition of matter, or any new and useful improvement thereof, may obtain a patent therefor, subject to the conditions and requirements of this title.
2. 35 U.S.C. § 100 (b) provides:
"The term 'process' means process, art or method, and includes a new use of a known process, machine, manufacture, composition of matter, or material."

in the process would not be patentable subject matter if considered in isolation. The Court of Customs and Patent Appeals held that the process is patentable subject matter, *Benson* being inapplicable since "[t]he present claims do not preempt the formula or algorithm contained therein, because solution of the algorithm, per se, would not infringe the claims." 559 F. 2d 21, at 23.

That decision seems to me wholly in conformity with basic principles of patent law. Indeed, I suppose that thousands of processes and combinations have been patented that contained one or more steps or elements that themselves would have been unpatentable subject matter.[3] *Eibel Process Co.* v. *Minnesota & Ontario Paper Co.*, 261 U.S. 45, is a case in point. There the Court upheld the validity of an improvement patent that made use of the law of gravity, which by itself was clearly unpatentable. See also, *e.g., Tilghman* v. *Proctor*, 102 U.S. 707.

The Court today says it does not turn its back on these well-settled precedents, *ante*, at—, but it strikes what seems to me an equally damaging blow at basic principles of patent law by importing into its inquiry under 35 U.S.C. §101 the criteria of novelty and inventiveness. Section 101 is concerned only with subject matter patentability. Whether a patent will actually *issue* depends upon the criteria of §§ 102 and 103, which include novelty and inventiveness, among many others. It may well be that under the criteria of §§ 102 and 103 no patent should issue on the proceeds claimed in this case, because of anticipation, abandonment, obviousness, or for some other reason. But in my view the claimed process clearly meets the standards of subject matter patentability of § 101.

In short, I agree with the Court of Custom and Patent Appeals in this case, and with the carefully considered opinions of that court in other cases presenting the same basic issue. See *In re Freeman*, —F. 2d—; *In re Richman*, 563 F. 2d 1026 (CCPA); *In re Castelet*, 562 F. 2d 1236 (CCPA); *In re Deutsch*, 553 F. 2d 689 (CCPA); *In re Chatfield*, 545 F. 2d 152 (CCPA). Accordingly, I would affirm the judgment before us.

---

3. In *Gottschalk* v. *Benson*, the Court equated process and product patents for the purpose of its inquiry: "We dealt there with a 'product' claim, while the present case deals with a 'process' claim. But we think the same principle applies." 409 U.S., at 67–68.

APPENDIX 5

DATA GENERAL CORP. v. DIGITAL COMPUTER CONTROLS, INC.

The exerpts in this appendix were taken from opinions in a trade secrecy case that dragged out over many years. If you read the material in the text on trade secrecy, you should have little trouble following the court's logic. A central issue in this dispute was whether or not Data General took adequate precautions to preserve the secrecy of its computer design.

The first opinion was one denying summary judgment (judgment reached without a trial, but merely on the pleadings together with affidavits and briefs submitted with the motion for summary judgment) and granting an order forbidding Digital Computer Controls from making use of the alleged trade secrets.

DATA GENERAL CORP. v. DIGITAL COMPUTER CONTROLS, INC., 297 A.2d 433 (Del. Ch. 1971).

Data General Corporation seeks an order preliminarily enjoining the defendant Digital Computer Controls from making use of claimed trade secrets allegedly contained in design drawings which accompany certain sales of plaintiff's Nova 1200 computer, defendant having acquired such a computer with accompanying drawings from one of plaintiff's customers.

The relevant facts . . . are as follows: During the past several years plaintiff has developed and marketed successfully small general-purpose computers to which they have given the name Nova, a large part of plaintiff's research and development budget for the past several years having been allocated to the development of such small computers, which, the parties agree, are the only ones of their type presently being profitably marketed, there having been no device on the market comparable to plaintiff's machines until defendant's entry on the scene.

When a sale of a Nova 1200 computer is made, plaintiff makes available at no extra cost to the customers who wish to do their own maintenance the design or logic drawings of the device sold, in this case a Nova 1200 computer. Such type of maintenance has been found to be desired by some customers to avoid periods of unproductive delay while waiting for repairs to be made by plaintiff's trained personnel.

Design drawings made available to customers are furnished subject to the terms of a nondisclosure clause contained in a paper which accompanies a purchase agreement. Furthermore, all drawings bear a legend to the effect that they contain proprietary information of the plaintiff which is not to be used by a purchaser for manufacturing purposes. However, the Nova 1200 is not patented, and its design drawings have not been copyrighted.

In April, 1971, ... the president of Digital purchased for his company from a customer of Data General, ... a Nova 1200 computer which the latter had earlier acquired from the plaintiff. Although the exact circumstances surrounding such sale are not entirely clear . . . , the . . . president, in consummating such purchase, acquired a set of design drawings of the Nova 1200, said drawings having been furnished to [the seller] by the plaintiff . . . . The corporate defendant thereafter proceeded to use such design drawings as a pattern for the construction of a competing machine which it is now about to market. . . .

[I]n order for the plaintiff to establish its right to relief here, it must demonstrate

1. the existence of a trade secret and that the corporate defendant has either
2. received the information within the confines of a confidential relationship and proposes to misuse the information in violation of such relationship, or
3. that the corporate defendant improperly received the information in question in such a manner that its confidential nature should have been known and it nonetheless proceeded [to use the information anyway].

Trade secrets have been defined in Restatement, Torts §757, comment h, as follows:

> A trade secret may consist of any formula, pattern, device or compilation of information which is used in one's business, and which gives him an opportunity to obtain an advantage over competitors who do not know or use it.

Defendants insist, however, that plaintiff has not maintained that degree of secrecy which will preserve its right to relief, either by publicly selling an article alleged to contain a trade secret, or by failing to restrict access to the design drawings for its device, arguing that matters of common knowledge in an industry may not be claimed as trade secrets.

It has been recognized in similar cases that even though an unpatented article, device or machine has been sold to the public, and is therefore subject to examination and copying by anyone, the manner of making the article, device or machine may yet constitute a trade secret until such a copy has been made.

Defendants contend, however, that the issuance by plaintiff of copies of design drawings to its customers was made without safeguards designed properly to maintain the secrecy requisite to the existence of a trade secret. In other words, it is contended that plaintiff's attempts to maintain secrecy merely consisted of

1. not giving copies of the design drawings to those customers who did not need them for maintenance of their computer,
2. obtaining agreements not to disclose the information from those customers who were given copies of the drawings, and
3. printing a legend on the drawings which contained the allegedly confidential information which identified the drawing as proprietary information, the use of which was restricted.

Plaintiff argues, however, that disclosure of the design drawings to purchasers of the computer is necessary properly to maintain its device, that such disclosure was required by the very nature of the machine, and that reasonable steps were taken to preserve the secrecy of the material released.

The previous material was taken from an opinion which, in part, denied the defendants motion for summary judgment. Summary judgment could have been granted if there were no real dispute as to the facts, and the defendants ought to prevail on issues of law. The judge decided that there was a real issue of fact whether or not secrecy had been preserved concerning the design of the Nova 1200 to warrant legal protection as a trade secret. The Supreme Court of Delaware affirmed that decision, and the case then went to trial. The next excerpt is from an opinion in the same case, but written some four years after the first. Such delays caused by procedural disputes are not rare in cases such as these.

DATA GENERAL CORP. v. DIGITAL COMPUTER CONTROLS, INC., 357 A.2d 105 (Del. Ch. 1975).

First of all, I am satisfied that plaintiff has developed and recorded in its logic drawings of the Nova 1200 concepts of a sufficiently novel nature to entitle each such design drawing to have been a trade secret as of the time of its conception, which property right, if shown to have been adequately withheld from general circulation and thus not freely published, may be, upon a proper showing, protected from unauthorized duplication and use although, of course, an imitator is always entitled to copy a device containing alleged trade secrets through a process of reverse engineering in which the use of protected design drawings are not employed.

Upon the sale and delivery of a Nova 1200 plaintiff's practice has been to deliver with each such machine, whether the buyer be an original equipment manufacturer or an end-user, a complete set of maintenance drawings containing the Nova 1200's logic design. And while other documents, such as a user's and a maintenance manual, promotional articles and brochures of a technical nature as well as advertising have been made generally available by plaintiff to its various established and would-be customers, trainees and vendors, and fallen into the hands of others, I am satisfied that such other documents do not contain sufficient logic design of the Nova 1200 to permit their being successfully used for the purpose of either duplicating such machine or in assembling a computer substantially identical to the Nova 1200. In other words use of the complete design of such device, which is found in plaintiff's maintenance documentation, is necessary in order for a person to recreate a simulacrum of the Nova 1200 from its existing documentation rather than through reverse engineering. However, each logic diagram made available to Data General's customers and others, including vendors and trainees, bears a legend . . . clearly stating that such drawings are not to be used for manufacture or sale of the items disclosed without written permission. And I am satisfied that [the agent of the defendant who acquired the drawings] not only read such legend but comprehended its purpose. Other precautionary measures of Data General designed to protect its alleged proprietary interest in its logic drawings of the Nova 1200 involved the use of standard forms of sales agreements, one being applicable to sales of original equipment manufacturers and the other to sales to end-users. Both forms of such contract, as well as special contracts, contain a provision to the effect that plaintiff's standard terms and conditions, as amended by the sales agreement itself, shall apply to any order filled in response to such agreement, and a form of such standard terms and conditions, which contains a statement of the proprietary nature of the data furnished with a Nova 1200, including information as to their stated restriction to being used for the installation, testing, operation and maintenance of the Nova 1200, is furnished to each customer entering a sales agreement as a prerequisite to obtaining a Nova 1200. In fact, maintenance documentation containing logic diagrams is not furnished to a buyer until he has agreed . . . to abide by the provision of the proprietary legends. In addition, plaintiff takes customary precautions contractually to bind its employees to secrecy about its trade secrets, and while plant security does not compare with that of [IBM], guards are present at plaintiff's plant. Next, of course, all trainees must sign a confidentiality agreement, and while additional sets of maintenance documentation for the Nova 1200 may be purchased for $100 each, such a purchase is tied into a requirement that the machine itself also have been purchased, a transaction which calls for the entry into a confidentiality agreement as to use of plaintiff's documentation. The only remaining classes of users of plaintiff's logic design, namely employees of customers and indirect customers not bound by the specific contract against the use of plaintiff's documentation, except for maintenance are, of course, on notice as to the prohibition against the proposed use of such drawings for competitive manufacturing of an identical device by reason of the aforesaid legend or notice affixed to each such document. And in the case of employees of customers there is a further guarantee of protection in that such person's employers are, of course, under contract not to disclose plaintiff's proprietary rights. Finally, I am satisfied the defendant's contention that plaintiff's other competitors have, in any event, widely used plaintiff's logic design is unsupported by the record, which shows that the only manufacturer other than defendant which has without a license been charged with having made use of plaintiff's Nova 1200 logic design . . . settled with plaintiff after suit was filed against it.

Having concluded that plaintiff has trade secrets reposing in the logic design of its Nova 1200, the next matter to be considered is whether or not such secrets are subject to protection by a state court of equity through the granting of injunctive relief and the award of damages.

The court concluded that state trade secret law was not preempted by any federal law pertaining to patents even if the device in question probably could be patented.

"The subject of a trade secret must be secret, and must not be of public knowledge or of a general knowledge in the trade or business." This necessary element of secrecy is not lost, however, if the holder of the trade secret reveals the trade secret to another 'in confidence, and under an implied obligation not to use or disclose it.' These others may include those of the holder's employees to whom it is necessary to confide it, in order to apply it to the uses for which it is intended.' Often the recipient of confidential knowledge of the subject of a trade secret is a licensee of its holder."

"The maintenance of standards of commercial ethics and the encouragement of invention are the broadly stated policies behind trade secret law. 'The necessity of good faith and honest, fair dealing, is the very life and spirit of the commercial world'."

As to the further contention that plaintiff can have no possible claim against defendant under the law of unfair competition from and after the disclosures contained in a patent involving the Nova 1200 . . . , I am satisfied that the granting of such patent which related to the ALU of the device was a disclosure of only one isolated part of the Nova 1200 and not of the design in general, the design of such part having been contained on one sheet of the Nova 1200's logic design documentation. Thus, the granting of such patent was not a full public disclosure making public plaintiff's total logic design of the Nova 1200.

As to plaintiff's right to relief, there is first of all a statute making it a misdemeanor for anyone . . . with an intent to appropriate a trade secret to his own use or to the use of another [to make or cause to be made a copy of an article which represents a trade secret].

And it is entirely appropriate that civil relief be granted in carrying out a duly expressed state policy even though such policy is contained in a criminal statute.

In its opinion of December 1971 in this same litigation this Court indicated that if plaintiff were to prevail at final hearing, it would only be entitled to permanent injunctive relief

> . . . during that undetermined period of time which would be required for defendants substantially to reproduce plaintiff's device without its accompanying drawings.

The evidence of record is to the effect, however, that such reverse engineering was not accomplished or even undertaken by defendant for the purpose of designing and manufacturing a minicomputer substantially identical to the Nova 1200 and that the D-116 was in fact designed and thereafter manufactured through reliance on plaintiff's Nova logic documentation. It is furthermore clear, in any event, . . . that although apparently irrelevant under the authority of [cases cited in this opinion] neither team engaged by defendant to reverse engineer the Nova 1200 after this action was filed succeeded in making an operable duplicate. Accordingly, a permanent injunction barring defendant from further use of both its Nova 1200 and D-116 logic drawings for the purpose of manufacturing a minicomputer substantially identical to the Nova 1200 will be granted . . . .

Finally, while evidence of damage suffered by plaintiff by reason of defendant's improper use of plaintiff's Nova 1200 logic design leading to the manufacture and sale of its D-116 was introduced at trial over the Court's protestations that in the interest of orderliness such issue should not be tried until it had been established that defendant was in fact liable to plaintiff under the law of trade secrets, I am now satisfied that not only because there is an absence from the record of basic evidence of such claimed damages in the form of books and records of original entry concerned with the manufacture and sale of the Nova 1200 as well as of the D-116, but for the further reason that plaintiff's claim is one for unliquidated damages as to which there is a wide difference as to the proper measure for determination of such damages, such issue should be referred to a jury sitting in Superior Court for its consideration and recommendation.

APPENDIX 6

MONARCH FEDERAL SAVINGS

This opinion represents a conscientious and scholarly effort by a New Jersey Superior Court to set out the principles involved in laying the foundation for computer-generated evidence. The court decided that a proper foundation had not been laid because of inadequate testimony concerning the kind and reliability of computer equipment used in preparing the evidence. Rather than entirely voiding the previous trial because of this deficiency and ordering a new trial, the Superior Court ordered that testimony be reopened to permit an opportunity to remedy the defective foundation. Presumably, of course, if it were not possible to provide testimony concerning the reliability of the computing equipment, then the previous result would be reversed and a new trial would be necessary.

MONARCH FEDERAL SAVINGS AND LOAN ASSOC. v. *GENSER,* 156 N.J. SUPER. 107(1977).

During the trial of the issues in this mortgage foreclosure action, plaintiff Monarch . . . requested that certain computer records be admitted into evidence under the business records exception to the hearsay rule . . . Defendants . . . (Gensers) objected to their admission on the ground that plaintiff failed to lay the necessary foundation. Plaintiff produced three foundation witnesses, and their testimony may be summarized as follows.

The first witness, Richard De Russo, assistant vice-president of the Wood-Ridge National Bank (Wood-Ridge), testified that Monarch maintains a lockbox deposition account with Wood-Ridge for processing of their mortgage accounts. The mortgagors forward their payment together with an IBM card to the bank. After the monies are received, processed and checked, the computer cards are forwarded to Financial Services, Inc. (Financial Services) and the checks are forwarded to Monarch. Any problems or questions with the account are handled by Monarch. This witness also indicated that the account was maintained in the regular course of the bank's business and that Wood-Ridge provides similar services for other banks.

The next witness, Otto Kieper, is the office manager of the mortgage department of Financial Services, a computer corporation . . . He testified that Financial Services . . . has computerized the accounts of Monarch. When an account is initially opened, Monarch forwards all the relevant information to Financial Services which is transferred into the computer. Thereafter, all transactions between Monarch and the mortgagor are processed through the individual account. Monarch receives a daily read-out for each transaction and a monthly read-out for each individual account. Every mortgagor receives monthly and yearly statements.

The records of the Gensers' account were marked for identification and identified by Kieper. He testified that this account, as well as the other accounts, are processed and maintained in the regular course of Financial Services' business.

The last witness, Victor Urbanovich, has been an employee of Monarch for the past 2½ years and presently is an assistant vice-president. He testified that he is familiar with the operation of Monarch's mortgage department. This witness identified and reviewed the monthly and yearly computer printouts produced by Financial Services and supplied to and maintained by Monarch for the Genser account. He further testified that this account was maintained in the regular course of business since March 1968. Every transaction on the Genser account from March 1968 to the present was recorded with and reflected in the records processed by Financial Services and maintained by Monarch. He also testified that after reviewing the records the Gensers failed to make the payment for April 1976 and that this account remains in default as of that date.

Based on this evidence, defendants maintained that a proper foundation has not been established for the admission of these records.

The issue before this court is one of first impression in this State: What is the proper foundation to support the authenticity of a computer print-out? The leading case in New Jersey on the admissibility of computer print-outs is *Sears, Roebuck & Co.* v. *Merla,* 142 *N.J. Super.* 205 (App. Div. 1976). In that case the Appellate Division reviewed the trial judge's refusal to admit a computer print-out as evidence of a defendant's indebtedness to Sears. In reversing the trial judge's decision the court held "that as long as a proper foundation is laid, a computer print-out is admissible on the same basis as any other business record." The *Merla* court, however, did not specify what type of foundation would be required to establish admissibility.

In New Jersey the admissibility of business records is governed by [the following rule]:

> A writing offered as a memorandum or records of acts, conditions or events is admissible to prove the facts stated therein if the writing or the record upon which it is based was made in the regular course of a business, at or about the time of the act, condition or event recorded, and if the sources of the information from which it was made and the method and circumstances of its preparation were such as to justify its admission.

[This rule] liberalized and modernized the common law prerequisites for admission of business records. Under the common law four elements were needed to be proven:

1. the entries must have been original entries made in the routine of business,
2. must have been made upon personal knowledge of the recorder or of someone reporting to him,
3. must have been made at or near the time of the transaction recorded, and
4. the recorder and his informant had to be shown to be unavailable.

The modern New Jersey approach has eliminated the common law requirement of unavailability of the recorder, and the requirement of personal knowledge of the recorder. [There are three conditions for admissibility]:

> First, the record must be made in the regular course of business. Second, it must be prepared within a short time of the act, condition or event being described. Third, the source of information and the method of preparation must justify allowing it into evidence.

In addition to [these] three elements, the courts of New Jersey have mandated that the informant be "under a 'business duty' to supply honest information to the entrant."

Although "the business entry exception to the hearsay rule . . . is generally limited to *business* records," our courts have applied this exception to "[r]ecords other than commercial payment records."

Only recently have the courts throughout this country faced the problem of admitting a new form of record—the computer print-out. Computer-kept records differ in some crucial respects from traditional business records. See generally Note, "Admissibility of Computer-Kept Business Records," 55 *Cornell L. Rev.* 1033 (1970). Despite these differences, courts have acknowledged that "[c]omputerized bookkeeping has become commonplace."

Although many courts have ruled upon the admissibility of computer print-outs, only some of them have addressed the question of what foundation is required.

The foundation requirements as set forth in these cases can be broken down into six elements. The first consideration is whether the foundation witnesses must have personal knowledge of the act or event recorded, or, more specifically, the need to produce the witness who originally supplied the information recorded on the computer tape. The majority of courts that have discussed this issue have determined that such personal knowledge is not necessary. . . .

The qualification of the foundation witness is the second consideration. Numerous cases in other jurisdictions have examined the issue of whether the witness in question is the custodian of the computer records or otherwise qualified to be the foundation witness . . . More recent decisions . . . have declared that there is no need for the preparer of the computer records to testify. In some cases, the courts have required that the supervisor of the computer-processing department testify . . . Witnesses have been found qualified to testify by reason of their expertise in computers, or by reason of their "training, experience and position to testify about the [computer] system." Other jurisdictions have gone so far as to eliminate any need for the witness' personal knowledge of the physical operations of the computer equipment and require only that the witness be generally familiar with the accounting and recording process. Furthermore, in one case, the witness was permitted to testify from company records rather than from his own general knowledge.

All of the cases which have dealt with the qualifications of the foundation witness involve statutes or case law which delineate the type of witness required. New Jersey eliminated its prior requirement of having a custodian or other qualified witness testify . . . No specific person must be called to supply the foundation testimony for the admission of business records. However, whoever testifies must be in a position to supply the foundation specified . . . , i.e., the regular course of business, the time of the making of the record and the event recorded, the sources of the information recorded, and, finally, the methods and circumstances of the computer record's preparation. . . . [I]n providing information as to the methods of preparation, the foundation witness should also be able "to testify as to the type of computer employed, the permanent nature of the record storage, and how daily processing of information to be fed into the computer was conducted, resulting in permanent records."

The third element of foundation testimony is proof that the computer records were made in the ordinary course of business.

In providing an adequate foundation, the fourth consideration is the time of preparation of the computer print-out. The requirement that the entry be made "at or about the time of the act . . . recorded," is satisfied so long as the input is placed into the computer "within a reasonable time after each act or transaction to which it relates." It is not required that the print-out itself be made at that time. Although the print-out can be made at some later time, it cannot be made specifically in preparation for trial or else it will not have been made in the regular course of business.

The fifth element of a proper foundation is the source of information from which the computer print-out was made. [C]ases . . . demand that the sources of information be specified. The original source of the computer program must be delineated, and the reliability and trustworthiness of the information fed into the computer must be established. The foundation witness should "describe in detail the sources of information upon which the print-out was based," explain, where necessary, the sources and meaning of any calculations, formulas or abbreviations appearing in the computer print-out, and show that the print-outs were not only prepared by information supplied by a certain source but were capable of being verified by that source.

The sixth, and perhaps the most important, element of foundation proof is the method and circumstances of the preparation of the computer printout. Most courts have required a complete and comprehensive description of the method of preparation. This description must include testimony as to

1. the competency of the computer operators;
2. the type of computer used and its acceptance in the field as standard and efficient equipment:
3. the procedure for the input and output of information, including controls, tests and checks for accuracy and reliability;
4. the mechanical operations of the machine; and
5. the meaning and identity of the records themselves.

The five factors listed are not intended to be exhaustive. A trial court may require further proof as is necessary to justify the admission of a computer record.

In conclusion, . . . a proper foundation for the admissibility of a computer print-out as a business record should be provided by a person who may lack personal knowledge of the events recorded but is sufficiently familiar with the computerized record and the methods under which they were prepared so as to testify that

1. the computer record, as opposed to the print-out, was made within a reasonable time after the happening of the event or transaction recorded;
2. the computer record and print-out were made in the regular course of business; and
3. the methods and circumstances . . . demonstrated that the computer and the print-out were reliable and trustworthy as to justify their admission.

Using the above principles to evaluate the foundation presented here, the court initially notes that in this case the actual route of the information from its source to the computer record is somewhat different from that in the previously cited cases. The mortgage payment, accompanied by a prepunched computer card, is sent by the mortgagee to the post office box of Wood-Ridge where the cards and the payments are matched and checked for the amounts. The checks are then forwarded to Monarch and the computer cards are sent to Financial Services. Financial Services processes these cards through its computer and obtains a daily read-out of the total daily payments, which read-out is then checked against the total amount on the checks received by Monarch. Financial Services then forwards the daily computer print-out to Monarch, which receives it on the next day and cross-checks the totals. Three witnesses were called to explain the procedure involved in processing these checks and computer cards.

Defendants, however, have raised several objections to the admission of these computer print-outs, including the qualifications of the foundation witnesses and the reliability of the computer itself. Throughout the testimony of these witnesses defendants objected that they did not have personal knowledge of the mortgage transactions recorded on the computer print-out. As I have previously noted, a foundation witness does not need to have personal knowledge of the transaction recorded. Therefore, as to all three witnesses this objection is without merit.

However, there is a question as to whether any of the three foundation witnesses was "familiar with the computerized records and methods under which they were made so as to satisfy the court that the methods, the sources of information, and the time of preparation render[s] [this] evidence trustworthy." The first witness was in position to testify as to the general practice of processing the mortgage checks and computer cards at Wood-Ridge since he had been the assistant vice-president of Wood-Ridge for thirteen years and was familiar with the business transactions and work of Wood-Ridge. He did not necessarily have to be the direct supervisor of the bank's processing of defendant's checks and computer cards.

Urbanovich, the third witness called, has been assistant vice-president of Monarch for the last ten years and was generally familiar with the workings of the mortgage department of the bank by reason of being in charge of the accounting at the bank.

The key foundation witness in this case was Kieper, the office manager of Financial Services, who is responsible for handling mortgage installment loans and has been in Financial Services employ for seventeen years. He neither is a computer expert nor did he set up the computer mechanics of this particular service. However, expertise in computers or setting up the particular program is not required under the reasoning and holding of this decison. The objection as to Kieper's lack of personal knowledge as to the relationship between Monarch and Financial Services is not meritorious since he has demonstrated a general familiarity with that relationship and that is all that will be required by this court.

There is a question, though, as to whether Kieper is sufficiently familiar with the method and circumstances of the computer print-out's preparation. A review of the testimony before this court reveals that adequate proof has been presented to show that the computer record was made within a reasonable time of the receipt of the mortgage payments and that the computer records and the print-outs were made in the ordinary course of business for Monarch and Financial Services. The problem arises when the testimony as to the actual preparation of the print-out is examined. Kieper testified as to what information was received by Financial Services to initiate a new mortgage account but he did not explain what Financial Services does with this information or how the computer program on a new account originates. Further testimony revealed the method by which the daily payment information is received from Wood-Ridge, the procedures for supplying daily, monthly and yearly read-outs, the method for checking totals and the fact that the information received from Wood-Ridge . . . is processed through the computer. He did not provide information on the type of computer used and its acceptance in the field as standard, efficient and accurate equipment. This witness did not testify as to the competency of those who program the computer and process the daily input, nor did he fully explain the input controls or the mechanics of the machines. In particular, Kieper had no knowledge of the procedure for handling "irregular payments" which came from Monarch.

On the evidence presented to this court, plaintiff has failed to lay the proper foundation. But in light of the fact that no judgment has yet been entered here and the conclusions reached in this opinion are novel in this State, plaintiff will be permitted on a date to be fixed by the court to reopen its case in order to have an opportunity to submit additional evidence to lay the proper foundation in accordance with the rulings herein.

APPENDIX 7

UNITED STATES v. RUSSO

This is a landmark case in the use of computer-generated evidence in a criminal trial. In addition to discussing the proper foundation for computer-generated evidence, the opinion also deals with the circumstances under which a summary of business records, as opposed to the entire set of records, can be used at trial, as well as what materials must be made available to a defendant and when they must be provided to help the defendant prepare his or her defense.

UNITED STATES v. RUSSO, 480 F.2D 1228 (6TH CIR. 1973).

II. The Computerized Statistical Evidence

Appellant has mounted a broad attack on the admission by the court of the 1967 annual statistical run of Blue Shield of Michigan. In the first place it is claimed that this evidence does not qualify as a business record under the Federal Business Records Act. That statute establishes the admissibility in federal courts of any writing or record, made as a memorandum or record of an act or transaction, as evidence of such act or transaction if made in the ordinary course of business. This is an exception to the hearsay rule. The uncontradicted testimony of two witnesses established that the 1967 statistical run was a regularly maintained business record of Blue Shield and was made in the ordinary course of business. It was also shown that this record was relied upon by the company in conducting its business, particularly with reference to its auditing and actuarial procedures. The appellant maintains that the annual statistical run is not the record of any act or transaction and that only the original DSR's should have been admitted to prove the "act" of payment for medical procedures.

Computer print-outs are not mentioned in the Federal Business Records Act. However, no court could fail to notice the extent to which businesses today depend on computers for a myriad of functions. Perhaps the greatest utility of a computer in the business world is its ability to store large quantities of information which may be quickly retrieved on a selective basis. Assuming that properly functioning computer equipment is used, once the reliability and trustworthiness of the information put into the computer has been established, the computer print-outs should be received as evidence of the transactions covered by the input. No evidence was introduced which put in question the mechanical or electronic capabilities of the equipment and the reliability of its output was verified. The procedures for testing the accuracy and reliability of the information fed into the computer were detailed at great length by the witnesses. The district court correctly held that the trustworthiness of the information contained in the computer printout had been established.

The appellant also maintains that the computer print-out should not have been received in evidence because it was not prepared at the time the acts which it purports to describe were performed or within a reasonable time thereafter . . . However, the evidence clearly shows that a record of payment was made at the time each DSR was paid by Michigan Blue Shield and that this record was referred to as the paid claims file. This file consisted of reels of magnetic tape which reflected every payment to a doctor in the year 1967. Since the computer print-out is just a presentation in structured and comprehensible form of a mass of individual items, it is immaterial that the print-out itself was not prepared until 11 months after the close of the year 1967. It would restrict the admissibility of computerized records too severely to hold that the computer product, as well as the input upon which it is based, must be produced at or within a reasonable time after each transaction to which it relates.

The Federal Business Records Act was adopted for the purpose of facilitating the admission of records into evidence where experience has shown them to be trustworthy. It should be liberally construed to avoid the difficulties of an archaic practice which formerly required every written document to be authenticated by the person who prepared it. The Act should never be interpreted so strictly as to deprive the courts of the realities of business and professional practices.

Appellant insists that the 1967 statistical record was a "summary" which is not admissible, citing *Melinder* v. *United States*, 281 F. Supp. 451 (W.D. Okla. 1968). That case involved an exhibit prepared by an Internal Revenue agent for use at the trial of an income tax case. It was not a record produced in the ordinary course of business and was merely a recapitulation of certain information which had not been introduced to verify it in the case. The annual statistical run of Blue Shield of Michigan is not a summary, since it contains a record of every claim paid by the organization during a given year. The information contained in it is arranged in a predetermined manner and classified according to medical procedures. However, all paid claims are included and all compensable procedures are covered. It is important to distinguish the entire print-out of the 1967 annual statistical run from a separate item of evidence consisting of a summary of portions of the print-out. The witness Smith did summarize portions of the annual statistical record and did relate these summaries to the annual statistical record and did relate these summaries to the individual doctor's profiles of the defendants. Nevertheless, the entire statistical run was produced by the prosecution was a business record prepared in the ordinary course of business long before the time of the trial. Although summaries may or may not be admissible in evidence according to the circumstances of a particular case, we hold that the computer print-out offered in evidence in this case was an original record and not a mere summary.

The appellant maintains that no proper foundation was laid for the admission of the 1967 annual statistical record. We disagree. The witnesses Smith and Mrachina were qualified as experts by education, training and experience and they showed a familiarity with the use of the particular computers in question. The mechanics of input control to assure accuracy were detailed at great length as was the description of the nature of the information which went into the machine and upon which its print-out was based. In *United States v. De Georgia*, 420 F.2d 889 (9th Cir. 1969), the computerized records of Hertz Corporation were admitted for the purpose of showing that a particular automobile was not involved in any rental or lease activity during a certain period of time. An employee of Hertz was permitted to testify, based on the computer information, that an automobile found in the custody of the defendant at the time of his arrest was stolen from the Hertz lot since it had not been rented or leased. As the opinion points out, the foundation for the admission of such evidence consists of showing the input procedures used, the tests for accuracy and reliability and the fact that an established business relies on the computerized records in the ordinary course of carrying on its activities. The defendant then has the opportunity to cross-examine concerning company practices with respect to the input and as to the accuracy of the computer as a memory bank and retriever of information. The concurring opinion in *De Georgia* emphasizes the necessity that the court "be satisfied with all reasonable certainty that both the machine and those who supply its information have performed their functions with utmost accuracy." This opinion goes on to say that the trustworthiness of the particular records should be ascertained before they are admitted and that the burden of presenting an adequate foundation for receiving the evidence should be on the parties seeking to introduce it rather than upon the party opposing its introduction. We believe that in this case the prosecution proved the essential elements upon which the district court could, and did, conclude that the annual statistical run . . . was a trustworthy record which was entitled to be received in evidence . . .

Appellant also complains that he was not given an opportunity to prepare his defense to the computerized material used by the prosecution. In *United States v. Stifel*, 433, F.2d 431 (6th Cir. 1970), . . . this Court held that if the Government uses highly sophisticated scientific evidence (in that case, neutron activation analysis) involving time-consuming and expensive laboratory tests, it must allow time for a defendant to make similar tests. The Manual for Complex and Multidistrict Litigation deals at some length with the use of computer evidence. Its admissibility is strongly defended where the records have been kept in the regular course of business and its reliability has been demonstrated. The Manual further states,

> It is essential that the underlying data used in the analyses, programs and programming method and all relevant computer inputs and outputs be made available to the opposing party far in advance of trial. This procedure is required in the interest of fairness and should facilitate the introduction of admissible computer evidence. Such procedure provides the adverse party and the court with an opportunity to test and examine the inputs, the program and all outputs prior to trial.

On March 22, 1971, appellant filed a request for particulars in which he sought information about the evidence which would be used in support of the charges against him. On April 27, 1971, the government filed its response and forwarded to the attorneys for appellant a number of documents relating to the request for particulars. [The documents forwarded included the statistical summary from Blue Shield.] So far as the record shows, no discovery steps were taken by the appellant between the time of the disclosure by the prosecution of the nature of this particular evidence and the beginning of the trial on September 14, 1971, despite the fact that Rule 16(b) [of the Federal Rules of Criminal Procedure] provides for discovery and inspection by a defendant in a criminal case. At the trial Charles Smith's testimony compared the number of claims made by Drs. Russo and Lieberwitz for five particular medical procedures with those made by all of the doctors in Michigan. This summary was prepared by the witnesses from two sources. The number of claims paid to Drs. Russo and Lieberwitz was determined from the individual doctor's profiles prepared for each one of the defendants concerning which there is no contention on appeal. The information as to the total number of claims paid all doctors in Michigan in the five categories . . . was based on the annual statistical run which was offered and accepted in evidence. In view of the enclosure of the identical summary in the letter of April 27, there was no surprise or sudden, unexpected production of this evidence. Mr. Smith was cross-examined vigorously as to the manner in which the annual statistical run was produced.

Furthermore, on the third day of the trial, . . . there was a discussion between the court and counsel concerning exhibits. The prosecuting attorney referred to the fact that he had furnished statistics to counsel for the defendant pursuant to the court's pretrial order and stated that statistics showing the volume of claims in certain categories by the defendants would be compared with the total volume of such claims paid to all doctors throughout Michigan. On September 24, 1971, the witness Smith was recalled for the purpose of testifying about individual doctor's profiles and the annual statistical run of his employer. The court recalled to the attorneys that there had been a previous discussion of this offer of proof and that he had requested attorneys to be prepared to offer authorities for their positions. When counsel for the appellant complained that the information included in the annual statistical run was exclusively in the control of Blue Shield the court reminded him that he had a right to get an order which would have permitted him to go into the plant and study the whole process, and had not done so. The court ruled that the summary evidence offered by the witness Smith could be introduced because the primary evidence upon which the summary was based was in the courtroom and available for inspection and use in cross-examination by appellant. The prosecuting attorney pointed out again that the original of the computer run for the 1967 annual statistical report was available to counsel for the defendants, that the doctors' profiles and the vouchers from which they were constructed were also available for examination by counsel.

In cross-examining the witness Smith on September 28, 1971, the defense for the first time asked about other information that Blue Shield might furnish from its computer for comparison with the statistics included in his testimony. At no time prior to the trial or after the September 14th conference with the court did the defense make any effort to require the prosecution or Blue Shield to make its computers available to the defendants or to an expert employed by them or even to provide other information from the computers which was not then available. The computerized annual statistical run was not introduced into evidence and presented to the jury until September 30, 1971. Defense counsel were given an opportunity to examine the exhibit and to cross-examine both Mr. Smith and Mr. Mrachina extensively concerning it. The prosecuting attorney stated that the reason for introducing the annual statistical run as an exhibit was to provide a foundation for the testimony of Mr. Smith. The court pointed out that the annual statistical run itself was not a summary but a primary and original record constantly used by the company and was admissible in support of the testimony relating to portions of the exhibit by the person under whose supervision it was prepared.

In *United States* v. *Kelly*, 420 F.2d 26 (2d Cir. 1969), despite a motion for discovery of scientific tests which would be relied upon, the Government failed to inform the defendant of a neutron activation test which it had performed and the defendant only became aware of it at the trial when the Government sought to introduce its exhibits. The defendant objected and requested a month's continuance to carry out its own neutron tests. The court held that fairness requires a disclosure, in advance, of the results of a scientific test in order to give the defendant an opportunity to conduct its own tests. The present case differs from *Kelly* in several respects. In the first place, in that case there was a motion for discovery as to scientific tests and secondly, there was a motion for a continuance to permit the defendants to conduct their own tests. Neither of these steps was taken by appellant. We conclude, as did the trial judge, that appellant had ample notice of the nature of the statistical evidence which the prosecution planned to use and chose to attempt to discredit this evidence by means of cross-examination rather than availing himself of discovery and the use of expert witnesses of his own choosing . . . Much of the objection to admission of the computerized statistics was held by the trial judge to go to the weight of the evidence rather than its admissibility. This ruling was correct in view of the language contained in [the Federal Business Records Act]:

> All other circumstances of the making of such writing or record, including lack of personal knowledge by the entrant or maker, may be shown to affect its weight, but such circumstances shall not affect its admissibility.

Appellant also complains that the computerized information did not bear directly on the question of guilt or innocence and encouraged the jury to draw unwarranted inferences. The trial court ruled, and we agree, that the testimony of Smith supported by computerized statistics, when considered in connection with the testimony of Dr. Thompson, furnished an inference from which the jury could properly conclude that the defendants did not actually perform the extremely large numbers of certain designated medical procedures for which they were paid in . . . 1967. It is also contended that the court failed to give a qualifying instruction with respect to the statistical evidence. The record discloses that the court instructed the jury that the summaries prepared by the witness Smith and admitted in evidence were not in and of themselves evidence or proof of any facts and were used only as a matter of convenience. The court further instructed that "If and to the extent that you find they are not in truth summaries of facts or figures shown by the evidence in the case, you may disregard them entirely." The court also gave a comprehensive instruction on the right to draw reasonable inferences from established facts . . .

GLOSSARY OF LEGAL TERMS

Action: another term for a lawsuit; a civil action would be a formal request of a court to redress some grievance against another party

Adjudication: the judgment or decision of a court

Admissible: a term used with respect to evidence. Evidence is admissible if the court will permit the trier of fact (usually the jury) to consider it in deciding the issues of the case.

Admission: An agreement by a party to a lawsuit that some fact is true for purposes of a suit.

Affidavit: a sworn statement taken before a person authorized to administer oaths

Answer: the formal response of a defendant in a civil suit to a complaint

Appeal: the process by which a party dissatisfied with the decision in a trial court will seek to have that decision overturned

Appellant: the party in a suit who initiates an appeal

Appellate court: a court of law, higher than a trial court, which decides questions of law raised in appeals, and exercises such other judicial functions as may be mandated by a constitution, state or federal, or a statute

Appellee: the party in a suit against whom an appeal is taken, usually the party that prevailed in the trial court

Attempt: an act beyond mere preparation directed toward the commission of a crime

Authority: a recognized source that supports a particular legal position; decisions of the highest court in a jurisdiction are usually the best authority in that jurisdiction

Best Evidence Rule: if the contents of a document are to be proved, then the original document, if available, must be offered as evidence; "documents" include not just written documents such as wills or contracts, but also such items as photographs, tapes, and phonograph records.

Bill: a proposed law that has been introduced into a legislative session, as opposed to a statute, which is what the bill becomes after it is passed and signed into law

Black letter law: a basic principle of law, all too often oversimplified so as to be false. *Warning:* Beware of "black letter" statements of law because they are often merely partial truths.

Breach: a violation of an agreement, a wrongful failure to perform as promised

Brief: a written statement to a court presenting the preparing party's legal arguments and citing authorities for its position
Burglary: breaking and entering with the intent to commit a felony
Business records exception: a rule of evidence that permits certain kinds of business records to be admitted into evidence, even though they would otherwise have to be excluded as hearsay

Case-in-chief: the presentation by a party at a trial (including the state in a criminal case) of his or her principal evidence
Case law: law as stated in the opinions of appellate courts, as opposed to statutory law, which is law passed by the legislature
Cause: a factor contributing to the happening of some event. An act is a **cause-in-fact** of an event E if E would not have happened but for the act, or if the act was a substantial factor in the occurrence of E (*see also* proximate cause).
Cause of action: a legally recognized basis for a lawsuit; grounds to bring an action
Certiorari: an order from a higher court to a lower court removing the case from the lower court to the higher court for review.
Chattel: virtually any property except real property (land and fixtures attached to it) and intellectual property
Civil relief: a judgment or order granted by a court in a civil suit in order to redress a grievance or right a wrong; this form of relief is to be distinguished from the punishment meted out to a convicted criminal under a state or federal penal code
Claim: 1) the assertion of a right; 2) a statement in a complaint that indicates why the plaintiff is entitled to relief from a court
Class action: a lawsuit in which many parties having essentially the same cause-of-action are joined to expedite litigation. *Note:* This is a highly technical area.
Code: a compilation of laws in force, usually organized by subject matter
Common Law: 1) Case law; 2) English law that formed the basis for our own system of law
Comparative negligence: a weighing of the relative responsibilities of the parties for injuries suffered in a negligence case and an assignment of liability based on the relative fault of each party
Complaint: the document a plaintiff files with a court to initiate his or her civil lawsuit; the complaint should state concisely the facts that give rise to his or her cause of action and any claim for relief.
Condition: a qualification to an agreement. An *express condition* is one that is set forth explicitly, while an *implied condition* is one that a court will assume to be present in any agreement for the sake of fairness, for example, a condition to deal in good faith. A

condition precedent is a condition which must be fulfilled in order to make an agreement binding, while a *condition subsequent* will void an already binding agreement if it is fulfilled.

Consequential damages: damages that result from an act, but are not the immediate result of the act

Consideration: something of sufficient value given in return for a promise that a court will recognize that a contract has been formed

Constitution: 1) the fundamental document upon which our system of law and government is based, the highest law of the land; 2) the fundamental document of state government (which cannot, however, contradict the United States Constitution)

Conspiracy: an illegal agreement between two or more persons to carry out some project harmful to the general welfare; if a crime is agreed to, there must be more conspirators than it takes to commit the crime itself

Contract: an agreement made upon consideration, which a court is willing to find legally binding

Contributory negligence: a negligent act by the plaintiff in a negligence suit, which contributed to his or her injury; contributory negligence will prevent recovery in some states

Conversion: the wrongful appropriation or taking of the property of another

Conveyance: a formal transfer of ownership of property to another

Copyright: a form of legal protection available from the United States government for original writings of an author

Corporation: a separate legal entity or person created by law by a group of persons, usually for carrying out a business or particular purpose; the distinguishing feature of a corporation is that it has an existence apart from those who brought it into being and can act as a person in the eyes of the law in its own right

Count: 1) a statement of one cause of action in a complaint (a complaint can state several causes of action, and, therefore, have several counts); 2) in criminal law, a charge of one distinct violation of the criminal law

Counterclaim: a claim by a defendant raised against the plaintiff

Court decision: a judgment of a court; the determination of the outcome of a case, as opposed to the reasoning or arguments the court gives in favor of its judgment

Court of appeals: an appellate court (see above)

Court of Customs and Patent Appeals: court of appeals that hears appeals from decisions of the Board of Patent Appeals, the administrative review board that hears cases involving denials of patents by the Patent Office

Court of equity: a court of law acting in equity, that is, a court seeking to fashion a remedy appropriate to a given situation where a remedy at law (usually money damages) does not give full relief. For example, a court order forbidding someone to conduct a business that is polluting the air in some neighborhood, or an order forbidding someone who obtained a trade secret illicity to use it or profit from it, would be actions a court would take in equity.

Crime: violations of the law that may incur prosecution by the state and punitive sanctions upon conviction

Cross-examination: questioning of a witness by the party opposing that party that called the witness

Damages: an award of money to a party for a wrong committed against him or her to compensate for the injury brought about by the wrong

Decision: a court decision (see above)

Decree: most generally, a judgment or decision of a court of equity

Defamation: a tort involving injury to a person's reputation through the spoken or written word

Defense: 1) a claim set forth by a defendant that, if true, would exonerate him or her of liability for the crime or tort of which he or she is accused; 2) that portion of a trial conducted by the defendant

Deposition: a form of discovery in which a witness is examined under oath, but outside the actual trial.

Dictum: a statement a judge makes in a written opinion, which is not necessary for his or her decision; such comments, also called *obiter dicta*, are useful as revelations of the judge's thinking on some matter of law, but are not binding as precedents

Direct examination: examination of a witness by the party that calls that witness

Disclaimer of warranty: a statement by a vendor or contractor that there is no guarantee made with respect to some aspect of the service or product sold

Discovery: procedure that takes place before trial, in which each party attempts to gather information to use at trial

Due care: measure of care that is required to avoid potential liability for negligence; it is usually measured by what a "reasonable person" would do under the circumstances

Due process of law: a broad term meant to describe the rules of procedural fairness that govern our legal system

Duty: an obligation owed to another

Element: a necessary factor in the make-up of a crime or tort; for example, if some action is missing an element of negligence, then that action cannot be in negligence. In any trial in which the defendant has been accused of a tort (crime), it is vital that the plaintiff (State) prove every element of the tort (crime) if the plaintiff is to prevail.

Equity: the fashioning of a remedy to fit a particular wrong, rather than inflexibly applying strict rules of law or just awarding money damages. Equity will, however, usually not be invoked unless money damages are inappropriate to the situation.

Error: a mistake of law. Generally, a party in a lawsuit must allege some error at the trial level as the foundation for an appeal.

Exclusionary Rule: the rule that evidence seized in violation of a defendant's constitutional rights cannot be introduced by the prosecution against the defendant

Execute a contract: legally formalize a contract

Exemplary damages: *see* Punitive damages

False light privacy: publishing a statement about an individual that will tend to portray a false and damaging image of that individual, even though the statement itself may be true

Felony: a serious crime, usually one punishable by more than one year in prison

Foundation: testimony or exhibits brought forward at trial to establish the admissibility of other evidence

Fraud: a tort (and sometimes also a criminal act) involving deceit and intentional misrepresentation on which another relies to his or her detriment

General intent: a form of intent in criminal law that embraces a lesser degree of moral culpability than specific intent.

Goods: a technical term of importance because the Uniform Commercial Code covers "transactions in goods"; generally, although too simplistically to be entirely accurate, goods include any tangible, movable object except money, investment securities, and various types of legal documents.

Grand jury: a body of citizens, acting under the authority of a court, who determine if sufficient grounds exist to formally charge someone with a crime

Headnote: a note that appears before the opinion in a case in some reporter series that summarizes some important point of law contained in the opinion; the headnotes are not part of the opinion.

Hearing: a general term covering a variety of court proceedings outside of an actual trial

Hearsay Rule: a rule of evidence that, in its general form, states that no out-of-court statement or writing can be introduced in court to prove the truth of what is asserted in the statement or writing. There are many exceptions to the Hearsay Rule; the statement of the rule itself and the formulation of the exceptions varies from jurisdiction to jurisdiction.

Holding: a conclusion of law, other than dictum, set forth in an opinion

Immunity: freedom from liability

Incidental damages: Expenses caused by a tort or breach of contract other than the primary loss or harm directly caused by the tort or breach; for example, the expense associated with reselling improperly rejected goods would be an item included under incidental damages.

Indictment: a formal accusation by a grand jury that the accused is guilty of a specified crime or crimes

Information: a formal accusation by a prosecuting attorney or other legal officer that the accused is guilty of a specified crime or crimes

Infringement: an improper and unauthorized use of intellectual property protected by a patent or copyright

Injunction: a court order directing a party to do or refrain from doing something, almost always issued as part of an action in equity

Instruction: a summary of some point of law given to the jury by a judge to serve as a guideline in their deliberations

Integration clause: a clause in a contract that declares that the written contract contains all of the terms of the agreement

Intent: in criminal law, the degree of culpability required as an element of a particular crime; crimes may be divided into crimes requiring specific intent, crimes requiring general intent, and crimes involving strict liability.

Interrogatory: a form of discovery involving the submission of written questions from one party to another

Judge: a public official empowered to decide legal issues in a court of law and to preside at trial and other judicial processes

Judgment: a determination by a court, a judicial decision

Jurisdiction: the legal authority to try a case or settle a question of law. If a court lacks jurisdiction in a matter, any decision it renders relative to that matter is generally of no effect. Jurisdiction is also used to refer to the geographical district within which a court exercises its authority; for example, the jurisdiction of the Supreme Court of Indiana will be the State of Indiana.

Jury: a group of citizens used in certain trials to decide questions of fact

Larceny: an unlawful taking of the property of another without an intent to return the same

Law: 1) the general body of case and statutory laws, which constitute the legal rules of our society; 2) a particular rule of law

Liability: an actual or potential legal obligation to pay or do something

Libel: a written defamation; this generally has been held to include a defamation using any public medium of communication, such as radio or television.

License: a permission to do something that would be tortious or illegal without that permission; the one who grants the license is called the *licensor*; the license is granted to the *licensee*.

Lien: a form of security device by which property is pledged for the payment of a debt; a lien attaches to the property when it has been established by any one of several means that the property will stand security for a debt.

Limitation of liability: a contractual clause that states that a party will not be liable beyond a certain amount in the event of breach of warranty or contract.

Limitation of Remedies: a contractual clause that states that an aggrieved party to the contract can seek a remedy only in certain specified allowable ways; often, too, even the permissible remedies must be exercised within some specified time or they are lost.

Liquidated Damages: specific monetary damages fixed at the time of contracting, which must be paid in the event of any breach; true liquidated damages are fixed independently of the actual damages that may have been suffered because of the breach

Litigate: institute, pursue, or contest a lawsuit

Looseleaf Service: a subscription service that provides information of various sorts concerning some particular area of law

Malpractice: the negligent or improper performance of professional obligations by a professional on behalf of a client

Mark for identification: A labeling of an item of evidence, usually by a number or letter, so that it can be referred to readily; the item is marked for identification before it is admitted.

Material Breach: a breach of contract so substantial that the aggrieved party is entitled to treat the contract as totally unperformed

Matter of law: something the judge at a trial should determine, as opposed to a jury question. For example, John is guilty of negligence as a matter of law if he is so clearly negligent that the issue of his negligence should be decided by the judge and not go to the jury at all.
Mens rea: a culpable state of mind required as an element of crimes requiring specific or general intent; criminal intent
"Mental steps" doctrine: a theory that no invention is patentable as a process if one of the steps in the process can be carried out with pencil and paper or a series of mental steps; the vitality of this theory is not clear.
Misdemeanor: a crime not rising to the level of a felony
Misrepresentation: a statement or action that misleads another, not necessarily intentionally
Mortgage: a form of pledging of real estate as security for a loan; the *mortgagor* is the one who pledges the real estate to the *mortgagee*
Motion: a request to a court

Negligence: a failure to use due care, a breach of a duty of care owed to another

Objection: an explicit and timely indication by a party at trial that he or she believes some action is being attempted or contemplated that he or she believes would constitute error
Opinion: a written statement supplying the rationale for a decision rendered by a court; not all decisions, however, are accompanied by opinions (*see also* Slip law)

Parol: oral
Parol Evidence Rule: the rule that a party may not introduce oral evidence that contradicts the terms of an unambiguous written agreement. Like the Hearsay Rule, this rule has many exceptions and is almost extinct in some jurisdictions.
Patent: a legal monopoly granted on a device or invention
Petitioner: one who requests something of a court or public official
Plaintiff: the party that initiates a lawsuit
Pleadings: the documents filed by the parties to a lawsuit at its inception, setting forth their basic positions on the matter being litigated
Pocket supplement (or **pocket part**): supplementary materials put out by the publisher of legal reference material to keep that material up-to-date
Precedent: a previous decision in a similar case in the same jurisdiction

Privilege: a special exemption

Privity: two parties are in privity if they deal directly with one another, for example, if Gloria buys goods directly from Bob

Promissory estoppel: a legal doctrine allowing someone to seek enforcement of a promise (or payment of appropriate damages) if he or she has justifiably relied on the promise to his or her detriment; a formal contract need not exist

Property: anything that can be owned

Proximate cause: a moderately vague concept used by courts to limit the scope of liability in negligence to bounds they consider reasonable; to be proximately caused by a negligent act, the harm must be sufficiently closely connected to the act.

Punitive damages (sometimes called *exemplary damages*): a monetary award to the plaintiff in a civil suit, not to compensate for actual losses suffered, but to punish the defendant in order to discourage similar wrongful behavior in the future. As a rule, punitive damages are only assessed when the tort committed by the defendant has been intentional or reckless. A few states also permit punitive damages under special circumstances for breach of contract.

Quasi-contract: a doctrine that enables a party to seek reasonable compensation for services or goods provided in good faith with the consent of the party to whom they are rendered, even though a formal contract does not exist

Reasoning: the rationale a court uses in arriving at its decision

Regulations: rules issued by an administrative agency; these often have the force of statutes and may even carry criminal penalties for violations

Relief: a redress fashioned by a court to right a wrong

Remand: to send back. If an appellate court finds error in the manner in which a trial court handled a case, it will remand the case to the trial court for a new trial or other action consistent with its opinion.

Remedy: a means recognized by law to redress a wrong or enforce a right

Reporter: a compilation of the opinions of a particular court, or group of courts. A reporter series may deal with the opinions of one particular court, courts in a particular geographic area, or opinions dealing with some special area of law. The *Computer Law Service Reporter* presents opinions dealing with computer-related law.

Request for particulars: a request for more information concerning the details of a complaint or indictment.
Rescission: a formal cancellation of an agreement with an attempt to place the parties in the positions they would have been in if there had been no agreement in the first place
Respondent: a party against whom a motion is filed
Restatements of the law: summaries of various areas of law prepared by panels of scholars and jurists under the auspices of the American Law Institute
Restitution: the return of something rendered, or its fair value
Reverse: a change of the decision of a court by a higher court, generally because of some reversible error (*see also* reversible error). When a higher court reverses, it generally remands the case to the lower court for action in keeping with its opinion.
Reversible error: an error by a trial judge, made in the course of a legal proceeding, sufficiently serious for a higher court to rule that the judge's decision in the case cannot stand. Reversible error is contrasted to *harmless error*, which is a mistake not presumed serious enough to substantially influence the outcome of the trial.
Right: a legally protected privilege or relationship
Ruling: a decision by a judge with respect to a motion or question of law

Search warrant: an order signed by a judicial officer permitting police to enter and search a specific place. The warrant must state with some particularity the place to be searched and the items to be seized.
Session laws: a compilation of the laws passed by a session of a state legislature
Slander: spoken defamation
"Slip" law (opinion): a copy of a law or court opinion published separately shortly after the law is passed or the opinion is announced.
Solicitation: the crime of inviting or encouraging someone to commit a specific crime
Specific intent: the highest form of culpability required for a crime; for specific intent to be present, an act must be done knowingly and purposely.
Specific performance: a court order to carry out the terms of a contract
Stare decisis: the legal doctrine that a court will be slow to overturn precedent unless there is a compelling reason.
Statute of Frauds: a rule of law, enacted statutorily in one form or another by most states, which declares that certain forms of con-

tracts or agreements must be in writing and signed by the party against whom they are to be enforced if they are to enforceable in a court of law

Statute of Limitations: a law setting a time period within which a suit must be instituted, with regard to a particular cause of action, from the time that action accrues or comes into being, or the right to such a suit will be forever barred; private statutes of limitations may be agreed upon by parties to a contract as well, as in a clause limiting remedies.

Statutes: laws formally enacted by a legislative body, at at least the state level

Strict liability: liability without regard to whether the defendant was negligent or blameworthy with regard to the act charged as wrongful

Strictly construed: interpreted literally

Subpoena: a court order to a witness to testify at a trial or some other judicial proceeding; administrative agencies and Congress can also issue subpoenas. Failure to obey a subpoena may result in a citation for contempt.

Substantial performance: a level of contractual performance such that there is no total breach; the contract has been essentially performed even if not fully and perfectly performed.

Summons: a court order, generally served by the sheriff, ordering a defendant to appear at a certain time in a proceeding instituted against him or her, under penalty of losing the suit by default if he or she fails to appear.

Supreme Court: 1) the United States Supreme Court, the highest judicial body of the United States; 2) the highest court in a state or territorial jurisdiction.

Syllabus: a summary of a court opinion prepared by the official reporter of court opinions; the syllabus is not, however, a part of the court's opinion

Theft: larceny

Theory: an argument or grounds proposed by a party why it should win a lawsuit

Tort: a civil wrong, other than breach of contract

Trade secret: a process, idea, or design not generally known, but known and used by a business with some economic interest in it; generally too, some element of novelty is required. The idea will not be considered a secret unless precautions have been taken to protect its secrecy.

Trespass: a general term denoting intentional interference with a person's body, property, or rights

True privacy: publicizing private facts of a harmful or offensive nature

Unavailable witness: grounds for "unavailability" of a witness vary from jurisdiction to jurisdiction. A dead witness is always unavailable; a witness who is merely ill may or may not be unavailable, as may a witness who simply refuses to cooperate

Unconscionability: a vague term used by courts to refuse enforcement of contractual clauses that seem particular unfair or oppressive

Uniform Commercial Code: a vitally important piece of model legislation enacted into law in every state except Louisiana (which is a Civil Code State, the only such state in the United States); the U.C.C. sets out rules governing most forms of commercial transactions.

Unliquidated damages: damages for which a definite monetary value has not yet been determined

Voir dire: the examination of prospective jurors in preparation for trial

Waiver: a voluntary relinquishment of a known right

Warranty: a guarantee

INDEX

Abandonment, 127
Abbreviations, case citation, 178
Absolute privilege. *See* Immunity
Acceptance, 29–30, 33–34
Access, 88, 89, 144, 146, 149, 150
Accuracy of personal data file, 77
Acquittal, directed verdict of, 171
Act, 66, 122, 124, 126
Action, 225
   for the price, 24–25
Adhesion, contract of, 35, 42
Administrative
   agencies, 3, 155
   regulations, 126, 180, 233
Admissibility, 163–164, 214–218
   passim, 219, 223, 225
Adversial nature of legal system, 4
Advertised risk of failure, 60
Advice
   legal, 144
   misguided, by seller, 65
Affirmation of fact in contract, 19
Agreements subsequent to contract, 34
Aiding and abetting, 142
Alarm limit, 105, 196, 199, 203–204
Algorithm, 80, 84, 87, 90, 101–108
   passim, 197, 198, 200, 205
Alteration, 146
Ambiguities, 16–17
Appeals, 173–175, 225
   Circuit Court of, 107, 225
Appellate court, 107, 225
Appropriation, improper, 89–90, 91, 113, 136–137, 187
Arizona computer fraud law, 146–147
"As is," 11
Asportation, 139, 148. *See also* Theft
Assertion of rights, timely, 39
Assimilative Crimes Act, 140
Association for Computing Machinery, 147
Assumption of risk, 55, 56, 60
Attempt to commit crime, 127, 225
Attorney role in negotiations, 42, 43
Author, 80
Authority, 125–126, 225

Authorized user, 150
Awareness of criminal act, 123

Bait and switch, 187
Balanced personal data file, 77
"Battle of the Forms," 17–18
Bender, David, 112, 130–131
Benson, Gary, 103. See also
   Gottschalk v. Benson
Bernhart, In re, 102–103
Best Evidence Rule, 167, 168, 225
Bias, 170
Blameworthiness, 123
Blue Cross, 75
Board of Patent Appeals, 102
Breach, 225
   of contract, 19–23, 30, 32, 91, 113, 134
   proof of, 51
   of warranty, 61
Broadcast, 68
Burglary, 137, 226
Business Record Exception, 166, 226
Buyer, 11, 25–26, 27–31

Calamari, John, 21
California trade secret law, 133–134
Cancellation of contract, 23–24, 37
Care, duty of, 46, 49, 50–52, 74
Case law, 2–3, 226
Cases-in-chief, 170–171, 226
Cause, 47–48, 52–53, 59, 226
Certiorari, 195, 226
Challenges, 170
Chattel, 64, 67, 226
Citations, format for, 177–182
Civil Code (Louisiana), 236
Civiletti, Benjamin, 145
Civil relief, 226
Classification of patents, 101–102
Coded message, program as, 83
Codes as security device, 74, 76
Common law, 121–122, 128, 131, 226
Common usage, 111
Comparative negligence, 55, 226
Compilation, 118, 192, 193
Computer, 147, 149
   as defined in S.240, 144
   fraud, 146–147

237

Computer-generated evidence, 213–218 *passim*, 219–224 *passim*
Conditions, 19, 20, 227
Conference, pretrial, 163
Confidentiality, 72, 74
Conflicting warranty terms, 35
Conformity
  to contract, 28–29
  to model or sample, 9
Congress, 85, 99, 129, 203
Consent of owner, 130
Consequences, natural, and intent, 122–123
Consequential damages, 14, 31, 67–68, 227
Consideration, 227
Conspicuousness of disclaimer, 35
Conspiracy, 126–127, 133, 142, 227
Constitution, 2, 79, 85, 99, 115–116, 157, 227
Constructive conditions. *See* Implied conditions
Consultant, bad advice from, 41
Contempt, 158, 235
Contingency fee, 159
Contract, 7–44, 56, 80, 109, 119, 183, 210, 227
  of adhesion, 35, 42
  breach of, 19–23, 30, 32, 91, 113, 134
  cancellation of, 23–24, 37
  defined, 7–8
  dilemmas, 8
  formation of, 7–8
  mistakes in wording of, 38–39
  reading list, 44
  remedies, 13–15, 23–36 *passim*
  vendor, typical, 9–18
Contributory negligence, 53–55, 227
Control, 67
  plan, program as, 82
  of property, 147
  system, 104
CONTU, 83, 114–119 *passim*
Conversion, 67–68, 135, 227
Copies, 192
Copying, 67, 87, 89, 130, 134, 149
Copyright, 79, 84–93, 107, 109, 113, 115, 207, 227
  application form, 94–98
  law, 85, 86, 92–93, 114, 116, 118, 192–194
  Office, 84, 85, 86, 92
  reading list, 120

Copyrightability, 84–86
Correction of defect, assurance of, 33
Cost
  of appeal, 172
  of obtaining patent, 117
  of program module, 119
  of restoration, 150
  of software development, 101
Counterclaim, 39–41, 227
Court, 3
  of Appeals, Circuit, 107, 227
  of Customs and Patent Appeals, 99, 102–106 *passim*, 227
  of equity, 210, 228
  order, 92
  Reporters, 177–179, 233
  Supreme, 85, 90, 99, 100, 101–102, 104, 106, 140, 235
Credit bureau, 72, 74
Credit card fraud, 137
Crime, 121–152, 228
  common law, 121–122, 128
  inchoate, 126–127
  nature of, 121–127
  reading list, 152
  state statutes, 131
Criminal
  activity, allegations of, 71
  negligence, 123
  trial, 171
Cross-examination, 172, 228
CRT, 74, 118
Customs and Patent Appeals, Court of, 99, 102–106 *passim*, 227
Custom-tailoring of software, 117

Damages, 21, 30, 113, 191, 210, 212, 228
  consequential, 14, 31, 67–68, 227
  in copyright cases, 92
  incidental, 31, 230
  punitive, 37, 233
  warranty, 32–33
Danger, 48, 57–60 *passim*
Data
  compilation, program as, 83, 87–88
  files, and defamation, 76–77
Davidson, Gordon, 168
Davis, Harold, 99
Deception, 140
Defamation, 68–76, 228
Defects, 30, 32, 33–34, 57, 58, 59, 62
Defense, 228
  of abandonment, 127

INDEX 239

to breach of contract, 39
to libel, 71
to negligence, 53-56
to strict liability, 59-60
Delinquency, erroneous notice of, 76
Denial
   of access, 150
   of allegations, 72-73
Deposition, 160-161, 228
Derivative work, 192, 193
Destruction of property, 141-142, 146, 149, 150
Detection
   of computer crimes, 155
   of infringement, 91, 107, 117
   of theft, 128, 138
Development on company time, 110
Device, 192
"Dialect" disguise for copying, 90
Diamond v. Bradley, 106
Diamond v. Diehr, 106
Dictionaries, law, 181
Difficulties which void contract, 42
Digests, law, 181
Directed verdict, 171
Direct examination, 172, 228
Directories, 181
Disclaimer, 35
   of liability, 48
   of warranty, 9-12, 17, 32, 48, 228
Discovery
   in patent law, 80
   pretrial, 75, 154-163, 172, 221, 222, 228
Disguised copying, 89-90
Disregard of trial testimony, 164
Documentation, 65, 117, 118, 149
Documents, request for production of, 160, 161-162
Downtime, 9, 14
Due care, 50, 228
Due process, 122, 228
Duty, 228
   of care, 46, 49, 50-52, 74
   fiduciary (to employer), 109
   to warn, 51

Electronic surveillance, 156
Element, 229
Embezzlement, 129, 135
Encyclopedias, law, 181
Equipment. *See* Hardware
Equity, 210, 229
Equity Funding case, 129

Error in trial, 174, 229, 234
Estoppel, promissory, 22, 233
Evidence, 16, 153-176. *See also* Discovery, pretrial
   computer-generated, 213-224 *passim*
   reading list, 176
Examinations, physical and mental, 160
Exclusionary rule, 156-157, 229
Exclusive rights in copyright, 194
Exhibit, 170
Expectation of privacy, 154-155
Expense. *See* Cost
Expertise, 49, 118, 128, 171, 215, 218
Expert witness, 172
Express conditions, 20, 226
Express warranty, 9-10, 11
"Extended notion" states (theft), 131

Facts, 2, 9, 74, 153, 173, 175
Failure to deliver, 27
Fair notice (of what is outlawed), 122
Fair use, 89, 194
False light privacy, 77, 229
False pretenses, 132
Federal and state crimes, 127
Federal Business Records Act, 219
Federal enclave, 139-140
Federal jurisdiction, 135-136, 145-146
Federal Register, 180
Federal Trade Commission, 126
Fee
   contingency, 159
   for program use, 117
Felony, 122, 229
Fenwick, William, 168
Fifth Amendment, 158, 162
Final instructions, 171
Financial instrument, 149
Finney, Jarvis, 138, 141
Firmware, 83, 106
First Amendment, 74
"Fishing expeditions," 161
"Fixed" work, 192
Florida computer crime law, 147-148
Folly, buyer's, 39, 41
Foreseeability, 52
Forgery, 137, 141
Foundation for evidence, 165, 168, 169, 213-218 passim, 220, 223, 229

Fourth Amendment, 139, 154
Fraud, 16, 37, 137-147 *passim*, 187, 229
Free speech, 73

Gaps in contracts, 18
General intent, 123-124, 125, 229
Good faith, 38, 126, 211
Goods, 229
   defective, 30, 32, 33-34, 57, 58, 59, 62
   description of, in contract, 9
   nonconforming, 29-30
   software as, 58
Gottschalk v. *Benson*, 103-104, 105, 124-125, 196-201 *passim*, 205, 206
Graham v. *John Deere Company*, 100
Grand Jury, 157-158, 229
Grounds for appeal, 173

Half-truths, 77
Hard copy, 68, 75, 90, 134, 155, 166
Hardware, 9, 34, 38, 42, 58, 116, 118, 119, 149
Harmless error, 174, 234
Harrassment, 161
Hazard. *See* Danger
Headnote, 229
Hearsay rule, 165-167, 168, 174, 213, 219, 230
Home-use software package, 118

IBM v. *Catamore Enterprises*, 183-191
Ideas, 64, 67, 79, 85, 86, 90, 101, 116, 193
Ignorance of statute or order, 126
Illegally obtained evidence, 156
Immunity, 230
   from libel suit, 71-72
   use (Grand Jury), 158
Impairment of value, substantial, 33
Implied
   conditions, 20, 226
   warranty, 10-11
Impracticability, technical, 51
Improper
   lawsuit, 160
   question, 161, 173
Inaccurate or inadequate software, 65
Incapacity, 124-125

Inchoate crimes, 126-127
Incidental damages, 31, 230
Incompetence, 51, 54
Inconsistent provisions, 190
Infringement, 87, 88-89, 91, 107, 108, 114-115, 117, 134, 230
Injunction, 210, 211, 230
Injury
   caused by malfunction, 46
   personal, 58, 61, 62, 64
   to society. *See* Crime, nature of
Installation, 15, 19
Instruction
   computer, 81
   to jury, 170, 171, 230
   manual, 65, 87, 118
Instrument, financial, 149
Insurance, liability, 57, 62
Integration clause, 15-18, 34, 230
Intellectual property, 147-150 *passim*. *See also* Ideas
Intention, 16, 48, 66, 70, 122-123, 124-126, 131, 135, 230
Interference with rights, 66
Internal Revenue Code (IRC), 179
Internal Revenue Service, 126
Interpretation of law, 2, 189
Interrogatories, 160, 161, 230
Invalidation, 107
Invalid statute, 124
Invasion of privacy, 76-77, 138
Inventor, 80
Inventory, 187
Irresponsibility, 66

Johnston, Thomas, 103
Jurisdiction, 3, 135-136, 145-146, 230
Jury, 170, 231

Knowledge, minimum standard of, 50

Labeling, 11, 60
Laches, 39
Languages, computer, and copying, 90
Larceny, 2, 129-130, 231. *See also* Theft
Law, 231
   business, 7
   computer-related, reading list, 6
   matters of, 153, 173, 231/2
   nature of, 1-4, 37

reviews, 180
school, purpose of, 4
sources of, 2-3
Lay person, 89, 171
Legal references, format of, 177-182
Legislation. *See* Statutes
"Legitimate interest" libel defense, 72
Liability, 39, 45, 47, 48, 52, 74, 183-191 *passim*, 231
  civil, 123
  insurance, 57, 62
  strict, 56-61, 124, 125, 235
License, 50, 109, 110, 116, 211, 231
Limitation
  of liability, 231
  of remedies, 13-15, 17, 231
Liquidated damages, 13, 231
Literary works, 192, 193
Looseleaf service, 181-182, 231
Loss, risk of, borne by lessor, 42
Louisiana, 9, 236
Lund, Charles, 132
Lund v. Commonwealth of Virginia, 132-133

Machine, 192
Mail fraud, 138
Maintenance, 9, 16
Malfunctions, liability and, 45-46, 48
Malice, 73, 122
Malicious mischief, 137
Malpractice, 49-51, 172, 231
Market value, 32, 133
Material breach of contract, 20-21, 231
Matter of law, 153, 173, 231/2
"Mental steps" doctrine, 102, 232
Minimum of knowledge standard, 50
Misappropriation, 89-90, 91, 113, 136-137, 187
Misdemeanor, 122, 232
Misfeasance, 187
Misleading software, 65
Mismatch of machine and needs, 33
Misrepresentation, 16, 37-38, 64, 232
Mistake
  in contract wording, 38-39
  as to law, 125-126
  negligent, 48
Mistaken belief as to contract provision, 37, 38
Misuse of product, 60
Mitigation of damages, 31

Mobility of employees, 91, 110-111, 113
Model Computer Crime Bill, 149-151
Model, conformity to, 9
Model Uniform Product Liability Act, 51, 62-63
Modification, 149, 150
Monarch Federal Savings v. Genser, 213-218
Monopoly, 99, 101

National Commission on New Technological Uses of Copyrighted Works. *See* CONTU
Natural consequences, intended, 122-123
Nature of law, 1-4
Needs, analysis of, 41
Negligence, 21, 45-56, 58, 61, 187, 232
Negligent misrepresentation, 64
Network, 149
Nonconforming goods, 29-30
Nondisclosure clause, 110, 111
Nonexclusive license, 110
Notice of copyright, 92, 93
Notification of defects by buyer, 33
Novelty, 100, 113, 206, 235
Nycum, Susan, 49, 142

Objection, 164, 173, 174, 232
Obvious danger, 59
Obviousness, 100, 107, 202
Omnibus Crime Act of 1968, 156
Opening statements, 170
Operating system, 12
Operators, computer, 48, 150
Opinion, legal, 2-3, 4, 177, 195, 232
Option to return equipment, 42
O'Reilly v. Morse, 195, 200, 202-204
Out-of-court settlement, 159

Packaging, 11
Parker, Donn, 129
Parker v. Flook, 105-106, 195-206
Patent, 79, 93, 99-109, 116-118 *passim*, 195, 207, 232
  Appeals, Board of, 102-104 *passim*, 197
  Appeals, Court of Customs and, 99, 102-106 *passim*, 227
  classification of, 101-102
  obtaining, 100-101

Office, 99, 102, 106
  reading list, 120
  standards for, 100
Peremptory challenges, 170
Performance,
  specific, 27–28
  substantial, 21
Perillo, Joseph, 21
Permission to enter, 160
Per quod libel, 70
Personal injury, 58, 61, 62, 64
Peters, Marybeth, 84–85
Phonograph record, program as 83–84
Photocopy as evidence, 168
Physical harm. *See* Personal injury
Plaintiff, 53, 232
Police, 154–155
Possession, rightful, 114, 135
Pranks, 66, 142, 146
Precedent, 232
Pre-emption, 104, 105, 108
Preliminary instructions, 170
President's Commission on the Patent System, 102, 118
Pretrial
  conference, 163
  discovery. *See* Discovery, pretrial
Prevention of injury, 62
Price-Anderson Act, 51
Print-outs, 166, 167, 169, 214, 216, 219
Prior art, 100, 105, 108, 202
Privacy, 76–77, 154–155
Private statements, 72
Privilege, 232/3
Privity, 57, 233
Probable cause, 154
Process, 85, 195
Production of documents, 160, 161–162
Profession, statements damaging, 71
Program, 58, 80–84, 149, 195
  modules, 119
  patents for, 106
Programmers, mobility of, 91
Promise, 7, 9, 10, 19, 34, 37, 42
Promissory estoppel, 22, 233
Proof. *See also* Detection
  of access, 88, 89
  of breach, 51
  of misappropriation, 113
  of value, 66

Property, 61–62, 72, 79, 131, 148, 149, 150, 233
Protection of software
  by contract, 111, 112, 119
  by copyright, 80, 84–93
  by patent, 99–109
  reading list, 120
  by trade secrecy, 112–113, 116, 119
Protective clauses, 34–35, 42
Protective devices, 48
Proximate cause, 47–48, 52, 233
Publication, 69, 73, 193
Public interest, 52, 73, 124
Public statements, 72
Public utilities, 151
Puffery in advertising, 64
Punitive damages, 37, 233
Purchaser. *See* Buyer

Qualified privilege, 72–73
Quasi-contract, 22–23, 233
Questions, improper, 161, 173

Real property, 64
Reasonable
  care, 50, 228
  expectation of privacy, 154–155
  form of evidence, 162
  liability, bounds of, 52
  mistake of fact, 125
  person, 49
  reliance, 38
  steps to protect own interests, 31
  time, 15, 30, 33, 39, 54, 169
Rebuttal, 171
Receiving stolen goods, 135
Recklessness, 124, 125
Recommendation, incorrect, by seller, 65
Records
  business, 162
  of negotiations, 42
Recovery, 27, 31, 61–62, 161
References, legal, 177–182
Registration of copyright, 86, 93
Regulations, administrative, 126, 180, 233
Reliability of evidence, 164
Reliance, reasonable, 38
Relief, 233
Remedies, 12, 13–15, 23–36 *passim*, 233

Reporter, court, 177-179, 233
Request for admissions, 160, 163
Resale of goods as contract remedy, 24
Rescission, 38, 39, 234
Restatement of the law, 234
Restatement Second of Torts
  conversion, 67
  danger, tests for, 60
  misrepresentation, 64
  strict liability, 56, 57-58, 59, 62
  trade secrets, 208
Restitution, 38, 234
Restrictive interpretation, 189, 235
Retraction, 75
Reversible error, 174, 234
Ribicoff, Abraham, 143, 145
Rightful possession, 114, 135
Rights, 159-160, 171, 194, 234
Risk, 37, 42, 55, 56, 58
Ross, Otho, 82
Rules
  of evidence, federal, 166
  of law, 2

"Salami technique" theft, 128-129
Sample, conformity to, 9
Sanctions, criminal, 121
Saying too much or too little, 63-65
"Science Court," 171
Search, 126, 154
  warrant, 138, 154-156, 234
Secrecy and patents, 107
Secret, trade. *See* Trade secret
Security, 74-75, 112, 146, 210
Seizure, 154
Self-serving data, 166
Seller, 9-11, 31-36
Services, 9, 36, 50, 132, 149
Settlement, out-of-court, 159
Slander, 68, 234
Slip opinion, 195, 234
Software, 26, 34, 38, 42, 49, 50, 54, 58, 149
  cost, 81
  failures, 14, 65
  protection. *See* Protection of software
Software Copyright Act (proposed), 115
Solicitation, 126, 234
Source program, 83
Sources of law, 2-3

Special orders, contract remedies, 24
Specifications, need for written, 41
Specific intent, 123, 130, 234
Specificity of product claim, 64
Specific performance, 27-28, 234
Standard of care. *See* Duty of care
Stare decisis, 234
State
  common law, 131
  constitutions, 2
  law variable in each, 5, 112, 127
  suits against, 75
State of the art, 51, 59-60. *See also* Prior art
Statute of limitations, 235
Statutes, 2, 121-126 *passim*, 133-148 *passim*, 235
  citation format, 179
Stealing. *See* Theft
Stolen property, recovery of, 72
Strict liability, 56-61, 124, 125, 235
"Striking similarities," 88, 90
String of symbols, program as, 84
S. 240, 143-146
Subpoena, 235
Substantial performance, 21, 235
Summary judgment, 209
Summary of business records, 219-224
Summons, 235
Supreme Court, 85, 90, 99, 100, 101-102, 104, 106, 140, 235
Surprise, 158, 161, 172
Syllabus, 195, 235
Synercom Technology v. *University Computing Company*, 86-87
System, 149

Talbott, Arthur, 103. See also *Gottschalk* v. *Benson*
Tax advantages to patent holder, 99
Technical impracticability, 51
Telephone
  abuse statutes, 137
  used to crash system, 142
  as tie-in to computer, 119
Tender, 30, 32
Term of copyright, 92
Testing by seller, 51-52, 54, 57
Tests, legal, for danger, 60-61
Theft, 66, 125, 127-136, 149, 150, 221, 235

"Thing of value," larceny of, 131, 132
Third parties, 61–62, 72
Time, computer, theft of, 131
Timeliness of notification, 15, 30, 33, 39, 54
Time-sharing, 33, 157
Title, 179
Torts, 37, 45–78, 79, 123, 134, 183–191 *passim*, 235
Trade secret, 67, 79, 91, 109–113, 116–117, 119, 131–132, 133–134, 147, 149, 160, 207–212 *passim*, 235
Transcript, trial, 173
Transferred intent, 124
Trespass, 65–66, 235/6
Trial, 1, 163–173
True privacy, 76–77, 236
Truth as defense to libel, 71, 76

Unbundling, 185
Unconscionable clause, 42, 34–35, 36, 111, 230
Understanding and libel, 69
Uniform Commercial Code (UCC), 9, 10–18 *passim*, 25, 29, 31, 32, 34–35, 36, 61, 236
United States Code
 citation format, 179
 deceptive practices, 140
 fraud, 138, 140
 interstate transportation of stolen goods, 136
 search, 156
 theft, 135, 136
United States v. *Jones*, 140–141
United States v. *Lester*, 136
United States v. *Russo*, 219–224

United States v. *Seidlitz*, 138–139
Unliquidated damages, 212, 236
Unwillingness
 to copyright, 93
 to prosecute, 129
 to patent, 108–109
Usefulness, 60, 100
Users, computer, 48, 150
Utilities, public, 151

Validity of patent, challenges to, 107
Value, 33, 66, 131, 133, 148–150
Vendor. *See* Seller
 contract, 9–18, 23–27
Verdict, 171
Voidability, 20
Voir dire, 170, 236

Waiver, 34, 155, 236
Ward v. *Superior Court of California*, 134
Warrant, search, 138, 154–156, 234
Warranty, 9–10, 118, 236
 breach of, 61
 damages, 32–33
 of Fitness for Purpose, 10, 32
 of Merchantability, 10–11, 32, 35, 57
Weizenbaum, Joseph, 82
Welfare of general public. See Public interest
Wire fraud, 138
"With all faults," 11–12
Withholding evidence, 158
Witnesses, examination of, 172–173
"Works for hire" doctrine, 91
Writing, 80, 85, 137

Zone of risk test, 52